Recommended Wayside & Country Inns

of Britain 2001

A Selection of Hostelries of Character for Food and Drink and, in most cases, Accommodation

with

The  Supplement for Pet-Friendly Pubs

and

Family Friendly Pubs Supplement

For Contents see Page 15

For Index of towns/counties see back of book

 FHG Publications
Paisley

Part of IPC Media

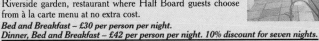
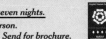

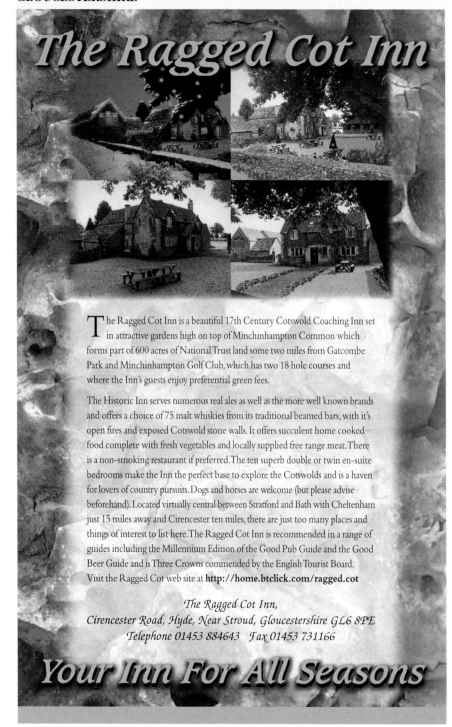

The Ragged Cot Inn

The Ragged Cot Inn is a beautiful 17th Century Cotswold Coaching Inn set in attractive gardens high on top of Minchinhampton Common which forms part of 600 acres of National Trust land some two miles from Gatcombe Park and Minchinhampton Golf Club, which has two 18 hole courses and where the Inn's guests enjoy preferential green fees.

The Historic Inn serves numerous real ales as well as the more well known brands and offers a choice of 75 malt whiskies from its traditional beamed bars, with it's open fires and exposed Cotswold stone walls. It offers succulent home cooked food complete with fresh vegetables and locally supplied free range meat. There is a non-smoking restaurant if preferred. The ten superb double or twin en-suite bedrooms make the Inn the perfect base to explore the Cotswolds and is a haven for lovers of country pursuits. Dogs and horses are welcome (but please advise beforehand). Located virtually central between Stratford and Bath with Cheltenham just 15 miles away and Cirencester ten miles, there are just too many places and things of interest to list here. The Ragged Cot Inn is recommended in a range of guides including the Millennium Edition of the Good Pub Guide and the Good Beer Guide and is Three Crowns commended by the English Tourist Board. Visit the Ragged Cot web site at **http://home.btclick.com/ragged.cot**

The Ragged Cot Inn,
Cirencester Road, Hyde, Near Stroud, Gloucestershire GL6 8PE
Telephone 01453 884643   Fax 01453 731166

Your Inn For All Seasons

Sparkford Inn

**High Street, Sparkford,
Near Yeovil,
Somerset BA22 7JN**

**Tel: 01963 440218
Fax: 01963 440358**

The Sparkford Inn is a homely and welcoming old coaching inn with en suite accommodation. Antique furniture and interesting old prints and photographs decorate the series of beamed bars and the carvery restaurant; there are log fires in the lounge bar and restaurant.

★ Large car park ★ Beer garden ★ Children's adventure play area
★ Free House - 5 real ales always available ★ No-smoking areas
★ Children welcome in the restaurant and in some areas in the bars.

Open daily Monday to Saturday 11am to 11pm – carvery lunch and snack menus 12 noon to 2pm.
Sundays open 12noon to 11pm –Sunday luncheon with speciality choice of roasts.
Specials boards in bars
Every evening including Sundays 7-10pm – à la carte menu and blackboard specialities

The Castle Hotel

Porlock, Somerset TA24 8PY

Tel: 01643 862504
Fax: 01643 862504

The Castle Hotel is a small, fully licensed family-run hotel in the centre of the lovely Exmoor village of Porlock. It is an ideal holiday location for those who wish to enjoy the grandeur of Exmoor on foot or by car. The beautiful villages of Selworthy and Dunster with its castle are only a short distance away.

There are 13 en suite bedrooms, all fully heated, with colour TV and tea/coffee making facilities.

The Castle Hotel has a well-stocked bar with Real Ale. Draught Guiness and Cider. A full range of Bar Meals are available at lunchtimes and Evenings or dine in our Restaurant.

Children and pets are most welcome. Family room available, cots available on request. Pool, Darts and Skittles all avaliable

❖ ❖ ❖ *Special Breaks available* ❖ ❖ ❖
Extremely low rates *Please contact Mr Bickerstaff on 01643 862504*

This charming, family-run 1700's country house is located in three acres of natural beauty between Exmoor and the Somerset coast, an ideal base to explore many renowned beauty spots. All bedrooms encompass the requirements of the modern traveller, with telephone, television and en suite facilities, each room retaining its individuality. The oak-panelled restaurant is the perfect setting to enjoy an evening of fine classical and West Country cuisine, accompanied by an impressive wine list. Simpler light meals, bar snacks, drinks and refreshments are available throughout the day in the comfortable bar, conservatory, colonnaded courtyard or underneath the largest Black Poplar in England.

**The Dragon House Hotel, Bilbrook,
Minehead, Somerset TA24 6HQ
Tel: 01984 640215 • Fax: 01984 641340
e-mail: info@dragonhouse.co.uk**

A warm welcome awaits you at

The Queens Head Inn

Egon Ronay

There are four double rooms, with own bathroom and colour TV, central heating, tea/coffee making facilities and telephone. Self-contained, motel-style, so that you are free to come and go as you wish. Relax in comfort in the friendly atmosphere of the low-beamed bars with part of the lounge area reserved for non-smokers. Well-behaved children are welcome in the lounge area. Your hosts, Michael and Norma Craggs, invite you to enjoy the superb menu available every lunchtime and evening, prepared from the finest and freshest food. There is also an excellent selection of real ales.

**North Street, Broad Chalke,
Salisbury SP5 5EN
Tel & Fax: 01722 780344**

THE BUCK INN

ETC/AA ★

Delightful Country Inn overlooking cricket green in quiet Wensleydale village. Relax in our comfortable en suite bedrooms, enjoy superb home cooked food and drink from our selection of five real ales. Ideal centre for exploring Herriot country. Private fly fishing available on River Ure and six golf courses within 20 minutes' drive. Good Pub Guide. CAMRA Good Beer Guide, Room at the Inn, Good Pub Food Guide.

**Thornton Watlass, Near Bedale
Ripon, North Yorkshire HG4 4AH
Tel: (01677) 422461 Fax: (01677) 422447**

AA and English Tourism Council
♦ ♦ ♦ GUEST ACCOMMODATION

Long Ashes Inn

Threshfield, Near Skipton, North Yorkshire BD23 5PN
Only 3 miles from picturesque Grassington
De-luxe en suite accommodation • Home-cooked food
Restaurant • Hand-pulled ales • Heated indoor pool
Special mid-week breaks
Idyllic setting perfect for exploring the Dales
Telephone for our colour brochure or visit our web site
to see photographs of our rooms etc.
Tel: 01756 752434   Fax: 01756 752937
E-mail : info@longashesinn.co.uk
www.longashesinn.co.uk

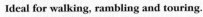

YE OLDE ORIGINAL ROSLIN INN

since 1827

Main Street, Roslin, Midlothian EH25 9LE

Tel: 0131-440 2384 Fax: 0131-440 2514

The 'Old Original' was in former times a temperance hotel but those seeking refreshment today may be assured that all four bars are well stocked with good beers, spirits and an interesting selection of fine wines. Substantial lunches are served in the comfortable lounge bar and the à la carte dinner menu attracts locals as well as tourists to a dining room graced by an absorbing collection of antiques and here one may dine memorably by candlelight. Six centrally heated, en suite bedrooms are available for letting, including two honeymoon suites; all have pleasing decor, television and tea and coffee-making facilities. Edinburgh is only seven miles away and there is a new leisure centre with a swimming pool nearby in Loanhead. AA, Les Routiers.

Nether Lochaber Hotel

Onich, Fort William,
Inverness-shire PH33 6SE
Tel: 01855 821235
Fax: 01855 821545

An ideal centre from which to explore Lochaber, the Ardnamurchan Peninsula and Glencoe. Traditional home cooking goes hand in hand with homely service, comfortable accommodation and private facilities. The inn stands on the shores of beautiful Loch Linnhe at Corran Ferry.

Other FHG holiday and accommodation guides

FHG Publications are available in most bookshops and larger newsagents but we will be happy to post you a copy direct if you have any difficulty. We will also post abroad but have to charge separately for post or freight.

The inclusive cost of posting and packing the guides in the UK is as follows:

£6.00

£5.50

£5.50

£6.00

£10.50

£4.50

£5.50

£4.50

£4.50

£6.50

Recommended

Wayside &Country Inns
of Britain 2001

A Selection of Hostelries of Character for Food and Drink and, in most cases, Accommodation

with

The BETA Supplement for Pet-Friendly Pubs

and
Family-Friendly Pubs Supplement

For Contents see Page 15
For Index of towns/counties see pages 169-170

FHG Publications
Paisley

Part of IPC Media

Other FHG Publications

Recommended Short Break Holidays in Britain
Recommended Country Hotels of Britain
Pets Welcome!
B&B in Britain
The Golf Guide: Where to Play/Where to Stay
Farm Holiday Guide England/Scotland/Wales/Ireland & Channel Islands
Self-Catering Holidays in Britain
Britain's Best Holidays
Guide to Caravan and Camping Holidays
Bed and Breakfast Stops
Children Welcome! Family Holiday and Attractions Guide

Acknowledgement
We thank The Sawrey Hotel, Cumbria and IPN
for the use of their pictures on our Outside Front Cover.

Cover design: Oliver Dunster, Focus Network

ISBN 185055 314 9
© IPC Media 2001

Cartography by GEO Projects, Reading
Maps are based on Ordnance Survey maps with the permission of
Her Majesty's Stationery Office, Crown Copyright reserved.

Typeset by FHG Publications Ltd. Paisley.
Printed and bound in Great Britain by William Clowes, Beccles, Suffolk

Distribution. Book Trade: WLM, Unit 11, Newmarket Court, Newmarket Drive, Derby DE24 8NW
(Tel: 01332 573737. Fax: 01332 573399).
News Trade: Market Force (UK) Ltd, 247 Tottenham Court Road, London WlP 0AU
(Tel: 020 7261 6809; Fax: 020 7261 7227).

Published by FHG Publications Ltd., Abbey Mill Business Centre,
Seedhill, Paisley PA1 lTJ (Tel: 0141-887 0428 Fax: 0141-889 7204).
e-mail: fhg@ipcmedia.com

US ISBN 1-55650-920-0
Distributed in the United States by
Hunter Publishing Inc., 130 Campus Drive, Edison, N.J., 08818, USA

Recommended Wayside & Country Inns is an FHG publication, published by
IPC Country & Leisure Media Ltd, part of IPC Media Group of Companies.

Recommended
Wayside & Country Inns
OF BRITAIN
CONTENTS

Guide to Tourist Board Ratings........17

ENGLAND

Bedfordshire 19	Lincolnshire 67
Berkshire 20	Merseyside 70
Buckinghamshire....................21	Norfolk 71
Cheshire................................22	Northumberland 75
Cornwall 25	Oxfordshire 77
Cumbria.................................30	Shropshire 80
Derbyshire 36	Somerset................................85
Devon....................................39	Staffordshire...........................92
Dorset....................................46	Suffolk 93
Durham 49	Surrey....................................95
Essex.....................................50	East Sussex 96
Gloucestershire 51	West Sussex 96
Hampshire 54	Warwickshire 97
Herefordshire 56	Wiltshire................................98
Isle of Wight..........................59	Worcestershire 101
Kent 61	East Yorkshire 102
Lancashire 63	North Yorkshire.....................103
Leicestershire 66	West Yorkshire 111

SCOTLAND

WALES

Aberdeen, Banff & Moray.......................115	North Wales 129
Argyll & Bute 116	Cardiganshire........................130
Ayrshire & The Island of Arran 117	Pembrokeshire 131
Borders...118	Powys 132
Dumfries & Galloway 120	South Wales 134
Dundee & Angus 121	
Edinburgh & Lothians...........................122	
Highlands...123	
Perth & Kinross 126	

Beta Guide to Pet-Friendly Pubs 137
Family-Friendly Pubs, Inns & Hotels Supplement............................151
Index of Towns/Counties 169
Map Section..173

Recommended

WAYSIDE & COUNTRY INNS OF BRITAIN 2001

PUBLISHER'S FOREWORD

A browse through the pages of *Recommended Wayside & Country Inns* is like a history lesson in miniature – the fascinating names being outdone by the equally fascinating history and the interesting snippets of information contained in the entries.

Though many of the establishments like to retain the character of yesteryear, they also offer a modern approach to service and hospitality. You will be delighted by the range and quality of the bar food, the real ales, many locally brewed, and the fine wines. Many also have separate diningrooms for more formal dining. Accommodation, ranging from comfortable to luxury, is usually available should you decide to spend the night.

Children are welcome in some inns and you may find special facilities for them such family rooms, smaller portions, play areas, and even adventure trails and Pets' Corners. More details can be found in our FAMILY-FRIENDLY PUBS supplement starting on Page 151.

Our selection of pubs, inns and small hotels is 'recommended" on the basis of reputation, written descriptions, facilities and long association rather than through personal inspection. We have included the separate 'PET-FRIENDLY PUBS' supplement which we hope will prove useful. We cannot accept responsibility for errors, misrepresentations or the quality of hospitality but we are always interested to hear from readers about their own experiences. Fortunately complaints are few, and rarely serious, but if you do have a problem which cannot be settled on the spot (the best solution, by the way), please let us know. We cannot act as intermediaries or arbiters, but we will record your complaint and follow it up with the establishment.

As far as we can establish, the details for all our entries are accurate as we go to press. We do suggest, however, that you confirm prices and other specific points while you are making enquiries and bookings.

Please mention *Recommended Wayside & Country Inns* when you make enquiries or bookings. Whether this latest edition is your touring companion, a source of holiday ideas or a handy outings guide, we hope that you will find high quality fare, good value and a warm welcome. *We would be happy to receive your recommendations and particulars of any pub or inn which you may judge worthy of inclusion – see page 150 for details.*

Anne Cuthbertson
Editor

Ratings You Can Trust

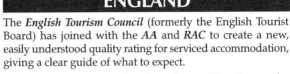

ENGLAND

The **English Tourism Council** (formerly the English Tourist Board) has joined with the **AA** and **RAC** to create a new, easily understood quality rating for serviced accommodation, giving a clear guide of what to expect.

HOTELS are given a rating from One to Five **Stars** – the more Stars, the higher the quality and the greater the range of facilities and level of services provided.

GUEST ACCOMMODATION, which includes guest houses, bed and breakfasts, inns and farmhouses, is rated from One to Five **Diamonds**. Progressively higher levels of quality and customer care must be provided for each one of the One to Five Diamond ratings.

HOLIDAY PARKS, TOURING PARKS and CAMPING PARKS are now also assessed using **Stars**. Standards of quality range from a One Star (acceptable) to a Five Star (exceptional) park.

Look out also for the new *SELF-CATERING* Star ratings. The more **Stars** (from One to Five) awarded to an establishment, the higher the levels of quality you can expect. Establishments at higher rating levels also have to meet some additional requirements for facilities.

NB Some self-catering properties had not been assessed at the time of going to press and in these cases the old-style KEY symbols will still be shown.

SCOTLAND

Star Quality Grades will reflect the most important aspects of a visit, such as the warmth of welcome, efficiency and friendliness of service, the quality of the food and the cleanliness and condition of the furnishings, fittings and decor.

THE MORE STARS, THE HIGHER THE STANDARDS.

The description, such as Hotel, Guest House, Bed and Breakfast, Lodge, Holiday Park, Self-catering etc tells you the type of property and style of operation.

> **In England, Scotland and Wales, all graded properties are inspected annually by Tourist Authority trained Assessors.**

WALES

Places which score highly will have an especially welcoming atmosphere and pleasing ambience, high levels of comfort and guest care, and attractive surroundings enhanced by thoughtful design and attention to detail

STAR QUALITY GUIDE FOR SERVICED ACCOMMODATION AND HOLIDAY PARKS

★★★★★ *Exceptional quality*
★★★★ *Excellent quality*
★★★ *Very good quality*
★★ *Good quality*
★ *Fair to good quality*

SELF-CATERING ACCOMMODATION

The *DRAGON GRADES* spell out the quality. They range from Grade 1 (simple and reasonable) to Grade 5 (excellent quality). The grades reflect the overall quality, not the range of facilities.

5 Night Bargains
from five superb
INNS OF TRADITION

Sunday to Thursday 5 nights DB&B from £165-£260pp (depending on season). Save up to £100pp off standard tariff prices. You can't afford to stay at home!

★ Green Farm Hotel, Thorpe Market, Norfolk (01263 833602)

★ Dornoch Castle, Dornoch Sutherland (01862 810216)

★ New Dungeon Ghyll, Great Langdale, Lake District (01539 437213)

★ The Red Lion, Hawshead, Lake District (015394 36213)

★ New Inn, Clapham, North Yorkshire (015242 51203)

Telephone the Inn of your choice direct – NOW!

For our current
Special Offers
please call
0800 917 3085
www.oldenglish.co.uk

FHG PUBLICATIONS

publish a large range of well-known accommodation guides. We will be happy to send you details or you can use the order form at the back of this book.

Bedfordshire

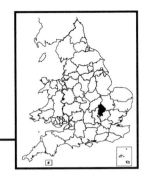

THE KNIFE & CLEAVER
The Grove, Houghton Conquest, Bedfordshire MK45 3LA
Tel: 01234 740387 • Fax: 01234 740900 • e-mail: knifeandcleaver.com
website: www.knifeandcleaver.com

Deep in the heart of rural Bedfordshire, this friendly country inn offers a warm welcome to locals and visitors alike, and proves equally popular with both. One of the main reasons for its enviable reputation is the quite exceptional Victorian-style conservatory restaurant, where the finest of fresh ingredients are prepared with care and imagination by first-class chefs and where the accompanying wine list has been selected with quality and value as the highest priorities. Nine well-appointed en suite bedrooms, all with power shower, satellite television and a full range of amenities, provide comfortable accommodation for those wishing to explore this lovely area. *ETC* ◆◆◆◆, *AA*.

9 BEDROOMS, ALL WITH PRIVATE BATHROOM; FREE HOUSE WITH REAL ALE; HISTORIC INTEREST; CHILDREN WELCOME, PETS BY ARRANGEMENT; BAR AND RESTAURANT MEALS; NON-SMOKING AREAS; AMPTHILL 2 MILES; S£££, D££

The **£** symbol when appearing at the end of the italic section of an entry shows the anticipated price, during 2001, for full Bed and Breakfast.

Normal Bed & Breakfast rate per person
(in single room)

Normal Bed & Breakfast rate per person
(sharing double/twin room)

PRICE RANGE	CATEGORY	PRICE RANGE	CATEGORY
Under £25	*S£*	**Under £25**	*D£*
£26-£35	*S££*	**£26-£35**	*D££*
£36-£45	*S£££*	**£36-£45**	*D£££*
Over £45	*S££££*	**Over £45**	*D££££*

This is meant as an indication only and does not show prices for Special Breaks,
Weekends, etc. Guests are therefore advised to verify all prices
on enquiring or booking.

Berkshire

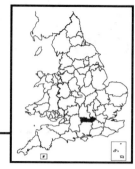

THE INN ON THE GREEN
The Old Cricket Common, Cookham Dean, Berkshire SL6 9NZ
Tel: 01628 482638 • Fax: 01628 487474 • e-mail: enquiries@theinnonthegreen.com
website: www.theinnonthegreen.com

Fashionable without being pretentious, this happy place is truly a resort of knowledgeable gourmets. The exceptional cuisine is a blend of traditional English and classical European fare; à la carte and table d'hôte dishes are offered seven days a week with Sunday lunchtime roasts a popular feature. Relaxation comes easily in the oak-beamed bar where a log fire blazes in winter months with a variety of real ales no doubt contributing to the mood. For a few days' break by the Thames, this is a well recommended venue; the en suite guest rooms an attractive amalgam of old-fashioned charm and modern conveniences. Excellent corporate facilities also exist. *ETC/AA/RAC* ◆◆◆◆, *AA Rosette, Which? Hotel Guide.*

8 BEDROOMS, ALL WITH PRIVATE BATHROOM; FREE HOUSE WITH REAL ALE; HISTORIC INTEREST; CHILDREN AND PETS WELCOME; BAR AND RESTAURANT MEALS; MAIDENHEAD 3 MILES; S££££, D££££.

THE DUNDAS ARMS
Station Road, Kintbury, Berkshire RG17 9UT
Tel: 01488 658263/658559 • Fax: 01488 658263 • e-mail: info@dundasarms.co.uk
website: www.dundasarms.co.uk

The inn's lovely position between the River Kennet and the canal makes it a most pleasant spot to stop for refreshment, and indeed for an overnight stay or weekend break. The comfortably furnished bedrooms are fully equipped with private bathroom, television and tea-making facilities, and enjoy relaxing views over the river. If your visit here is purely for refreshment, you will be delighted by the excellent bar food menu, which features really interesting "specials" alongside traditional favourites such as ploughmans and steak and kidney pie, and by the range of well kept real ales. For more leisurely dining, menus in the restaurant make full use of fresh local produce, and there is also an excellent wine list. *CAMRA.*

5 BEDROOMS, ALL WITH PRIVATE BATHROOM; FREE HOUSE WITH REAL ALE; CHILDREN WELCOME; BAR MEALS, RESTAURANT EVENINGS ONLY; NON-SMOKING AREAS; HUNGERFORD 3 MILES; S££££, D££.

THE BELL AT BOXFORD
Lambourn Road, Newbury, Berkshire RG20 8DD
Tel: 01488 608721 • Fax: 01488 608749 • e-mail: bell.boxford@excite.co.uk

The smart exterior of this traditional country inn between Newbury and Lambourn will attract the attention of passers by, maybe and possibly disciples of the turf. To venture within is to discover homely comforts in the form of log fires and real ales as well as bags of character. Widely recommended, the international fare on offer in the candlelit restaurant is a lure in itself, there being a mouth-watering choice of reasonably-priced dishes on the à la carte menu, not forgetting the daily 'blackboard specials'. Excellent accommodation is available at this hostelry run in distinguished style by Paul and Helen Lavis, bedrooms having en suite facilities, direct-dial telephone and modern appointments.

11 BEDROOMS, ALL WITH PRIVATE BATHROOM; FREE HOUSE WITH REAL ALE; CHILDREN AND PETS WELCOME; BAR AND RESTAURANT MEALS; NON-SMOKING AREAS; READING 16 MILES; S££££, D££.

Buckinghamshire

THE PLOUGH
Hyde Heath, Near Amersham, Buckinghamshire HP6 5RW
Tel: 01494 783163

In a tranquil position on the gentle slopes of the Chiltern Hills and actually in the famed Chiltern Hundreds, this homely inn is only a mile or so west of Chesham and a leisurely drive from the urban hassle of Greater London. The Plough is just the place to recharge the batteries through the medium of excellent refreshment and good company. There is a most interesting and varied selection of dishes on offer at lunchtime and in the evening, all of which are home-cooked to order using only fresh produce. After satisfying ourselves in style and at surprisingly moderate cost, we found the return to the concrete jungle something of a penance. *CAMRA.*

NO ACCOMMODATION; REAL ALE; CHILDREN AND PETS WELCOME; BAR MEALS; CHESHAM 2 MILES.

PLEASE MENTION THIS GUIDE WHEN YOU WRITE

OR PHONE TO ENQUIRE ABOUT ACCOMMODATION

IF YOU ARE WRITING, A STAMPED, ADDRESSED

ENVELOPE IS ALWAYS APPRECIATED

Cheshire

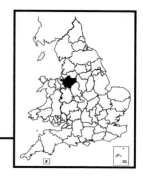

SYCAMORE INN

Sycamore Road, Birch Vale, High Peak, Cheshire SK22 1AB
Tel: 01663 742715 • Fax: 01663 747382 • e-mail: sycamoreinn@aol.com
website: www.sycamoreinn.co.uk

Picturesquely situated by the River Sett overlooking the valley, this friendly free house is ideally placed to visit the Peak District, as well as being a short train journey to Manchester. This family orientated pub restaurant, which has an excellent reputation for food and cask conditioned ales, is a children's paradise. It has a pets' corner and adventure trail playground which keep them fully occupied. The two sizeable restaurants have a non-smoking area as well as offering excellent home-cooked food and a good choice of wines, with a special children's menu. The guest bedrooms offer full en suite facilities, satellite television, tea and coffee makers. *Egon Ronay.*

8 BEDROOMS, ALL WITH PRIVAYE BATHROOM; FREE HOUSE WITH REAL ALE; CHILDREN AND PETS WELCOME; BAR AND RESTAURANT MEALS; NON-SMOKING AREAS; HAYFIELD 1 MILE; S££, D£.

CHURCH HOUSE INN

Church Street, Bollington, Macclesfield, Cheshire SK10 5PY
Tel: 01625 574014 • Fax: 01625 576424

Convenient for Chester and Manchester and for the unspoiled scenery of the Peak District National Park, this charming hostelry makes the most of an tranquil and relaxing situation. Delightfully decorated and efficiently run by hosts, Stephen and Julie Robinson, the inn provides good food, ale and company in a warm, unhurried atmosphere, a subtle amalgam of Victorian values and modern practicality. All food is freshly cooked to order; generous portions beautifully presented and at the most reasonable prices, too! En suite bedrooms are tastefully furnished, each with tea/coffee facilities, television and trouser press. *Egon Ronay.*

5 BEDROOMS, ALL WITH PRIVATE BATHROOM; FREE HOUSE WITH REAL ALE; CHILDREN WELCOME; BAR MEALS; NON-SMOKING AREAS; MACCLESFIELD 3 MILES; S££, D£.

FHG PUBLICATIONS

publish a large range of well-known
accommodation guides.

We will be happy to send you details or you can use
the order form at the back of this book.

CHESHIRE CAT
Whitchurch Road, Christleton, Chester, Cheshire CH3 6AE
Tel: 01244 332200 • Fax: 01244 336415 • website: www.thecheshirecat.co.uk

Here at the Cheshire Cat we take pride in the quality of our food and drink, offering a superb selection of great food all day, every day and in generous portions too. And what's more, as we are a traditional inn you can also enjoy our cask-conditioned ale and wide selection of quality wines from around the world. Comfortable, traditionally decorated and individual in character, each of our bedrooms (including one four-poster and one family room) offers you a slightly different experience to treasure. Each room has en suite bathroom or shower, colour TV, telephone with modem facility and tea/coffee making facilities. Whether you are here for a relaxing meal, a sociable drink or an overnight stay, we are confident that you will find the Cheshire Cat is the ideal setting. *ETC/AA* ★★★.

14 BEDROOMS, ALL WITH PRIVATE BATHROOM; VINTAGE INNS HOUSE WITH REAL ALE; HISTORIC INTEREST; CHILDREN WELCOME; BAR AND RESTAURANT MEALS; NON-SMOKING AREAS; CHESTER CITY CENTRE 1.5 MILES; S£££, D££.

CHOLMONDELEY ARMS
Cholmondeley, Malpas, Cheshire SY14 8HN
Tel: 01829 720300 • Fax: 01829 720123 • e-mail: cholmondeleyarms@circom.net
website: www.cholmondeleyarms.co.uk

Perfect for those seeking somewhere a little bit different, this appealing pub was until 1982 the village school. People come from far beyond the area to sample the Cholmondeley cuisine, with a fine range of starters, main courses such as home-made pies, curries and filled savoury pancakes, and a mouth-watering selection of speciality puddings. Overnight guests are accommodated in the school house, just a step across the playground, where individually styled bedrooms offer tea and coffee facilities, colour television, radio alarm, hairdryer and direct-dial telephone as well as smart decor and furnishings and supreme comfort. This unique establishment is to be found on the A49, next to the park and gardens of Cholmondeley Castle. *ETC* ◆◆◆

6 BEDROOMS, ALL WITH PRIVATE BATHROOM; FREE HOUSE WITH REAL ALE; CHILDREN AND PETS WELCOME; BAR AND RESTAURANT MEALS; CHESTER 16 MILES, NANTWICH 8; S£££, D££.

THE PHEASANT INN
Higher Burwardsley, Tattenhall, Cheshire CH3 9PF
Tel: 01829 770434 • Fax: 01829 771097

For 300 years the lovely half timbered and sandstone Pheasant Inn has stood atop the Peckforton Hills, gazing out over the Cheshire Plain to distant Wales. Panoramic views are to be enjoyed from most of the nicely decorated bedrooms, which are complete with en suite bathroom, colour television, radio alarm, hairdryer and beverage making facilities. Accommodation is in the beautifully converted barn, tucked quietly away from the convivial bar with its huge log fire, and the Bistro Restaurant which enjoys a well-deserved reputation for fine fare, well presented and served with cheerful efficiency. Weekend mini-breaks are a popular feature of this commendable establishment. *ETC* ★★, *AA Listed*.

10 BEDROOMS, ALL WITH PRIVATE BATHROOM; FREE HOUSE WITH REAL ALE; HISTORIC INTEREST; CHILDREN WELCOME; BAR AND RESTAURANT MEALS; NON-SMOKING AREAS; CHESTER 9 MILES; S££££, D£££.

Cornwall

THE WELLINGTON HOTEL
The Harbour, Boscastle, Cornwall PL35 0AQ
Tel: 01840 250202 • Fax: 01840 250621 • e-mail: vtobutt@enterprise.net
website: www.wellingtonboscastle.co.uk

This historic 16th century coaching inn is situated by the Elizabethan harbour and is surrounded by National Trust countryside. It is ideally situated for walking, touring and golfing holidays, and close to glorious sandy beaches, beautiful wooded valleys and dramatic moorland. The Wellington Hotel is a free house and offers real ales, pub grub, open fires and beams; the fine Anglo-French restaurant specialises in regional cuisine and seafood. There are ten acres of private woodland walks and pets are very welcome. *AA/RAC* ★★. *See also Colour Advertisement on page 2.*

16 BEDROOMS, ALL WITH PRIVATE BATHROOM; FREE HOUSE WITH REAL ALE; HISTORIC INTEREST; PETS WELCOME; BAR AND RESTAURANT MEALS; TINTAGEL 3 MILES; S££, D££.

THE EARL OF ST VINCENT
Egloshayle, Cornwall PL27 6HT
Tel: 01208 814807 • e-mail: earl@globalnet.co.uk

Dating from the Middle Ages, this friendly pub is named after Sir John Jervis, the Earl of St Vincent, who was Lord Nelson's commanding officer. Among many attractive features are colourful floral displays and a collection of old clocks. A comprehensive menu is available lunchtimes and evenings.

NO ACCOMMODATION; ST AUSTELL BREWERY HOUSE WITH REAL ALE; BAR MEALS; BODMIN 7 MILES.

For details of Tourist Board Gradings in England, Scotland and Wales see page 17

THE COPLEY ARMS
Hessenford, Torpoint, Cornwall PL11 3HJ
Tel: 01503 240209 • Fax: 01503 240766

Over the Tamar Bridge from historic Plymouth, it is just a short drive along the A387 to this idyllic spot, the home of the lovely old Copley Arms. Here one will find friendly hospitality in the best Cornish tradition, along with excellent food and drink. There is a tempting selection of bar meals or one may dine informally in a pleasant restaurant. This is an first rate touring location within easy reach of Looe and Polperro on one hand and Plymouth Hoe and naval dockyards on the other. En suite bedrooms are available to overnight guests, all rooms having colour television and tea/coffee making facilities. *AA*.

5 BEDROOMS, ALL WITH PRIVATE BATHROOM; ST AUSTELL BREWERY HOUSE WITH REAL ALE; HISTORIC INTEREST; CHILDREN AND PETS WELCOME; BAR AND RESTAURANT MEALS; NON-SMOKING AREAS; LISKEARD 6 MILES; S£££££, D£££££.

SHIP INN
Lerryn, Lostwithiel, Cornwall PL22 0PT
Tel: 01208 872374 • Fax: 01208 872614
website: www.cornwall-online.co.uk/shipinn-lerryn

This charming and traditional Cornish country inn can be found in what must surely be the prettiest riverside village in Cornwall. The wooded river banks were the inspiration for Kenneth Grahame's *The Wind in the Willows*. Popular with walkers and sailors alike, it offers a warm welcome to all. A log fire and central heating ensure year round comfort and make this a cosy choice for an out of season break. The attractive guest rooms all have en suite bathrooms, beverage-making facilities, colour television and radio. One bedroom is on the ground floor, making it ideal for elderly or disabled visitors. Excellent home-cooked fare is available in the restaurant lunchtimes and evenings, when you can choose from our extensive menu which also includes a good choice for vegetarians; an extensive wine list will complement any meal. The bar offers a choice of real ales and a large selection of malt whiskies. Conveniently situated for the coast, valleys and moors of central and east Cornwall. *Good Pub Guide*.

4 BEDROOMS, ALL WITH PRIVATE BATHROOM; FREE HOUSE WITH REAL ALE; CHILDREN AND PETS WELCOME; RESTAURANT MEALS; NON-SMOKING AREAS; LOSTWITHIEL 3 MILES; S££, D££.

ROYAL OAK INN
Duke Street, Lostwithiel, Cornwall PL22 0AG
Tel: 01208 872552 • website: www.angelfire.com.ky/royaloak/royaloak.html

Full of character and with two beautifully kept bars, one of which does duty as a restaurant where splendid and reasonably priced meals are served nightly, the 13th century Royal Oak is tucked away just off the main road. An underground tunnel is said to connect its cellar to the dungeons of nearby 12th and 13th century Restormel Castle, providing a smuggling and, possibly, an escape route. No-one will surely wish to escape from this warmly welcoming hostelry with its log fire and tfriendly atmosphere. Overnight guests are accommodated in attractively decorated bedrooms, all appointed with en suite facilities, television, radio and tea-makers. *RAC* ★★.

6 BEDROOMS, ALL WITH PRIVATE BATHROOM; FREE HOUSE WITH REAL ALE; HISTORIC INTEREST; CHILDREN AND PETS WELCOME; BAR AND RESTAURANT MEALS; BODMIN 5 MILES; S£££, D££.

FOUNTAIN INN
Cliff Street, Mevagissey, Cornwall PL26 6QH
Tel: 01726 842320 • e-mail: billymoore@cwcom.net

The oldest inn in the quaint Cornish coastal village of Mevagissey, the 'Fountain' dates from the 15th century. Its Smugglers Bar takes its name from a tunnel that linked with the harbour and where rum and brandy were smuggled in from France. The front bar with its original oak beams, slate floor and fireplace is somewhat unusual in the modern world being bereft of juke box or fruit machine; gentle entertainment is regularly provided by piano. Good solid sustenance is dispensed in the bars at lunchtime or in the restaurant in the evenings, specialities being prime steaks and fresh, locally caught fish. Well-appointed overnight accommodation is available. *RAC, Brittany Ferries.*

3 BEDROOMS,ALL WITH PRIVATE BATHROOM/SHOWER; ST AUSTELL BREWERY HOUSE WITH REAL ALE; HISTORIC INTEREST; CHILDREN AND PETS WELCOME; BAR LUNCHES, RESTAURANT EVENINGS ONLY; ST AUSTELL 5 MILES; S£, D£££.

CRUMPLEHORN MILL
Polperro, Cornwall PL13 2RJ
Tel: 01503 272348 • Fax: 01503 272914 • e-mail: AndrewCrumplehorn@msn.com
website: www.crumplehorn-inn.co.uk

A complex created out of old farm buildings in 1972, the hotel, bars, restaurant and self-catering facilities exhibit character and an enlightened appreciation of the worthwhile things of life. Crumplehorn Mill has, in part, been transformed into a most attractive free house with a notable à la carte restaurant and traditional bar snacks. Food is freshly prepared and represents excellent value for money. Many are the fascinating stories featuring the inn, especially of the days of 'Good Queen Bess' when a tally of treasures acquired by privateers from France and Spain was counted here. The hotel provides accommodation in suites and bedrooms, matched only, perhaps, by the splendid self-catering flats and penthouse apartment. *CTB, SECTA Approved, CAMRA.*

B&B OR SELF-CATERING FOR 2-8 PERSONS; FREE HOUSE WITH REAL ALE; HISTORIC INTEREST; CHILDREN AND PETS WELCOME; BAR MEALS, RESTAURANT EVENINGS ONLY (OCT –JULY); NON-SMOKING AREAS;LISKEARD 6 MILES; S££, D££.

THE CORNISH ARMS
Pendoggett, Port Isaac, North Cornwall PL30 3HH
Tel: 01208 880263 • Fax: 01208 880335

A delightful 16th century Coaching Inn in the small rural village of Pendoggett, just one mile from the coast. Anyone who makes The Cornish Arms a base for exploring the area will not be disappointed by the attractive accommodation or the warmth of welcome extended. Whilst retaining the character of a traditional coaching inn, The Cornish Arms offers all modern amenities in every bedroom; colour and satellite TV, telephone, tea and coffee making facilities, etc. The highly recommended restaurant specialises in locally caught seafood and an extensive range of other dishes. Complement your meal with wine from the extensive cellars of The Cornish Arms. Pendoggett Special Bitter is famous for its strength – the locals won't touch it, it's so strong. With Bass straight from the barrel, together with other real ales, you will see why it is worth visiting The Cornish Arms. ETC/RAC ★★.

8 BEDROOMS, 7 WITH PRIVATE BATHROOM; FREE HOUSE WITH REAL ALE; HISTORIC INTEREST;
CHILDREN AND PETS WELCOME; BAR MEALS, RESTAURANT EVENINGS ONLY PLUS SUN. LUNCH;
NON-SMOKING AREAS; WADEBRIDGE 8 MILES, POLZEATH 6, PORT ISAAC 1; S£££, D££.

PORT GAVERNE INN AND GREEN DOOR COTTAGES
Near Port Isaac, Cornwall PL29 3SQ
Tel: 01208 880244 • Fax: 01208 880151 • e-mail: pghotel@telinco.co.uk

This well-known Cornish Coastal Inn offers eight comfortably renovated beamed character cottages, sleeping two to six persons; each with central heating throughout; spacious lounge with log burner, completely equipped fitted kitchen, colour TV, telephone, free parking, enclosed sheltered garden. Two large flats sleep eight – elevated position on cliff, overlooking the Cove. Central heating/washing machine/tumble dryer/dishwasher/colour TV/direct-dial telephone. No meters, everything included in the price. Convenient to the fully licensed, internationally recognised Port Gaverne Inn. Port Isaac half-a-mile; beach 50 yards. Golf, fishing, sailing, riding nearby. Cornish Coastal Path passes the door. Open all year. Pets welcome in the Inn and Self Catering Accommodation. ♥♥♥♥ *Commended*. *See also Colour Advertisement on page 2.*

8 SELF-CATERING COTTAGES (SLEEP 2/6); PETS WELCOME; WADEBRIDGE 5 MILES.

DRIFTWOOD SPARS HOTEL
Trevaunance Cove, St Agnes, Cornwall TR5 0RT
Tel: 01872 552428/553323

Situated only a hundred yards from the beach, the building which is now the popular Driftwood Spars Hotel is over 300 years old and has seen active service as a tin miners' store, a chandlery, a sailmaker's workshop and a fish cellar. But nowadays the emphasis is strictly on providing guests with good food, ale and atmosphere. There are three bars – one has a children's room – serving a selection of real local ales, including one brewed on the premises, and appetising home-cooked food; there is also an upstairs dining area. Driftwood Spars offers 18 bedrooms, all with private facilities, colour television, telephone, and tea-making equipment; some with stunning sea views. Open all day during the holiday season. Please telephone or write for brochure. *See also Colour Advertisement on page 2*

18 BEDROOMS, ALL WITH PRIVATE FACILITIES; FREE HOUSE WITH REAL ALE; HISTORIC INTEREST; CHILDREN WELCOME; BAR AND RESTAURANT MEALS; NEWQUAY 12 MILES, TRURO 8, REDRUTH 7; S££, D££.

CORNISHMAN INN
Tintagel, Cornwall PL34 0DB
Tel: 01840 770238 • Fax: 01840 770078
e-mail: jeremy@cornishmaninn.freeserve.co.uk

A simple but heartwarming pleasure is to sit on the terrace of this traditional wayside hostelry surrounded by blooms that would be the envy of Kew Gardens, enjoying a glass of one's favourite nectar and perhaps, one of the home-made 'specials' from the comprehensive menu. Should the sun not oblige, there are three charismatic bars featuring a proud display of rural bygones. Within easy reach of the mythical home of King Arthur at Tintagel Castle and a romantically rugged coast, the inn has all the attributes of a wonderful holiday base with the coastal footpath, several surfing beaches and facilities for golf and boating near at hand. *ETC* ◆◆◆

10 BEDROOMS, ALL WITH PRIVATE BATHROOM; FREE HOUSE WITH REAL ALE; HISTORIC INTEREST; CHILDREN WELCOME; BAR LUNCHES, RESTAURANT EVENINGS ONLY; NON-SMOKING AREAS; CAMELFORD 4 MILES; S££, D££.

NEW INN
Veryan, Truro, Cornwall TR2 5QA
Tel: 01872 501362 • Fax: 01872 501078

Set in a picturesque village on the Roseland Peninsula, the New Inn is a small granite pub, originally consisting of two cottages and was built in the 16th century. Visitors are welcome to enjoy the atmosphere in our local village bar and we are locally renowned for our good food and cask ales, a wide range of food being served in the bar. Accommodation consists of spacious and comfortable rooms - one single with shared facilities, and one double and one twin en suite. St Austell and Truro are nearby, and we are situated close to the beautiful sandy beaches of Pendower and Carne.

3 BEDROOMS, 2 WITH PRIVATE BATHROOM; REAL ALE; HISTORIC INTEREST; BAR MEALS; MEVAGISSEY 7 MILES.

Cumbria

THREE SHIRES INN
Little Langdale, Ambleside, Cumbria LA22 9NZ
Tel: 015394 37215 • Fax: 015394 37127 • e-mail: ian@threeshiresinn.co.uk
website: www.threeshiresinn.com

The three shires in question are the old counties of Cumberland, Westmorland and Lancashire, and for over a century the inn has provided a welcome resting place for travellers in this most scenic area. True peace and relaxation can be found here, the roar of traffic and the bustle of city and town but a distant memory. However long or short one's stay, the warm welcome accorded to all visitors will ensure lasting memories - and a heartfelt desire to return at the earliest possible opportunity! The prettily furnished bedrooms afford delightful views over the valley, and guests can also relax in their own television lounge and lounge bar. Appetites large and small are amply catered for in the restaurant and public bars, and a wide range of traditional ales, wines and spirits are dispensed with friendly courtesy. *ETC/AA* ★★.

10 BEDROOMS, ALL WITH PRIVATE BATHROOM; FREE HOUSE WITH REAL ALE; HISTORIC INTEREST; CHILDREN WELCOME, PETS IN PUBLIC BAR ONLY; BAR MEALS, RESTAURANT EVENINGS ONLY; NON-SMOKING AREAS; AMBLESIDE 5 MILES; S££, D££.

SAWREY HOTEL
Far Sawrey, Near Ambleside, Cumbria LA22 0LQ
Tel & Fax: 01539 443425

This recommended port of call is interesting for a variety of reasons. It was originally three separate buildings, the central part dating from about 1700. The bar was created out of the old stables and is named after the ghost of a monk who spent his time rescuing fallen women – with disastrous results! The old beams are believed to be from ships wrecked nearby, some possibly from the scattered Armada. One mile from Windermere car ferry and with a vast number of country pursuits to be enjoyed, Sawrey Hotel backs up its inn traditions with excellent cuisine in restaurant and bar and first-class accommodation. *ETC/RAC* ★★. *See also Colour Advertisement on page 3.*

18 BEDROOMS, ALL WITH PRIVATE BATHROOM; FREE HOUSE WITH REAL ALE; HISTORIC INTEREST; CHILDREN AND PETS WELCOME; BAR LUNCHES, RESTAURANT EVENINGS ONLY; NON-SMOKING AREAS; HAWKSHEAD 2 MILES; S££, D££

DRUNKEN DUCK INN
Barngates, Ambleside, Cumbria LA22 0NG
Tel: 015394 36347 • Fax: 015394 36781 • e-mail: info@drunkenduckinn.co.uk
website: www.drunkenduckinn.co.uk

Dating from the 16th century, this unique establishment was known originally as the 'Barngates Inn'. Its present name appears to have been acquired less than a century ago when a barrel on stillage in the cellar slipped its hoops and the contents seeped into the ducks' feeding ditch. Thus was born a name which is as memorable and unusual as the inn itself. Veritably, this is a mellow place with the bars offering a variety of real ales, including the inn's own popular brews, and over 60 whiskies. The restaurant has a relaxed and informal atmosphere. At night the candlelit rooms provide a perfect setting for the excellent, imaginative food and good selection of wines. Set in 60 acres of enchanting Cumbrian scenery and with all the pleasures of Lakeland within easy reach, the Drunken Duck offers splendid accommodation, guest rooms being furnished in traditional style but with such modern conveniences as en suite facilities, colour television and hair dryer. Definitely, delightfully different! *ETC/AA* ◆◆◆◆, *Silver Award*.

11 BEDROOMS, ALL WITH PRIVATE BATHROOM; FREE HOUSE WITH REAL ALE; HISTORIC INTEREST; CHILDREN WELCOME, PETS WELCOME IN PUB ONLY; BAR MEALS, RESTAURANT EVENINGS ONLY; AMBLESIDE 2 MILES; S££££, D£££.

THE QUEEN'S HEAD INN
Askham, Penrith, Cumbria CA10 2PF
Tel & Fax: 01931 712225 • website: www.SmoothHound.co.uk/hotels/thequeen.html

Dating from the 17th century, the Queen's Head retains many of its original features such as a wealth of exposed beams. Situated in the idyllic village of Askham in the heart of the Lake District National Park, it provides a base for fell walking, country pursuits and touring the Lakes. Ullswater and Lowther Castle are close by, as is Haweswater, home to England's only pair of breeding golden eagles. The Queens offers an olde worlde interior with low ceilings, brass and copper memorabilia, open fires, real ales and our own resident ghost. A comprehensive à la carte menu and daily changing specials are served in either the bar areas or the dining room. Recent extensive alterations have provided three comfortable en suite rooms with shower, colour television and tea and coffee making facilities. They are named after the thoughts and efforts that provided them: Faith, Hope and Charity; the Lowther Suite offers a master bedroom, seating area (can be transformed to twin room) and bathroom. *See also Colour Advertisement on page 5*.

3 BEDROOMS, ALL WITH PRIVATE BATHROOM; REAL ALE; BAR AND RESTAURANT MEALS; PENRITH 4 MILES.

THE BLACKSMITH'S ARMS
Talkin Village, Brampton, Cumbria CA8 1LE
Tel: 016977 3452 • Fax: 016977 3394

The Blacksmith's Arms offers all the hospitality and comforts of a traditional country inn. Enjoy tasty meals served in the bar lounges, or linger over dinner in the well-appointed restaurant. The inn is personally managed by the proprietors, Anne and Donald Jackson, who guarantee the hospitality one would expect from a family concern. Guests are assured of a pleasant and comfortable stay. There are five lovely bedrooms, all en suite and offering every comfort. Peacefully situated in the beautiful village of Talkin, the inn is convenient for the Borders, Hadrian's Wall and the Lake District. There is a good golf course, walking and other country pursuits nearby. *See also Colour Advertisement on page 4*.

5 BEDROOMS, ALL WITH PRIVATE BATHROOM; FREE HOUSE; HISTORIC INTEREST; CHILDREN WELCOME; BAR AND RESTAURANT MEALS; NON-SMOKING AREAS; CARLISLE 9 MILES, BRAMPTON 3; S££, D£.

Please mention
Recommended WAYSIDE & COUNTRY INNS
when seeking refreshment or accommodation
at a Hotel mentioned in these pages.

CAVENDISH ARMS
Cartmel, Cumbria LA11 6QA
Tel: 015395 36240 • Fax: 015395 36243 • e-mail: thecavendish@onlineuk.com

Situated near Grange-over-Sands, Cartmel is a charming village based around Cartmel Priory Church, founded in 1188. The town square, complete with 18th century market cross, is surrounded by ivy covered walls, old shops and pubs. The Cavendish is the only inn offering accommodation in the village, part of which dates from the 16th century, and accommodation is provided in seven double bedrooms, one with four-poster bed and all en suite with tea/coffee making facilities and TV. Meals are available in our à la carte restaurant, which is non-smoking, and we have "special menu" nights every three/four weeks. We have a varied menu which offers unusual specials and our Sunday roasts are prepared over a spit. We cater for small parties, and are open Christmas Day for lunch.

7 BEDROOMS, ALL WITH PRIVATE BATHROOM, FREE HOUSE WITH REAL ALE; BAR AND RESTAURANT MEALS; NON SMOKING AREAS; CHILDREN WELCOME; NEWBY BRIDGE 4 MILES.

SUN HOTEL & 16TH CENTURY INN
Coniston, Cumbria LA21 8HQ
Tel: 015394 41248 • Fax: 015394 41219 • e-mail: thesun@hotelconiston.com
website: www.SmoothHound.co.uk/hotels/sun

The Sun is a superbly located 11 bedroom hotel designed to overlook the village and enjoy panoramic mountain views. With a large private garden, patio, comfortable lounge and extensive restaurant menu and wine-list, the hotel offers comfortable en suite accommodation in a peaceful and informal setting. Better still, when built in 1902 it was attached to the end of a 16th century pub! Now a free house with real ales and real fires in a classic Lakeland setting of beamed ceiling, flagged floor and old range, where you can enjoy the best of both worlds right at the heart of South Lakeland. *See also Colour Advertisement on page 4.*

11 BEDROOMS, ALL WITH PRIVATE BATHROOM; FREE HOUSE WITH REAL ALE; CHILDREN AND PETS WELCOME; BAR FOOD, RESTAURANT EVENINGS ONLY; NON-SMOKING AREAS; AMBLESIDE 6 MILES; S£££, D££..

The **£** symbol when appearing at the end of the italic section of an entry shows the anticipated price, during 2001, for full Bed and Breakfast.

Normal Bed & Breakfast rate per person (in single room)

PRICE RANGE	CATEGORY	PRICE RANGE	CATEGORY
Under £25	S£	**Under £25**	D£
£26-£35	S££	**£26-£35**	D££
£36-£45	S£££	**£36-£45**	D£££
Over £45	S££££	**Over £45**	D££££

Normal Bed & Breakfast rate per person (sharing double/twin room)

This is meant as an indication only and does not show prices for Special Breaks, Weekends, etc. Guests are therefore advised to verify all prices on enquiring or booking.

BOWER HOUSE INN
Eskdale, Holmrook, Cumbria CA19 1TD
Tel: 019467 23244 • Fax: 019467 23308 • e-mail: info@bowerhouseinn.freeserve.co.uk
website: www.bowerhouseinn.co.uk

A 17th century inn of considerable character, the Bower House is as popular with the locals as it is with tourists, always a good recommendation for any establishment. Decor and furnishings throughout are tasteful and designed with an eye to comfort as well as style, and all guest rooms have private facilities, colour television and telephone. Cuisine is of a consistently good standard, with fresh produce from nearby farms featuring extensively in skilfully prepared and well presented dishes, and the wine cellar should satisfy the most demanding palate. Mature gardens make a fine setting for this gem of an inn. *ETC/AA* ★★.

24 BEDROOMS, ALL WITH PRIVATE BATHROOM; FREE HOUSE WITH REAL ALE; HISTORIC INTEREST; CHILDREN WELCOME; BAR MEALS, RESTAURANT EVENINGS ONLY; GOSFORTH 6 MILES; £££.

THE BURNMOOR INN
Boot, Eskdale, Cumbria CA19 1TG
Tel: 019467 23224 • Fax: 019467 23337 • e-mail: enquiries@burnmoor.co.uk

Situated in this stunning valley close to amazing walks, including Scafell, Harter and Gable to name but a few. Both you and your hounds can enjoy en suite luxury in one of our nine bedrooms, all with tea and coffee making facilities and comfortable furnishings. We offer good food in both restaurant and bar where you can enjoy one of our real ales (CAMRA Guide) and discuss your next day's assault. Dogs welcome to lie by the fire in the bar. We do not make a charge for well behaved dogs. Special bargain breaks available October to April. Resident Proprietors: Harry and Paddington Berger. *ETC* ◆◆◆

9 BEDROOMS, ALL WITH PRIVATE BATHROOM; FREE HOUSE WITH REAL ALE; HISTORIC INTEREST; CHILDREN AND PETS WELCOME; BAR MEALS, RESTAURANT EVENINGS ONLY; NON-SMOKING AREAS; RAVENGLASS 6 MILES; S££, D££.

Please mention *Recommended Wayside & Country Inns*
when enquiring about accommodation featured in these pages.

QUEEN'S HEAD HOTEL
Main Street, Hawkshead, Cumbria LA22 0NS
Tel: 015394 36271 • Freephone: 0800 137263 • Fax: 015394 36722
e-mail: enquiries@queensheadhotel.co.uk • website: www.queensheadhotel.co.uk

The 16th century Queen's Head, set in the traffic-free village of Hawkshead on the edge of Esthwaite Water, has a wonderful atmosphere, with low oak-beamed ceilings, panelled walls and a warm log fire whenever necessary. The friendly bar and separate dining room are noted for high quality food, with many locally and organically produced ingredients and a comprehensive wine list. Beer is hand-pulled from the wood. The attractive en suite bedrooms, some with four-poster beds, have colour television, tea and coffee making facilities, hairdryer and telephone. The village was the home of Beatrix Potter and is an excellent centre for fishing, bowling, riding, water skiing, cycling and walking. *ETC/AA* ★★ *and Silver Award. See also Colour Advertisement on page 3.*

13 BEDROOMS, ALL WITH PRIVATE BATHROOM; HARTLEYS HOUSE WITH REAL ALE; HISTORIC INTEREST; CHILDREN WELCOME; BAR AND RESTAURANT MEALS; AMBLESIDE 4 MILES; ££.

THE SWAN HOTEL
Thornthwaite, Keswick, Cumbria CA12 5SQ
Tel: 017687 78256 • website: www.swan-hotel-keswick.co.uk

A family-run 17th century former coaching inn set in idyllic surroundings twixt lake and mountains. Here you will experience a true sense of beauty, history and relaxation, cossetted by polite, friendly staff catering to your every need. Enjoy an open fire, lake walks, imaginative home-cooking and real ales. Excellent restaurant and bar food. Winter and spring breaks from 3 nights Thursday to Sunday £65. *ETC* ★★. *See also Colour Advertisement on page 4.*

22 BEDROOMS, ALL WITH PRIVATE BATHROOM; FREE HOUSE; HISTORIC INTEREST; CHILDREN AND PETS WELCOME; BAR MEALS, RESTAURANT EVENINGS ONLY; NON-SMOKING AREAS; KESWICK 3 MILES; S££, D££.

COLEDALE INN
Braithwaite, Near Keswick, Cumbria CA12 5TN
Tel: 017687 78272

A friendly, family-run Victorian Inn in a peaceful hillside position above Braithwaite, and ideally situated for touring and walking, with paths to the mountains immediately outside our gardens. All bedrooms are warm and spacious, with en suite shower room and colour television. Children are welcome, as are pets. Home-cooked meals are served every lunchtime and evening, with a fine selection of inexpensive wines, beers and Coledale XXPS and Yates real cask ale. Open all year except midweek lunches in winter. Tariff and menu sent on request. *ETC* ◆◆◆.

12 BEDROOMS, ALL WITH PRIVATE SHOWER/WC; FREE HOUSE WITH REAL ALE; CHILDREN AND PETS WELCOME; BAR AND RESTAURANT MEALS; NON-SMOKING AREAS; CARLISLE 30 MILES, COCKERMOUTH 10, KESWICK 2; S£, D££.

OUTGATE INN
Outgate, Near Hawkshead, Cumbria LA22 0NQ
Tel: 015394 36413 • Fax: 015394 36171

Situated in the heart of the Lake District, with its craggy fells, peaceful lakes and spectacular scenery which inspired William Wordsworth and Beatrix Potter, this 18th century inn lies between the lakes of Coniston and Windermere. Accommodation is provided in two double and one twin bedded room, all with en suite facilities. Meals are served either in our restaurant or in the bar, and a full English breakfast is available.

3 BEDROOMS, ALL WITH PRIVATE BATHROOM; HAWKSHEAD 1 MILE.

WHITE LION HOTEL
Patterdale, Penrith, Cumbria CA11 0NW
Tel: 01768 482214

This old world country inn with a friendly atmosphere is situated on Lake Ullswater, near Helvellyn, an ideal centre for walking, fishing and sailing. The seven cosy letting bedrooms are mostly en suite with all facilities. Traditional beers and good home-made food are served. Whatever the reason for visiting the White Lion, you will always leave with the memory of a good time. Open all year. *ETC* ◆◆◆.

7 BEDROOMS, ALL WITH PRIVATE BATHROOM; REAL ALES; CHILDREN AND DOGS WELCOME; BAR MEALS; WINDERMERE 12 MILES; S££, D££.

BULL HOTEL
Main Street, Sedbergh, Cumbria LA10 5BL
Tel: 015396 20264 • Fax: 015396 20212 • e-mail: thebull@hotels.activebooking.com
website: www.thebull.activebooking.com

Ideally situated for excursions to both the Lake District and Yorkshire Dales, the Langdale and Winder Bars of this homely and charmingly decorated hotel invariably buzz with convivial conversation, whilst the splendid Baugh Fell Restaurant is an obviously popular rendezvous in the evenings; the straightforward menu is of excellent quality and complemented by a worthy selection of well-chosen wines. With so many lovely walks to be enjoyed in the vicinity, this is a recommended place in which to stay and is within easy access from the M6. The en suite accommodation represents exceptional value for money. Children under 16 sharing their parents' room are subject to certain reductions and special meals for youngsters are served at lunchtime and early evenings. *ETC* ◆◆◆◆.

15 BEDROOMS, ALL WITH PRIVATE BATHROOM; WHITBREADS HOUSE WITH REAL ALE; CHILDREN AND PETS WELCOME; BAR MEALS, RESTAURANT EVENINGS ONLY; NON-SMOKING AREAS; KENDAL 9 MILES; S££, D££.

PLEASE MENTION THIS GUIDE WHEN YOU WRITE
OR PHONE TO ENQUIRE ABOUT ACCOMMODATION.
IF YOU ARE WRITING, A STAMPED,
ADDRESSED ENVELOPE IS ALWAYS APPRECIATED.

FHG PUBLICATIONS

publish a large range of well-known accommodation guides.

We will be happy to send you details or you can use

the order form at the back of this book.

Derbyshire

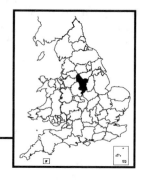

THE DOG AND PARTRIDGE COUNTRY INN
Swinscoe, Ashbourne, Derbyshire DE6 2HS
Tel: 01335 343183 • Fax: 01335 342742

Mary and Martin Stelfox welcome you to a family-run seventeenth century inn and motel set in five acres, five miles from Alton Towers and close to Dovedale and Ashbourne. We specialise in family breaks, and special diets and vegetarians are catered for. All rooms have private bathrooms, colour television, direct-dial telephone, tea-making facilities and baby listening service. It is ideally situated for touring Stoke Potteries, Derbyshire Dales and Staffordshire moorlands. The restaurant is open all day, and non-residents are welcome.Open Christmas and New Year. *ETC* ★★.

29 BEDROOMS, ALL WITH PRIVATE BATHROOM; FREE HOUSE; HISTORIC INTEREST; CHILDREN WELCOME; BAR AND RESTAURANT MEALS; NON-SMOKING AREAS; ASHBOURNE 3 MILES; S££, D££.

THE WALTZING WEASEL
New Mills Road, Birch Vale, High Peak, Derbyshire SK22 1BT
Tel & Fax: 01663 743402 • e-mail: w-weasel@zen.co.uk
website: www.w-weasel.co.uk

There are pub names of infinite variety but this one must take the biscuit for originality. This is, in fact, a dyed-in-the-wool traditional country inn that is without the need of gimmicks to attract lovers of good food and drink. Bang in the heart of the Peak District, the inn possesses a restful ambience induced by subdued lighting, antiques and mullioned windows through which there are fine views of Kinder Scout. Wholesome fare is served in a cosy restaurant and those seeking first rate accommodation in this lovely area have handsome en suite bedrooms at their disposal, all with colour television, direct-dial telephone and tea and coffee making facilities. *AA.*

8 BEDROOMS, ALL WITH PRIVATE BATHROOM; FREE HOUSE WITH REAL ALE; HISTORIC INTEREST; CHILDREN AND PETS WELCOME; BAR MEALS, RESTAURANT EVENINGS ONLY; NON-SMOKING AREAS; HAYFIELD 1 MILE; S££££, D££££.

THE CHARLES COTTON HOTEL
Hartington, Near Buxton, Derbyshire SK17 0AL
Tel: 01298 84229 • Fax: 01298 84301

The Charles Cotton is a small comfortable hotel lying in the heart of the Derbyshire Dales, pleasantly situated in the village square of Hartington, with nearby shops catering for all needs. It is renowned throughout the area for its hospitality and good home cooking. Pets and children are welcome; special diets are catered for. The Charles Cotton makes the perfect centre to relax and enjoy the area, whether walking, cycling, pony trekking, brass rubbing or even hang-gliding. Open Christmas and New Year.

16 BEDROOMS; FREE HOUSE WITH REAL ALE; HISTORIC INTEREST; CHILDREN WELCOME; BAR AND RESTAURANT MEALS; NON-SMOKING AREAS; ASHBOURNE 9 MILES; ££.

Please mention *Recommended Wayside & Country Inns*
when enquiring about accommodation featured in these pages.

THE CASTLE HOTEL
Castle Street, Castleton, Hope Valley, Derbyshire S33 8WG
Tel: 01433 620578 • Fax: 01433 622902 • website: www.peakland.com/thecastle

A delightful blend of 17th century character and 20th century comforts, the Castle is an ideal base for a relaxing break in the heart of the Peak District National Park. This is just how one imagines the perfect English country inn – low beams, cheerful log fires, friendly conversation and good ales – and the management and staff take great pride in upholding the noble traditions of English hospitality. Food is good and plentiful, and can be enjoyed all day every day. Should accommodation be required, a choice of delightfully furnished bedrooms is available, each en suite and with a full range of amenities. This splendid establishment is within convenient reach of many sporting activities and places of interest. Our vision: to be consistently consistent in our excellent guest care and our passion for fantastic food. *AA* ★★★.

9 BEDROOMS, ALL WITH PRIVATE BATHROOM; REAL ALE; HISTORIC INTEREST; CHILDREN AND PETS WELCOME; BAR AND RESTAURANT MEALS; NON-SMOKING AREAS; SHEFFIELD 16 MILES; S£££, D£.

THE MANIFOLD INN
Hulme End, Hartington, Derbyshire SK17 0EX
Tel: 01298 84537

The Manifold Inn is a 200-year-old coaching inn now owned by Frank and Bridgette Lipp. It offers warm hospitality and good pub food at sensible prices. This lovely mellow stone inn nestles on the banks of the River Manifold opposite the old toll house that used to serve the turnpike and river ford. All guest accommodation is in the old stone blacksmith's shop in the secluded rear courtyard of the inn. The bedrooms have en suite showers, colour television, tea/coffee making facilities and telephone. *ETC* ◆◆◆

5 BEDROOMS, ALL WITH PRIVATE SHOWER/TOILET; FREE HOUSE WITH REAL ALE; BAR MEALS AND DINING ROOM; NON-SMOKING AREAS; BUXTON 10 MILES, ASHBOURNE 10, BAKEWELL 10, LEEK 8; S££, D££.

POACHERS ARMS HOTEL
Castleton Road, Hope, Derbyshire S33 6SB
Tel: 01433 620380 • Fax: 01433 621915 • e-mail: reservations@poachers.co.uk
website: www.poachers-arms.com

Conveniently placed for all types of countryside recreation, this little inn-cum-hotel is worth a visit for the excellent food and well-kept real ales alone, although discerning holidaymakers have already discovered the full worth of the accommodation offered. Under the personal supervision of hosts, Philip and Linda Wood, comforts abound, guest rooms having private bath/shower, colour television, radio and tea and coffee-making facilities amongst their excellent appointments. Set in the heart of the Peak District, this is an ideal base for exploring the many places of interest and attractions in the surrounding area. *ETC* ◆◆◆

6 BEDROOMS, ALL WITH PRIVATE BATHROOM; FREE HOUSE WITH REAL ALE; CHILDREN AND PETS WELCOME; BAR AND RESTAURANT MEALS; NON-SMOKING AREAS; HATHERSAGE 4 MILES; S£££, D££.

The beautiful 200' spire of the Church of St Oswold at Ashbourne, Derbyshire

Devon

THE TORS
Belstone, Near Okehampton, Devon EX20 1QZ
Tel: 01837 840689

The Tors is a village pub in the true English tradition - good beer, good food, plus a warm welcome. It is also 1000 feet up on Dartmoor, at the heart of the village of the Belstone, making it an ideal port of call for walkers, riders, or anyone exploring the moor by car. The menu reflects the traditional atmosphere - good platefuls of the best of English food, evening grills using local meat are a speciality. Dogs and well behaved children are welcome, but please leave your muddy boots and waterproofs in the porch! Bed and Breakfast available. *CAMRA Recommended. AA Listed.*

2 BEDROOMS, BOTH WITH PRIVATE BATHROOM; FREE HOUSE WITH REAL ALE; CHILDREN AND PETS WELCOME; BAR MEALS, RESTAURANT EVENINGS ONLY; NON-SMOKING AREAS; OKEHAMPTON 2 MILES; S£, D£.

THE PALK ARMS INN
Hennock, Bovey Tracey, Devon TQ13 9QS
Tel: 01626 836584

The Palk Arms is a traditional country pub with log fires, real ales, darts, bar billiards and other pub games; village shop and post office downstairs. Bar meals are available during the week, and the restaurant (22 covers) is open from Friday night to Sunday night (bookings preferred) and enjoys seven-mile views across the Teign Valley to Exeter Racecourse and Haldon Hill. There are three bedrooms (one with four-poster) and a residents' sitting room, and the inn is ideal for weekend breaks and short stays. The Palk Arms is situated inside Dartmoor National Park (guided tours available) ,with fishing on three 70-acre lakes a mile away and also birdwatching and walks. Fishing licences and equipment are available in the shop. Newton Abbot races three miles, nearest beach at Teignmouth (seven miles). We welcome pets and smokers.

3 BEDROOMS; FREE HOUSE WITH REAL ALE; HISTORIC INTEREST; CHILDREN AND PETS WELCOME; BAR MEALS, RESTAURANT WEEKENDS ONLY; NON-SMOKING AREAS; EXETER 13 MILES, TORQUAY 8; S£, D££.

THE POACHER'S POCKET
Redball, Burlescombe, Near Tiverton, Devon EX16 7JY
Tel: 01823 672286

Retaining all the character of yesteryear, this tidy little hostelry dates from the 17th century. Whether your visit be long and lingering or short and sweet, you may be sure of a warm welcome from hosts, Graeme and Gillian Yeo, aided in practical terms by a real log fire in the bar. A delicious variety of home-cooked meals are served daily, and can be enjoyed either in the restaurant, or, more informally, in the lounge bar. Direct on the A38 between Junctions 26 and 27 of the M5 and within easy reach of Exmoor and several areas of outstanding beauty, this former coaching inn provides excellent accommodation at very reasonable rates in double, twin or family rooms.

8 BEDROOMS, ALL WITH PRIVATE BATHROOM; FREE HOUSE WITH REAL ALE; HISTORIC INTEREST; CHILDREN WELCOME; BAR MEALS, RESTAURANT EVENINGS ONLY; NON-SMOKING AREAS; TIVERTON 10 MILES; S££, D£.

THE NEW INN
High Street, Clovelly, Near Bideford, Devon EX39 5TQ
Tel: 01237 431303 • Fax: 01237 431636

This unspoilt heritage village is filled with colourful flower-strewn cottages that seem to tumble over one another down the steep and narrow cobbled street which descends towards the tiny harbour. To stay at the New Inn in the heart of the village is to wake up to the sights and sounds of a seafaring way of life that has changed little over the last hundred years. Each of the hotel bedrooms is beautifully decorated. The magic touch of a talented interior designer is to be seen everywhere. The restaurant serves local and regional specialities. This really is a short break paradise. *ETC* ★★.

8 BEDROOMS, ALL WITH PRIVATE SHOWER/BATH; REAL ALE; HISTORIC INTEREST; CHILDREN WELCOME; BAR AND RESTAURANT MEALS; BARNSTAPLE 19 MILES; S£££, D£££.

The **£** symbol when appearing at the end of the italic section of an entry shows the anticipated price, during 2001, for full Bed and Breakfast.

Normal Bed & Breakfast rate per person (in single room)		Normal Bed & Breakfast rate per person (sharing double/twin room)	
PRICE RANGE	CATEGORY	PRICE RANGE	CATEGORY
Under £25	S£	**Under £25**	D£
£26-£35	S££	**£26-£35**	D££
£36-£45	S£££	**£36-£45**	D£££
Over £45	S££££	**Over £45**	D££££

This is meant as an indication only and does not show prices for Special Breaks, Weekends, etc. Guests are therefore advised to verify all prices on enquiring or booking.

HOOPS INN
Horns Cross, Near Clovelly, Bideford, Devon EX39 5DL
Tel: 01237 451222 • Fax: 01237 451247 • e-mail: sales@hoopsinn.co.uk
website: www.hoopsinn.co.uk

This lovingly cared for, picturebook, thatched country inn blends 13th century charm with 20th century luxury and extends a warm welcome to its guests. Relax by one of the open log fires to soak up the olde worlde atmosphere while enjoying a real ale or wine before dining on the best of local fish, game or meat, including house favourites: seafood platters, half shoulder of lamb in onion gravy, crackly pork, or traditional steak and kidney pudding. All bedrooms are en suite, individually furnished and well appointed. The superior rooms under the old thatch have romantic antique canopy beds. Special golfing breaks available. The Hoops is a splendid base for a combined sea, country or touring holiday, with opportunities for walking, cycling, fishing, golf, together with historic gardens, houses, and the world-famous fishing village of Clovelly on the doorstep, and Dartmoor and Exmoor within easy reach. *RAC ★★ and Merit Award, Restaurant 3 Ribbons, Which? Good Pub Guide, CAMRA.*

12 BEDROOMS, ALL WITH PRIVATE BATHROOM; REAL ALES; HISTORIC INTEREST; RESTAURANT MEALS; NON-SMOKING AREAS; BIDEFORD 5 MILES.

EXMOOR SANDPIPER INN
Countisbury, Near Lynmouth, Devon EX35 6NE
Tel: 01598 741263 • Fax: 01598 741358 • e-mail: exmoorsandpiper@demon.co.uk

This fine old coaching inn, reputedly dating in part from the 13th and 15th centuries, lies in a beautiful setting amidst rolling moors, high above Lynmouth on the coastal road with the dramatic backdrop of Exmoor. Bedrooms are designed for your every comfort, with tea-making, colour television and bathroom en suite. After a traditional English breakfast, discover the magic of Exmoor by car or on foot, along Doone Valley following the river to the majestic Watersmeet, or further to the Valley of Rocks and beyond to the Devon/Somerset borders. Delicious five-course dinners include smoked salmon, seafood platters with lobster, steaks and a delicious selection of sweets. Brochure on request. *ETC/RAC ★★*

16 BEDROOMS, ALL WITH PRIVATE BATHROOM; FREE HOUSE WITH REAL ALE; HISTORIC INTEREST; CHILDREN AND PETS WELCOME; BAR AND RESTAURANT MEALS; NON-SMOKING AREAS; LYNTON 2 MILES; ££££.

THE COTT INN
Dartington, Totnes, Devon TQ9 6HE
Tel: 01803 863777 • Fax: 01803 866629

This rambling thatched inn is one of the oldest in the country (AD 1320), and is certainly one of the most beautiful. A free house, the inn is on the Buckfastleigh to Totnes road and travellers will find ample room to park their cars and relax for a while in an atmosphere of timeless charm. The cottage-style bedrooms are spotless, and in addition to bed and breakfast, special terms are offered for short breaks. A superb hot and cold buffet table offers excellent refreshment at lunchtime, and during the evening there is an à la carte menu presenting home-cooked dishes using local produce.

5 BEDROOMS, ALL WITH PRIVATE BATHROOM; FREE HOUSE WITH REAL ALE; HISTORIC INTEREST; WELL-BEHAVED CHILDREN AND PETS WELCOME; BAR LUNCHES, RESTAURANT EVENINGS ONLY; NON-SMOKING AREAS; TOTNES 2 MILES; S££££, D££.

THE ROYAL OAK INN
Dunsford, Near Exeter, Devon EX6 7DA
Tel: 01647 252256

Enjoy a friendly welcome in our traditional Country Pub in the picturesque thatched village of Dunsford. Quiet en suite bedrooms are available in the tastefully converted cob barn. An ideal base for touring Dartmoor, Exeter and the coast, and the beautiful Teign Valley. Real ale and home-made meals are served. Well behaved children and dogs are welcome. Please ring Mark or Judy Harrison for further details. *Tourist Board Listed Approved, CAMRA, Good Pub Guide.*

8 BEDROOMS, 5 WITH PRIVATE BATHROOM; FREE HOUSE WITH REAL ALE; CHILDREN WELCOME; BAR FOOD; EXETER 6 MILES, MORETONHAMPSTEAD 4; £.

BRIDGE INN
Bridge Street, Hatherleigh, Devon EX20 3JA
Tel: 01837 810947 • Fax: 01837 810614 • e-mail: thebridgeinn@writme.com
website: www.bridge.great-pubs.com

An unspoiled country market town of true Devonian character, Hatherleigh is worth a place on any touring itinerary of the area. Not least of its attractions is this charming 16th century inn on the banks of the River Lew. Cosy overnight accommodation is available at most reasonable rates and the friendly proprietors extend a warm welcome to visitors of all ages. The inn has a beer garden and a skittle alley and is especially noteworthy for its high standard of home cooking; the à la carte menu will surprise and delight diners. Good bar snacks are available in the attractive stone-faced bar.

6 BEDROOMS, ALL WITH PRIVATE BATHROOM; FREE HOUSE WITH REAL ALE; HISTORIC INTEREST; CHILDREN AND PETS WELCOME; BAR AND RESTAURANT MEALS LUNCHTIMES WEEKDAYS, ALL DAY WEEKENDS; OKEHAMPTON 7 MILES; S££, D£.

THE FOREST INN
Hexworthy, Dartmoor, Devon PL20 6SD
Tel: 01364 631211 • Fax: 01364 631515

A haven for walkers, riders, fishermen, canoeists, or anyone just looking for an opportunity to enjoy the natural beauty of Dartmoor. The restaurant specialises in home-cooked foods using local produce wherever possible. As an alternative, there is an extensive range of snacks which can be enjoyed in the more informal setting of the Huccaby Room. With the emphasis on Devon beers and cider, you have the opportunity to quench your thirst after the efforts of the day with a drink in the bar or relaxing on the chesterfields in the lounge area, which is complete with a log fire for winter evenings. Short breaks available. *ETC* ◆◆◆, *Good Beer Guide.*

10 BEDROOMS, ALL EN SUITE OR WITH PRIVATE BATHROOM; FREE HOUSE WITH REAL ALE; HISTORIC INTEREST; CHILDREN AND PETS WELCOME; BAR MEALS, RESTAURANT EVENINGS ONLY; NON-SMOKING AREAS; ASHBURTON 7 MILES; S££, D££.

Please mention *Recommended Wayside & Country Inns*
when enquiring about accommodation featured in these pages.

MILDMAY COLOURS INN
Holbeton, Plymouth, Devon PL8 1NA
Tel: 01752 830248 • Fax: 01752 830432 • website: www.mildmay-colours.co.uk

A magnet for real ale buffs and racing enthusiasts, this old inn was built in 1617 and is set in a beautiful village near superb beaches and with Dartmoor and the fine city of Plymouth within easy reach. Golf, fishing, horse riding, sailing and walking the Devon Coastal Path are local activities to be enjoyed. Renamed in memory of the steeplechasing legend, the late Anthony Mildmay, it offers a choice of locally brewed beers. There is a large bar with an extensive menu, and a popular à la carte restaurant known for its delicious home cooking. Excellent en suite accommodation is available in tastefully decorated bedrooms. *ETC* ★★★

8 BEDROOMS, ALL WITH PRIVATE BATHROOM; FREE HOUSE WITH REAL ALE; HISTORIC INTEREST; CHILDREN AND PETS WELCOME; BAR MEALS, RESTAURANT SATURDAY EVENINGS AND SUNDAY LUNCHTIMES; NON-SMOKING AREAS; YEALMPTON 3 MILES; S££, D£.

THE SPORTSMAN'S INN AND RESTAURANT
Exeter Road, Ivybridge, Devon PL21 0BQ
Tel: 01752 892280 • Fax: 01752 690714

The South Hams of Devon is a holiday playground 'par excellence' with a vast variety of pleasures to enjoy – zoos, wild life parks, places of historic interest, steam trains and numerous golf courses to say nothing of the lure of Dartmoor and the Torbay resorts. There is no better place to seek first-class refreshment and accommodation than this enlightened hostelry, situated on the fringe of Dartmoor and midway between Exeter and Cornwall. Resident owners, Doh and Bill Hibbert, have created a widely acclaimed reputation here for their first-rate cuisine which covers a mouthwatering selection of starters, fish dishes and grills. The ideal touring base, the 'Sportsman's' boasts superbly equipped guest rooms. *AA/RAC* ★★, *Les Routiers.*

18 BEDROOMS, ALL WITH PRIVATE BATHROOM; FREE HOUSE WITH REAL ALE; CHILDREN WELCOME, PETS IN BAR ONLY; BAR AND RESTAURANT MEALS; NON-SMOKING AREAS; PLYMOUTH 10 MILES; S£££, D££.

RISING SUN HOTEL
Harbourside, Lynmouth, Devon EX35 6EQ
Tel: 01598 753223 • Fax: 01598 753480
website: www.risingsunlynmouth.co.uk

This fourteenth century smugglers' inn overlooking the harbour and river is steeped in history, with oak panelling, crooked ceilings, thick walls, and uneven oak floors. All the bedrooms have recently been refurbished to a very high standard. The excellent restaurant specialises in local game and seafood. It is claimed that R.D. Blackmore wrote part of his novel Lorna Doone whilst staying at The Rising Sun. The poet Shelley spent his honeymoon in 1812 in a cottage, now named after him, which is part of the hotel. It has a four-poster bed and a comfortable sitting room, and is ideal for a special holiday occasion. Guests can relax in the beautifully landscaped garden and free fishing is available on the hotel's private stretch of salmon river. *AA* ★★ *and Two Rosettes for Food, Johansens "Inn of the Year 1991", Egon Ronay, Les Routiers Casserole Award, Which? Good Hotel Guide Recommended, Good Pub Guide.*

16 BEDROOMS, ALL WITH EN SUITE SHOWER/BATHROOM; FREE HOUSE; HISTORIC INTEREST;
BAR AND RESTAURANT MEALS; NON-SMOKING AREAS; BARNSTAPLE 20 MILES, MINEHEAD 17; S££££, D££££.

BLACKCOCK INN
Molland, South Molton, Devon EX36 3NW
Tel & Fax: 01769 550297 • e-mail: blackcockinn@tinyworld.co.uk

On the southern fringe of Exmoor and romantically remote, this homely, stone-built inn, set in a picturesque valley, extends a real Devon welcome to families. Excellent real ales and home-cooked bar and restaurant meals are served seven days a week. Children are welcome and there is a beer garden, an indoor heated swimming pool and a family and games room; free live entertainment is provided on Saturday evenings. Accommodation is provided in delightfully equipped cottages situated just behind the pub where there is a caravan and camping site. An idyllic retreat with coarse fishing available nearby.

4 BEDROOMS, ALL WITH PRIVATE BATHROOM; FREE HOUSE WITH REAL ALE; HISTORIC INTEREST; CHILDREN AND PETS
WELCOME; BAR AND RESTAURANT MEALS; NON-SMOKING AREAS; SOUTH MOLTON 6 MILES; S££, D£££.

THE SMUGGLERS
North Morte Road, Mortehoe, North Devon EX34 7DR
Tel & Fax: 01271 870891

Situated in the pretty village of Mortehoe The Smugglers offers luxury accommodation from twin rooms to family suites; all our rooms are en suite. We offer home-cooked meals and full English breakfasts. Licensed bar with beer garden. Satellite TV. Well trained pets welcome. *See also Colour Advertisement on page 5.*

7 BEDROOMS, ALL WITH PRIVATE BATHROOM; FREE HOUSE WITH REAL ALE; HISTORIC INTEREST; CHILDREN AND PETS WELCOME; BAR AND RESTAURANT MEALS; NON-SMOKING AREAS; ILFRACOMBE 4 MILES; S££, D£££.

ROCK INN AT HAYTOR
Haytor Vale, Newton Abbot, Devon TQ13 9XP
Tel: 01364 661305 • Fax: 01364 661242 • e-mail: inn@rock-inn.co.uk
website: www.rock-inn.co.uk

In a sheltered and secluded setting on the fringe of Dartmoor, this charming, 18th century coaching inn has a friendly welcome for all and is recommended for its excellent accommodation and refreshment. Who would "o'er the moors so free"? Above rises Haytor Rock, 1490 feet above sea level and beyond lie Dartmoor's heathy slopes and wooded valleys teeming with wildlife. Free fresh air promotes hearty appetites that the splendid Rock Inn is well qualified to cater for, the imaginative and varied, chef-inspired dishes temptingly presented. With brasswork, oak furniture and log fires, the bars are full of character; invariably they buzz with convivial conversation and on fine days one may enjoy a glass of one's fancy outside and take in the panorama of a verdant, rolling countryside. Guest rooms are delightfully furnished; all have en suite facilities, colour television with satellite channel, in-house video, radio, direct-dial telephone, mini-bar and tea and coffee-makers. Special weekend and seasonal breaks are organised. There are numerous sporting and leisure opportunities in the area quite apart from walking the moors. These include horse riding, river fishing, especially for Dart salmon, and golf, whilst the south coast resorts with all their attractions are within easy reach. *AA* ★★

9 BEDROOMS, ALL WITH PRIVATE BATHROOM; FREE HOUSE WITH REAL ALE; HISTORIC INTEREST; CHILDREN WELCOME; BAR AND RESTAURANT MEALS; NON-SMOKING AREAS; TORQUAY 9 MILES; S££££, D££.

KING'S ARMS INN
Tedburn St Mary, Near Exeter, Devon EX6 6EG
Tel: 01647 61224 • Fax: 01647 61324 • e-mail: reception@kingsarmsinn.co.uk
website: www.kingsarmsinn.co.uk

Just off the A30 and well placed for close acquaintance with the myriad pleasures of Devon's homely towns and incomparable countryside and with Exeter and the south coast not far distant, this historic and visually appealing hostelry dates back to the early 17th century. Originally known as the 'Taphouse Inn', it is said that King Charles II and his entourage stayed here whilst journeying to Cornwall in the mid-1600's and in recognition of his patronage, the King granted permission for the inn's name to be changed and accordingly to display his coat of arms. A right royal welcome is still extended to visitors with initiative enough to divert from the busy A30 to enjoy good food, drink and, if need be, accommodation in a typical Devon pub. *ETC* ★★★, *AA, RAC, Ashley Courtenay.*

8 BEDROOMS, 2 WITH PRIVATE BATHROOM; FREE HOUSE WITH REAL ALE; HISTORIC INTEREST; CHILDREN WELCOME, GUIDE DOGS ONLY; BAR AND RESTAURANT MEALS; NON-SMOKING AREAS; EXETER 7 MILES; S£/££, D£/££.

Dorset

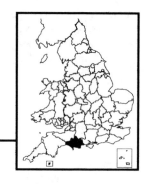

ANVIL HOTEL & INN
Salisbury Road, Pimperne, Blandford, Dorset DT11 8UQ
Tel: 01258 453431 • Tel and Fax: 01258 480182

A long, low thatched building set in a tiny village deep in the Dorset countryside two miles from Blandford – what could be more English? And that is exactly what visitors to the Anvil will find – a typical old English hostelry dating from the sixteenth century, set in an English country garden and offering good old-fashioned English hospitality. A mouth watering menu with delicious desserts is available in the charming beamed restaurant with log fire, or in the attractive fully licensed bar. All bedrooms have private facilities, direct dial telephones and Teasmaids. Ample parking. *ETC* ★★, *Good Food Pub Guide, Les Routiers Silver Key Award, Housekeeping Casserole Award.*

11 BEDROOMS, ALL WITH PRIVATE BATHROOM; FREE HOUSE; HISTORIC INTEREST; CHILDREN AND PETS WELCOME; BAR AND RESTAURANT MEALS; NON-SMOKING AREAS; BOURNEMOUTH 26 MILES, SALISBURY 24, POOLE 16; D£££.

THE POACHERS INN
Piddletrenthide, Dorchester, Dorset DT2 7QX
Tel: 01300 348358 • Fax: 01300 348153 • website: www.thepoachersinn.co.uk

This delightful Country Inn is set in the heart of the lovely Piddle Valley, within easy reach of all Dorset's attractions. All rooms are en suite and have colour television, tea/coffee making facilities and telephone. For relaxation there is an outdoor swimming pool and a riverside garden. Half board guests choose from our à la carte menu at no extra cost. Brochure with full details on request. *ETC/AA* ◆◆◆. *See also Colour Advertisement on page 5.*

18 BEDROOMS, ALL WITH PRIVATE FACILITIES; CHILDREN AND PETS WELCOME; NON-SMOKING AREAS; DORCHESTER 8 MILES; S££, D££.

KING'S ARMS INN
East Stour Common, Near Gillingham, Dorset SP8 5NB
Tel: 01747 838325

This lovely old inn nestling in the lush beauty of the Blackmore Vale is of direct appeal to country lovers seeking rest and relaxation. Its situation just west of Shaftesbury (Hardy's "Shaston") is near perfect and the welcome from the Langton family heartwarming. There are fine views all around and one may explore a pastoral landscape on foot or horseback amidst a maze of small roads, footpaths and bridleways; fishing and clay pigeon shooting may also be enjoyed locally. An excellent centre from which to visit the Dorset coast, Longleat, Cheddar, Stonehenge and numerous other places of interest, the 'Kings Arms' offers splendid en suite accommodation with everything one needs for a rejuvenating break. *ETC* ◆◆◆, *AA.*

3 BEDROOMS, ALL WITH PRIVATE BATHROOM; FREE HOUSE WITH REAL ALE; CHILDREN WELCOME, PETS ALLOWED IN BAR; BAR LUNCHES AND RESTAURANT MEALS; NON-SMOKING AREAS; GILLINGHAM 2 MILES; S££, D£££.

Please mention *Recommended Wayside & Country Inns*
when enquiring about accommodation featured in these pages.

THE SCOTT ARMS
Kingston, Corfe Castle, Dorset BH20 5LW
Tel: 01929 480270 • Fax: 01929 481570

Situated on the Isle of Purbeck, close to the Dorset Coastal Path, the Scott Arms is a traditional 18th century inn with a character all of its own. With exposed oak beams, open fireplaces, friendly atmosphere and a truly breathtaking view of Corfe Castle from our beer garden, it is easy to see why this inn has been popular for many years. We offer a superb menu every lunchtime and evening featuring our extensive specials board. To complement the food we have a selection of well-kept traditional ales, lagers, fine wines and spirits. Country inn accommodation is available at reasonable rates, with all the amenities you would expect, including en suite facilities, tea/coffee making, hairdryer, colour television, and, of course, our full English breakfast. For that added hint of luxury, our bedrooms have four-poster beds.

2 BEDROOMS, BOTH WITH PRIVATE BATHROOM; SCOTTISH & NEWCASTLE HOUSE WITH REAL ALE; HISTORIC INTEREST; CHILDREN WELCOME; BAR AND RESTAURANT MEALS; NON-SMOKING AREAS; SWANAGE 5 MILES; S££££, D££££.

MILL HOUSE HOTEL
Lulworth Cove, West Lulworth, Dorset BH20 5RQ
Tel: 01929 400404 • Fax: 01929 400508 • e-mail: dukepayne@aol.com

The Mill House Hotel is situated within the heart of Lulworth Cove overlooking the Mill Pond and only a short walk from the sea. It provides a convenient location for guests to explore this part of Dorset which is a designated Area of Outstanding Natural Beauty. There are nine en suite bedrooms (double, twin and family), all tastefully furnished in country house style, with direct-dial telephone, radio, colour television and hospitality tray. The residents' lounge offers magnificent sea views over Lulworth Cove and the surrounding countryside, while the Mill House Bar has a cosy atmosphere and a door leading into the garden. Jenny Hen's Tearoom provides a full range of meals and snacks during the day. Local attractions include Corfe Castle, Bovington Army Tank Museum and the resorts of Poole, Swanage and Weymouth.

9 BEDROOMS, ALL WITH PRIVATE BATHROOM; CHILDREN WELCOME; WAREHAM 10 MILES; ££

The **£** symbol when appearing at the end of the italic section of an entry shows the anticipated price, during 2001, for full Bed and Breakfast.

Normal Bed & Breakfast rate per person (in single room)		Normal Bed & Breakfast rate per person (sharing double/twin room)	
PRICE RANGE	CATEGORY	PRICE RANGE	CATEGORY
Under £25	S£	**Under £25**	D£
£26-£35	S££	**£26-£35**	D££
£36-£45	S£££	**£36-£45**	D£££
Over £45	S££££	**Over £45**	D££££

This is meant as an indication only and does not show prices for Special Breaks, Weekends, etc. Guests are therefore advised to verify all prices on enquiring or booking.

THE LANGTON ARMS

Tarrant Monkton, Near Blandford Forum, Dorset DT11 8RX
Tel: 01258 830225 • Fax: 01258 830053 • e-mail : info@thelangtonarms.co.uk
website: www.thelangtonarms.co.uk

This charming 17th century thatched inn stands peacefully and picturesquely close to the village church, a scene that has changed little over the years. Conforming to most people's concept of the typical English country hostelry, The Langton Arms perpetuates the compelling vision in its friendly bars where there is a choice of real ales and home-made light meals. A Bistro Restaurant situated in a converted stable serves an interesting selection of dishes from Wednesdays to Saturday evenings at reasonable prices. This is a delightful part of 'dreamy Dorset' ideal for gentle exploration. Several guest rooms ranged round an attractive courtyard await those wishing to tarry awhile. Each has its own entrance, en suite bathroom, colour television and beverage-maker. *AA QQQ.*

6 BEDROOMS, ALL WITH PRIVATE BATHROOM; FREE HOUSE WITH REAL ALE; HISTORIC INTEREST; CHILDREN AND PETS WELCOME; BAR AND RESTAURANT MEALS; NON-SMOKING AREAS; BLANDFORD FORUM 4 MILES; S£££££, D££.

The rural charm of Pamphill, Dorset

Durham

SWALLOW EDEN ARMS HOTEL
Rushyford, Co. Durham DL17 0LL
Tel: 01388 720541 • Fax: 01388 721871 • e-mail: info@swallowhotels.com
website: www.swallowhotels.com

Originally a 17th century coaching inn called the 'Wheatsheaf' when the advent of the Darlington to Newcastle railway line reduced its requirement, the building was purchased by the Eden family who converted it into a fine manor house. Change begets change; today, features so endearing to the image of a favourite inn – traditional styling and period furniture – characterise a warm and welcoming hotel renowned for the superb, award-winning food served in the Lord Eldon Restaurant, magnificently appointed accommodation and fabulous Leisure Club. Surrounded by lovely countryside, the hotel achieves the highest marks for comfort: each bedroom has a private bathroom, satellite television, direct-dial telephone, ironing facilities, hairdryer and tea and coffee-makers. This is a wonderful place for family parties and children. Never a dull moment manifests itself here with leisure amenities including a heated, indoor swimming pool, sauna, spa bath, fitness room, solarium, plunge pool, impulse shower, bar and cocktail lounge. There are many places of natural interest within easy reach, among them the Hamsterley Forest, Teesdale, Weardale, the North York Moors and with Cleveland's Heritage Coast on the doorstep. For the historian, delightful Durham City is within half-an-hour's drive and there is a fascinating open-air museum at Beamish, where time stands still. A real 'Garden of Eden'! *ETC* ★★★, *AA Rosette*.

45 BEDROOMS, ALL WITH PRIVATE BATHROOM; WHITBREAD HOUSE; CHILDREN WELCOME; BAR MEALS, RESTAURANT EVENINGS ONLY; NON-SMOKING AREAS; DURHAM 10 MILES; S£££££, D£££££.

The £ symbol when appearing at the end of the italic section of an entry shows the anticipated price, during 2001, for full Bed and Breakfast.

Normal Bed & Breakfast rate per person (in single room)		Normal Bed & Breakfast rate per person (sharing double/twin room)	
PRICE RANGE	CATEGORY	PRICE RANGE	CATEGORY
Under £25	S£	**Under £25**	D£
£26-£35	S££	**£26-£35**	D££
£36-£45	S£££	**£36-£45**	D£££
Over £45	S££££	**Over £45**	D££££

This is meant as an indication only and does not show prices for Special Breaks, Weekends, etc. Guests are therefore advised to verify all prices on enquiring or booking.

Essex

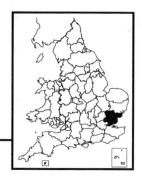

THE PELDON ROSE INN
Mersea Road, Colchester, Essex CO5 7QJ
Tel: 01206 735248 • Fax: 01206 735055 • e-mail: thepeldonroseinn@aol.com
website: www.colchester-essex.com

One's lasting memory of this attractive, pink-washed pub is usually the friendly welcome one has received, for whether calling in for a meal or a drink, every effort is made to ensure that all one's requirements are cheerfully and efficiently catered for. Single and double rooms are available, and are equipped with television and coffee making facilities. Throughout the week top quality home-cooked fare is supplied lunchtime and evenings in the beamed bar, the dining room, and during the warmer months, the large conservatory and gardens which overlook the pond which is reputed to be over 1000 years old.

3 BEDROOMS; FREE HOUSE WITH REAL ALE, HISTORIC INTEREST; CHILDREN WELCOME; BAR AND RESTAURANT MEALS; NON-SMOKING AREAS; COLCHESTER 5 MILES; S££, D£.

Gloucestershire

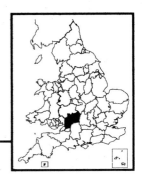

THE OLD NEW INN
Bourton-on-the-Water, Gloucestershire GL54 2AF
Tel: 01451 820467 • Fax: 01451 810236 • e-mail: old_new_inn@compuserve.com

Dating from the early 18th century, this traditional country inn is situated in the heart of the Cotswolds and is an ideal centre for a country holiday – golf, fly or coarse fishing, and horse riding can all be arranged nearby. All rooms are en suite, and all have television and tea/coffee making facilities. There is also a comfortable residents' lounge, and three bars where guests can enjoy a drink and a chat. A comprehensive table d'hôte menu is served each evening and light lunches and bar meals are available daily; packed lunches can be provided if required. An interesting feature is the model village at the rear of the inn, a one-ninth size replica of the actual village, built by local men in 1937. *ETC/AA* ★★.

12 BEDROOMS, ALL WITH PRIVATE BATHROOM; BASS HOUSE WITH REAL ALE; HISTORIC INTEREST; CHILDREN WELCOME; BAR AND RESTAURANT MEALS; NON-SMOKING AREA; STOW-ON-THE-WOLD 4 MILES; S£££, D£££.

WILD DUCK INN
Drakes Island, Ewen, Near Cirencester, Gloucestershire GL7 6BY
Tel: 01285 770310 • e-mail: wduckinn@aol.com

Nestling in delightful, unspoilt Gloucestershire countryside, this is an old inn of outstanding character, with original beams and inglenook open fires giving a traditional atmosphere of warmth and friendliness. Food is of the highest quality, with an extensive menu operating at lunchtime and in the evenings. Bar lunches are also available. Three bedrooms have four-posters and overlook the delightful, award-winning garden. All ten rooms have private bath en suite, colour television, tea/coffee making facilities and telephone, making this a desirable overnight or weekly holiday base, in addition to being an enchanting place to quench one's thirst. Access, Visa, Amex accepted. *RAC* ★★★, *AA Rosette, Les Routiers, Egon Ronay.* **See also Inside Back Cover.**

10 DOUBLE BEDROOMS, ALL WITH PRIVATE BATHROOM; HISTORIC INTEREST; FREE HOUSE WITH REAL ALE; BAR AND RESTAURANT MEALS; CHIPPENHAM 18 MILES, CHELTENHAM 16, SWINDON 16, TETBURY 9, CIRENCESTER 3, KEMBLE STATION 1; D£££.

LAMB INN
Great Rissington, Cheltenham, Gloucestershire GL54 2LP
Tel: 01451 820388 • Fax: 01451 820724

Overlooking the picturesque Windrush Valley and in the peaceful heart of the Cotswolds, this comfortable and cosy inn is a welcoming sight. Within you will find a friendly welcome from hosts, Paul and Jacqueline Gabriel, backed up by excellent food, traditional ales and wines from around the world. The bar food is home-made and includes delicious soups, sandwiches and pies whilst a wider choice may be enjoyed in a separate dining room. Parts of the inn are up to 300 years old and bedrooms, individually designed to reflect their character, are decorated in pretty, chintzy style. Among six lovely suites, all with en suite facilities, colour television and tea and coffee-makers, is one with a king-size bed and another with a four-poster.

14 BEDROOMS, ALL WITH PRIVATE BATHROOM; FREE HOUSE WITH REAL ALE; HISTORIC INTEREST; CHILDREN AND PETS WELCOME; BAR AND RESTAURANT MEALS; NON-SMOKING AREAS; GLOUCESTER 8 MILES; S££/£££, D££.

THE RAGGED COT INN
Cirencester Road, Hyde, Near Stroud, Gloucestershire GL6 8PE
Tel: 01453 884643 • Fax: 01453 731166
website: http://home.btclick.com/ragged.cot

The Ragged Cot Inn is a beautiful 17th Century Cotswold Coaching Inn set in attractive gardens high on top of Minchinhampton Common which forms part of 600 acres of National Trust land some two miles from Gatcombe Park and Minchinhampton Golf Club, which has two 18 hole courses and where the Inn's guests enjoy preferential green fees. The Historic Inn serves numerous real ales as well as the more well known brands and offers a choice of 75 malt whiskies from its traditional beamed bars, with its open fires and exposed Cotswold stone walls. It offers succulent home cooked food complete with fresh vegetables and locally supplied free range meat. There is a non-smoking restaurant if preferred. Superb double or twin en suite bedrooms make the Inn the perfect base to explore the Cotswolds and is a haven for lovers of country pursuits. Central for Stratford and Bath with Cheltenham just 15 miles away and Cirencester ten miles, there are just too many places and things of interest to list here. The Ragged Cot Inn is recommended in a range of guides including the Millennium Edition of the Good Pub Guide and the Good Beer Guide. 👑👑👑 *Commended. **See also Colour Advertisement on page 6.***

BEDROOMS WITH PRIVATE BATHROOM; FREE HOUSE WITH REAL ALE; HISTORIC INTEREST; BAR AND RESTAURANT MEALS; NON-SMOKING AREAS; CIRENCESTER 10 MILES.

FALCON INN
Painswick, Gloucestershire GL6 6UN
Tel: 01452 814222 • Fax: 01452 813377 • e-mail: bleninns@clara.net

Being situated right on the popular Cotswold Way, this fine 16th century coaching inn and posting house is a particular favourite with walkers and touring parties who appreciate the ambience of the bars with their stone floors, wood panelling and log fires; there is even a special drying room for ramblers should the weather disappoint. The inn has a fascinating history, having, in its time, served as a courthouse, the venue for cockfights and as an important coaching inn with stage coaches leaving regularly for destinations throughout the country. It also claims the world's oldest bowling green in the grounds. Excellent accommodation awaits guests, facilities being on a par with those offered by the restaurant which is renowned for its superb fare. *ETC* ★★, *CAMRA, AA, Good Pub Guide.*

12 BEDROOMS, ALL WITH PRIVATE BATHROOM; FREE HOUSE WITH REAL ALE; HISTORIC INTEREST; CHILDREN AND PETS WELCOME; BAR AND RESTAURANT MEALS; NON-SMOKING AREAS; STROUD 3 MILES; S£££, D££.

ROSE AND CROWN INN
Nympsfield, Stonehouse, Gloucestershire GL10 3TU
Tel: 01453 860240 • Fax: 01453 860900

With the ancient Cotswold Way footpath nearby inviting excursions into a landscape of outstanding scenic beauty, this old coaching inn is a recommended retreat at lunchtime or after a day's sightseeing. With its origins in the 16th century, the inn has attractive, beamed bars which, although modernised, still retain their time-honoured ambience. Its reputation for providing the best of home-made food is well deserved; the dining room, candlelit in the evenings, presents a wide choice of dishes; something for all ages and tastes, including vegetarian dishes. There is a large garden and a safe play area for children. First-class accommodation comprises twin and double-bedded rooms with a high standard of amenities. *AA, RAC, CAMRA, The Circle, Les Routiers.*

3 BEDROOMS, ALL WITH PRIVATE BATHROOM; FREE HOUSE WITH REAL ALE; HISTORIC INTEREST; CHILDREN WELCOME; BAR AND RESTAURANT MEALS; NON-SMOKING AREAS; NAILSWORTH 3 MILES; S£££, D£££.

THE PLAISTERERS ARMS
Abbey Terrace, Winchcombe, Near Cheltenham, Gloucestershire GL54 5LL
Tel & Fax: 01242 602358

Set in the heart of historic Winchcombe (the capital of Mercia in the Middle Ages), and close to Sudeley Castle, the Plaisterers Arms is an unusual split-level Cotswold stone inn with oak-beamed ceilings and a wonderful traditional atmosphere. The inn serves a varied selection of hand-pulled real ales and a wide range of meals, including delicious home-made pies, daily specials and a traditional roast lunch on Sundays. Upstairs are five well appointed and attractively decorated en suite bedrooms, all with colour television and tea/coffee facilities. At the rear is a large beer garden with attractive patios which overflow with spectacular floral displays during spring and summer. *See also Colour Advertisement on page 5.*

5 BEDROOMS, ALL WITH PRIVATE BATHROOM; USHERS OF TROWBRIDGE HOUSE WITH REAL ALE; BAR MEALS; NON-SMOKING AREAS; CHELTENHAM 8 MILES; S££, D£.

Hampshire

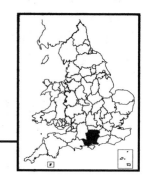

THE COMPASSES INN
Damerham, Near Fordingbridge, Hampshire SP6 3HQ
Tel: 01725 518231 • Fax: 01725 518880

A perfect example of the traditional English country inn, The Compasses offers excellent value for money and a really warm welcome. Superb accommodation is available, with a choice of single, double and family rooms and a four-poster room. All are en suite, with television and tea and coffee making facilities. Great pride is taken in both the quality and variety of food and drink, with freshly produced food, an extensive wine list, a selection of over 100 malt whiskies and several real ales. The Compasses is situated in the heart of rural Wessex and offers excellent opportunities for exploring the New Forest, South Coast and many other local attractions. *ETC/AA* ◆◆◆

6 BEDROOMS, ALL WITH PRIVATE BATHROOM; FREE HOUSE WITH REAL ALE; HISTORIC INTEREST; CHILDREN WELCOME, PETS BY ARRANGEMENT; BAR AND RESTAURANT MEALS; NON-SMOKING AREAS; FORDINGBRIDGE 3 MILES; S£££, D££.

THE GEORGE HOTEL
High Street, Odiham, Hook, Hampshire RG29 1LP
Tel: 01256 702081 • Fax: 01256 704213

To step over the threshold of The George is like entering a living history lesson - at every turn one's gaze meets a reminder of its noble past. Here, an Elizabethan wall painting; there, wattle and daub walls and original timber framing; in the oak-panelled Cromwell's Seafood Restaurant superbly preserved stone flags and an intricately carved fire surround. Rest assured, however, that all modern amenities are available in the individually styled bedrooms (some with four-posters). Dining here is a particular pleasure, candlelight and attentive service complementing the imaginative menus and excellent wine list. And afterwards, relax in the friendly bars, whose popularity with locals bears testimony to the fine quality of their ales! *ETC* ★★, *AA*.

28 BEDROOMS, ALL WITH PRIVATE BATHROOM; FREE HOUSE WITH REAL ALE; HISTORIC INTEREST; CHILDREN AND PETS WELCOME; BAR AND RESTAURANT MEALS; NON-SMOKING AREAS; FAREHAM 4 MILES. S££££, D££££.

SHIP AND BELL HOTEL
London Road, Horndean, Hampshire PO8 0BZ
Tel: 01705 592107 • Fax: 01705 571644

Situated on the site of the original Gales brewery, parts of which may still be seen in the bars, this former coaching inn of the 17th century has changed little in exterior appearance over the years, whilst the bars and restaurant remain basically the same but with a practical attitude to the requirements of a modern age. It is in the matter of accommodation that improvements are most evident, all rooms being furnished with twin or double beds and with full en suite facilities, colour television with satellite channels, direct-dial telephone and tea and coffee-makers amongst their thoughtfully planned appointments. One may eat generously and well in the bars or a restaurant renowned for its excellent home-cooked fare. *ETC* ◆◆◆.

14 BEDROOMS, ALL WITH PRIVATE BATHROOM; GALES HORNDEAN HOUSE WITH REAL ALE; HISTORIC INTEREST; CHILDREN WELCOME; BAR AND RESTAURANT MEALS; NON-SMOKING AREAS; HAVANT 5 MILES; D££.

YE OLDE GEORGE INN
Church Street, East Meon, Near Petersfield, Hampshire GU32 1NH
Tel: 01730 823481 • Fax: 01730 823759

This lovely character inn consists partly of a pair of converted 15th century cottages complete with original inglenook fireplaces, exposed brickwork and beams. The George complements the historic village with its famous church in every way. The bar welcomes you with its old pine tables, open fires, horse brasses and a selection of excellent ales and wines, and quality selection of home-cooked dishes on blackboard menus. Night time sees the Inn at its best, with polished tables and horse brasses reflecting the warm glow of candles and firelight. The desire may arise to linger longer in this charming place. *ETC* ◆◆◆

5 BEDROOMS, ALL WITH PRIVATE BATHROOM; HALL & WOODHOUSE HOUSE WITH REAL ALES; HISTORIC INTEREST; CHILDREN AND PETS WELCOME; BAR AND RESTAURANT MEALS; NON-SMOKING AREAS; PETERSFIELD 5 MILES; S££, D£.

Herefordshire

THE GREEN MAN
Fownhope, Herefordshire HR1 4PE
Tel: 01432 860243 • Fax: 01432 860207

This ancient black and white timbered inn provides an ideal base for exploring the beautiful surrounding countryside and nearby places of interest. There are two bars, an oak-beamed restaurant, a buttery for bar snacks and a large attractive garden. The resident proprietors place great emphasis upon the quality of food and an informal and friendly atmosphere. An extensive bar food menu is available mornings and evenings; afternoon teas and dinners à la carte are served in the restaurant. Bedrooms all have colour television/satellite, radio alarm, direct-dial telephone, tea/coffee making equipment, central heating and many extras. Indoor swimming pool, sauna, steam room, jacuzzi, and gym. *ETC/AA/RAC* ★★, *Egon Ronay*. **See also Outside Back Cover.**

20 BEDROOMS, ALL WITH PRIVATE BATHROOM; FREE HOUSE WITH REAL ALE; HISTORIC INTEREST; CHILDREN WELCOME; BAR FOOD, RESTAURANT EVENINGS ONLY; NON-SMOKING AREAS; GLOUCESTER 24 MILES, MONMOUTH 22, ROSS-ON-WYE 9, HEREFORD 7; S£££, D££.

RHYDSPENCE INN
Whitney-on-Wye, Near Hay-on-Wye, Herefordshire HR3 6EU
Tel: 01497 831262 • Fax: 01497 831751

This picturesque black-and-white timbered inn can claim to be both the first and last in England, standing as it does on the border between Herefordshire and Powys. Indeed it can trace its intriguing history back to the time when it offered food and sustenance to Welsh cattle drovers on their way to the English markets. Today it is popular with both locals and visitors, providing an excellent selection of traditional and more unusual bar and restaurant meals, accompanied by an extensive choice of wines, beers and spirits. Those fortunate enough to be able to linger awhile in this captivating spot will find immaculate en suite bedrooms, tastefully furnished and decorated in traditional style. *AA* ★★ 73%..

7 BEDROOMS, ALL WITH PRIVATE BATHROOM; FREE HOUSE WITH REAL ALE; HISTORIC INTEREST; BAR AND RESTAURANT MEALS; NON-SMOKING AREAS; HAY-ON-WYE 4 MILES; S£££, D£££.

THE TALBOT
New Street, Ledbury, Herefordshire HR8 2DX
Tel: 01531 632963 • Fax: 01531 633796

Take a step back in time to this owner-run historic inn which offers a warm and friendly welcome. It has an original oak-panelled restaurant and an old world bar with log fire, where guests can enjoy an excellent choice of refreshments, including well-kept ales. A regularly changing menu available lunchtimes and evenings will satisfy most tastes and budgets. Ideally placed for visiting historic Malvern and the Wye Valley, the Talbot makes a good base whether on business or touring, and however long or short your stay you will be assured of warm hospitality and first-class service. Good value accommodation is offered in double, twin and family bedrooms, all en suite. *ETC* ★★.

7 BEDROOMS, 6 WITH PRIVATE BATHROOM; WADWORTHS HOUSE WITH REAL ALE; HISTORIC INTEREST; CHILDREN AND PETS WELCOME; BAR MEALS, RESTAURANT EVENINGS ONLY; NON-SMOKING AREAS; HEREFORD 12 MILES; S£££, D££.

THE NEW INN
Market Square, Pembridge, Leominster, Herefordshire HR6 9DZ
Tel: 01544 388427

The last battle of the Wars of the Roses was fought just a few miles from here at Mortimers Cross, and the treaty which gave England's crown to the Yorkist leader is believed to have been signed in the courtroom of this fourteenth century inn. Two ghosts are said to haunt the Inn: one a girl who appears only to women; the other a red-coated soldier armed with a sword. Comfortable accommodation is available, and a good breakfast is included in the rate for a nicely furnished, spick and span bedroom. A varied and interesting menu is offered at most reasonable prices in the bar, which has a log fire to warm it on chillier days, and the attractive lounge area is a popular venue for cosy evening dinners.

6 BEDROOMS; FREE HOUSE WITH REAL ALE; HISTORIC INTEREST; CHILDREN WELCOME, PETS IN BEDROOMS ONLY; BAR MEALS, RESTAURANT EVENINGS ONLY; NON-SMOKING AREAS; KINGTON 6 MILES; S£, D£.

For details of Tourist Board Gradings in England, Scotland and Wales see page 17

THE NEW INN
St Owen's Cross, Near Ross-on-Wye, Herefordshire HR2 8LQ
Tel: 01989 730274

With its black and white timbered facade decorated with colourful hanging baskets, this one-time coaching inn dates from around 1540 and its time-hallowed character is epitomised by its many beams and huge inglenook fireplaces. Owners, Nigel and Jane Donovan, have been at the New Inn for ten years and have a fine reputation for supplying outstanding food and drink; the majority of the dishes on the extensive menu being home-made and prepared from fresh local produce. On fine days, there are few better places in which to relax with a glass of one's fancy than in the spacious beer garden with views stretching across undulating countryside towards the Black Mountains. For a revivifying break away from so-called civilization, the inn has two well-appointed four-poster bedrooms.

2 BEDROOMS, BOTH WITH PRIVATE BATHROOM; FREE HOUSE WITH REAL ALE; HISTORIC INTEREST; CHILDREN AND PETS WELCOME; BAR AND RESTAURANT MEALS; NON-SMOKING AREAS; ROSS-ON-WYE 5 MILES; S£££, D£££.

THE INN ON THE WYE
Kerne Bridge, Goodrich, Near Ross-on-Wye, Herefordshire HR9 5QS
Tel: 01600 890872 • Fax: 01600 890594 • e-mail: gkgardiner.attheinn@virgin.net
website: thetheinnonthewye.co.uk

A beautifully restored 18th century coaching inn with views of Goodrich Castle on the banks of the River Wye. Our ten en suite bedrooms, some with four-poster beds, have colour television, telephone and the usual facilities. As well as the à la carte and bar snack menus offering home-cooked food we also serve a traditional roast on Sundays. Peaceful country walks, idyllic scenery, close to local attractions - we are the ideal base for touring, walking, fishing, canoeing, golfing, etc. Families are welcome, pets by arrangement. Children's play area, beer garden and large car park. Open all day, seven days a week. *RAC* ◆◆◆

10 BEDROOMS, ALL WITH PRIVATE BATHROOM; FREE HOUSE WITH REAL ALE; HISTORIC INTEREST; CHILDREN AND PETS WELCOME; BAR AND RESTAURANT MEALS; NON-SMOKING AREAS; ROSS-ON-WYE 4 MILES; S£££, D£.

Isle of Wight

SPYGLASS INN
The Esplanade, Ventnor, Isle of Wight PO38 1JX
Tel: 01983 855338

Yo, ho, ho and a bottle of what you fancy – to go with your choice of freshly prepared fare from the extensive menu and served in a nautical environment. This fine seafront hostelry is renowned for its magnificent cuisine with seafood, naturally, a speciality of the house. One of the most famous inns on the delectable island, the Spyglass is a happy, friendly place to visit with entertainments and special events held regularly. Conviviality reigns in the bar, a mood to which a glass or two of the fine real ales contributes not a little. Bed and breakfast accommodation is provided in three self-contained suites comprising a double bedroom with bathroom en suite and a lounge and patio with wide sea views. Your hosts are Neil, Stephanie and Rosie Gibbs. *Egon Ronay Recommended.*

3 SUITES; FREE HOUSE WITH REAL ALE; HISTORIC INTEREST; NON-SMOKING AREAS; SHANKLIN 3 MILES; D££.

The £ symbol when appearing at the end of the italic section of an entry shows the anticipated price, during 2001, for full Bed and Breakfast.

Normal Bed & Breakfast rate per person (in single room)		*Normal Bed & Breakfast rate per person (sharing double/twin room)*	
PRICE RANGE	CATEGORY	PRICE RANGE	CATEGORY
Under £25	S£	**Under £25**	D£
£26-£35	S££	**£26-£35**	D££
£36-£45	S£££	**£36-£45**	D£££
Over £45	S££££	**Over £45**	D££££

This is meant as an indication only and does not show prices for Special Breaks, Weekends, etc. Guests are therefore advised to verify all prices on enquiring or booking.

BUGLE HOTEL
The Square, Yarmouth, Isle of Wight PO41 0NS
Tel: 01983 760272 • Fax: 01983 760883

A mere stone's throw from the yacht harbour, this delectable, 17th century listed Inn-cum-hotel is one of the most interesting in the idyllic Isle. Immersed in maritime history, it has innate character expressed in the oak-panelled walls, beams and blazing log fires of the Poachers Lounge Bar, whilst keeping pace with modern trends, the Galleon Bar has a large television screen showing leading sporting events, and live entertainment is held here several times a week. Both bars provide excellent food and real ales and the restaurant is renowned for its appetising cuisine, courtesy of course, of the spectral female figure which is reputed to haunt the kitchens. A splendid place in which to stay, the 'Bugle' provides first-rate en suite accommodation. *ETC* ★★

10 BEDROOMS, 8 WITH PRIVATE BATHROOM; WHITBREAD HOUSE WITH REAL ALE; HISTORIC INTEREST; CHILDREN AND PETS WELCOME; BAR AND RESTAURANT MEALS; NON-SMOKING AREAS; NEWPORT 9 MILES; S£££, D££.

The harbour at Yarmouth, Isle of Wight

Kent

THE OLD COACH HOUSE
Dover Road (A2), Barham, Kent CT4 6SA
Tel: 01227 831218 • Fax: 01227 831932

Halfway between the historic city of Canterbury and the Channel port of Dover, here is a first-class opportunity to enjoy the flavour of France without recourse to ferry or tunnel. Under the expert care of chef/patron, Jean-Claude Rozard, this early 17th century coaching inn is the venue for the happy marriage of fine Continental cuisine and English rural charm. Run on the relaxed lines of a French country auberge, the Old Coach House is widely acknowledged by bon viveurs and specialised feature writers for its outstanding fare, dishes featuring, in particular, local game in season and fresh turbot, bass, grilled lobster and Dover sole. *ETC* ★★, *RAC*.

10 BEDROOMS, ALL WITH PRIVATE BATHROOM; FREE HOUSE WITH REAL ALE; HISTORIC INTEREST; CHILDREN WELCOME, PETS BY ARRANGEMENT; RESTAURANT LUNCHTIME BOOKINGS ONLY, EVENINGS; NON-SMOKING AREAS; CANTERBURY 6 MILES; S£££, D££.

FLYING HORSE INN
Boughton Aluph, Near Ashford, Kent TN25 4HH
Tel: 01233 620914

Deep in the fertile 'Garden of England', this 15th century hostelry with its oak beams and crackling log fires in winter is a real gem. The comfortable and romantic Minstrel Bar with its sunken wells is a big attraction, the ideal place to relax in good company with one's choice from a large selection of real ales. Everything is in traditional vein at this happy retreat, even to the cricket played on the village green opposite. There is an excellent range of gourmet meals available seven days a week in both the bar and dining room. A really homely place in which to stay, the inn has centrally heated bedrooms, all with hot and cold water, colour television and tea and coffee-making facilities.

3 BEDROOMS; FREE HOUSE WITH REAL ALE; HISTORIC INTEREST; CHILDREN WELCOME; BAR AND RESTAURANT MEALS; NON-SMOKING AREAS; ASHFORD 4 MILES; S£, D£.

THE RINGLESTONE INN & FARMHOUSE HOTEL
Near Harrietsham, Maidstone, Kent ME17 1NX
Tel: 01622 859900 • Fax: 01622 859966 • e-mail: bookings@ringlestone.com
website: www.ringlestone.com

Since the early 1600s this unique inn has offered a "ryghte joyouse and welcome greetynge to ye all", and still today its original brick and flint walls, sturdy oak beams, inglenooks and traditional wooden furniture reflect the relaxed atmosphere of less hurried times. The Ringlestone offers superb "help yourself" buffet lunches, cream teas and interesting evening menus, featuring the best of local produce. Those in search of refreshment will savour the selection of well-kept real ales and the interesting range of English country fruit wines – something really different! Set in two acres of peaceful gardens deep in the lush Kent countryside, this truly welcoming inn upholds the finest traditions of English inn-keeping. *ETC/AA* ◆◆◆◆ *and Gold Award.*

3 BEDROOMS, ALL WITH PRIVATE BATHROOM; FREE HOUSE WITH REAL ALE; HISTORIC INTEREST; CHILDREN WELCOME; BAR AND RESTAURANT MEALS; NON-SMOKING AREAS; MAIDSTONE 7 MILES; S££££, D££££.

THE HARROW HILL HOTEL
Warren Street, Near Lenham, Maidstone, Kent ME17 2ED
Tel: 01622 858727 • Fax: 01622 850026

Situated high on the North Downs of Kent amidst lush farmland, The Harrow was once a resting place for pilgrims en route to Canterbury. Now a comfortable country inn, it offers visitors good food and a comfortable night's stay in centrally heated en suite bedrooms, all provided with modern necessities such as telephone, colour television, and clock radio. Eating here is popular with residents and locals alike, either in the lounge bar or in the quieter, secluded restaurant overlooking the garden. The Harrow is conveniently situated for visiting historic Canterbury and the Cinque Ports, as well as being within a short drive of the Channel ports and the Tunnel. *ETC* ◆◆◆, *AA.*

14 BEDROOMS, ALL WITH PRIVATE BATHROOM; FREE HOUSE WITH REAL ALE; HISTORIC INTEREST; CHILDREN WELCOME; BAR AND RESTAURANT MEALS; NON-SMOKING AREAS; LENHAM 2 MILES; S£££, D££££.

THE ST CRISPIN INN
The Street, Worth, Kent CT14 0DF
Tel: 01304 612081 • Fax: 01304 614838

Traditional Kentish country pub set in an area of outstanding natural beauty. Large garden and covered patio. 28-seater restaurant with a fine selection of wines and real cask ales and open log fire. Six rooms en suite. Families always welcome. Plenty of parking space. Many golf clubs in the locality. *Twice winner of Kent Country Pub of the Year, Egon Ronay recommended.*

6 BEDROOMS WITH PRIVATE BATHROOM; REAL ALES; CHILDREN WELCOME; RESTAURANT MEALS; SANDWICH 1 MILE.

Please mention *Recommended Wayside & Country Inns*
when enquiring about accommodation featured in these pages.

Lancashire

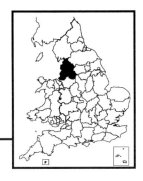

OWD NELL'S CANALSIDE TAVERN
Guy's Thatched Hamlet, St Michael's Road, Bilsborrow, Lancashire PR3 0RS
Tel: 01995 640010 • Fax: 01995 640141 • e-mail: guyshamlet@aol.com
website: www.guysthatchedhamlet.co.uk

Here's one for collectors of the unusual and the idyllic – a thatched oldtime refreshment house tucked away by the side of the Lancaster Canal. Open all day dispensing the best of home made country tavern fayre, Owd Nell's is renowned for its range of tempting bar dishes designed to serve all palates and pockets, as well as its great selection of cask-conditioned ales. This gem is just one unit in the complex that is Guy's Thatched Hamlet, where guests can step back in time and enjoy the good things in life in a relaxed and unfussy atmosphere. Superb overnight accommodation with the highest modern standards is provided in Guy's Lodgings, comprising en suite rooms with colour television, telephone and tea and coffee making facilities. For dining "par excellence", guests just have to follow their noses to the adjacent Guy's Eating Establishment, where the emphasis is on tasteful informality, the variety of dishes ranging from freshly made pizza to a succulent sirloin steak. Without venturing beyond this quaint and attractive complex one may confirm the time warp illusion by strolling through the old world elegance of Spout Lane and School House Square to visit the craft shops. Our own cricket ground with thatched pavilion can be hired, and there is crown green bowling. Other amenities include conference rooms and a licensed pavilion. Golf (two miles) can be arranged. Short breaks are available – ring for further information.

53 BEDROOMS, ALL EN SUITE; FREE HOUSE WITH REAL ALE; CHILDREN WELCOME; BAR AND RESTAURANT MEALS; NON-SMOKING AREAS; M6/M55 3 MILES, GARSTANG 3; S£££, D£.

The **£** symbol when appearing at the end of the italic section of an entry shows the anticipated price, during 2001, for full Bed and Breakfast.

Normal Bed & Breakfast rate per person (in single room)		Normal Bed & Breakfast rate per person (sharing double/twin room)	
PRICE RANGE	CATEGORY	PRICE RANGE	CATEGORY
Under £25	S£	**Under £25**	D£
£26-£35	S££	**£26-£35**	D££
£36-£45	S£££	**£36-£45**	D£££
Over £45	S££££	**Over £45**	D££££

This is meant as an indication only and does not show prices for Special Breaks, Weekends, etc. Guests are therefore advised to verify all prices on enquiring or booking.

For details of Tourist Board Gradings in England, Scotland and Wales see page 17

THE ROEBUCK
Garstang Road, Bilsborrow, Lancashire PR3 0RN
Tel: 01995 640234

Set in peaceful, pleasant surroundings, The Roebuck derives its name from the herds of wild deer that used to roam Bleasedale forest in the 16th century. With log fires, wooden beams and memorabilia, it has the idyllic charm of yesteryear, rarely found these days. As well as a wide choice of cask conditioned ales and fine wines available by the glass or bottle, there is an extensive chalkboard menu, which features imaginative food that changes with the seasons, beautifully presented at reasonable prices. There are over 40 main courses to choose from including fresh fish, the house speciality, and the chef's dish of the day, plus an interesting selection of hot and cold snacks is also on offer. Desserts are all tempting and delicious. The Roebuck is open all day, every day for food and drink. Local attractions include Lancaster Canal, Beacon Fell and Trough of Bowland.

NO ACCOMMODATION; REAL ALES; BAR MEALS; PRESTON 2 MILES.

OLD BELL INN
Huddersfield Road, Delph, Oldham, Lancashire OL3 5EG
Tel: 01457 870130 • Fax: 01457 876597

This pleasant, stone-built 18th century coaching house has played host to several famous personages over the years, Queen Victoria and Charles Dickens amongst them. Old beams, leaded light windows and open fires in the bar immediately induce a feeling of well-being, confirmed and compounded by recourse to the restaurant where the menu reflects flair and variety; an appetising selection of snacks is available in the bar. Conveniently placed as a quiet retreat within easy reach of the many commercial and industrial centres of the North West, the hostelry provides excellent accommodation with some rooms having the luxury of four-poster beds.

14 BEDROOMS, ALL WITH PRIVATE BATHROOM; FREE HOUSE WITH REAL ALE; HISTORIC INTEREST; CHILDREN WELCOME; BAR MEALS, RESTAURANT EVENINGS ONLY; OLDHAM 4 MILES; S£££££, D££.

HARK TO BOUNTY INN
Slaidburn, Near Clitheroe, Lancashire BB7 3EP
Tel: 01200 446246 • Fax: 01200 446361 • e-mail: harktobounty@btclick.com
website: www.hark-to-bounty.co.uk

Dating back to the 13th century, this old inn was known as 'The Dog' until 1875. Entertaining the local hunt, the entertainment was interrupted by the persistent baying of the favourite dog of the local squire who was heard to exclaim 'Hark to Bounty' and the name has stuck ever since. In the heart of the scenic Forest of Bowland, the inn was once the seat of the Bowland Forest Court and anyone giving it a trial today will pronounce a most favourable verdict in respect of accommodation, cuisine and service. A popular haunt of locals and tourists alike, the oak beamed bar provides excellent bar meals and real ale with more substantial fare served in a highly commended restaurant.

9 BEDROOMS, ALL WITH PRIVATE BATHROOM; SCOTTISH COURAGE HOUSE WITH REAL ALE; HISTORIC INTEREST; CHILDREN AND PETS WELCOME; BAR AND RESTAURANT MEALS; CLITHEROE 7 MILES; S£, D£.

THURNHAM MILL HOTEL AND RESTAURANT
Thurnham, Near Lancaster, Lancashire LA2 0BD
Tel: 01524 752852 • Fax: 01524 752477

This unique port of call with its outstanding Canalside Restaurant was originally a 16th century cloth mill. Unusual in that the mill wheel was driven by canal rather than river water, it was rebuilt in 1829 and in more modern times, turbines and then electricity became the energy source. Today, much energy is expended in providing first-class accommodation and food for family holiday-makers. On sunny days, meals are served on the canalside terrace with garrulous ducks and the occasional passing narrowboat for company. The Millers Tavern with its beams and flagstone floor is a popular meeting place and those constrained to stay overnight in such charming surroundings will be enchanted by the beautifully appointed guest rooms, some of which are of family size. *ETC* ★★.

18 BEDROOMS, ALL WITH PRIVATE BATHROOM; JOHN SMITHS HOUSE WITH REAL ALE; HISTORIC INTEREST; CHILDREN AND PETS WELCOME; BAR AND RESTAURANT MEALS; NON-SMOKING AREAS; LANCASTER 5 MILES; S£££, D££.

PLEASE MENTION THIS GUIDE WHEN YOU WRITE

OR PHONE TO ENQUIRE ABOUT ACCOMMODATION

IF YOU ARE WRITING, A STAMPED, ADDRESSED

ENVELOPE IS ALWAYS APPRECIATED

Leicestershire
including Rutland

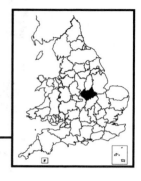

GEORGE HOTEL
Belton, Loughborough, Leicestershire LE12 9UH
Tel: 01530 222426

The character of this well-regarded mid-18th century hostelry remains redolent of the day when ostlers hurried to change the teams of horses as carriages pulled in the secure rest and refreshment for their occupants travelling between Burton and Nottingham. Today, conveniently situated for the East Midlands Airport and within easy access of the Peak District National Park, Charnwood and Sherwood Forests, it continues to perform its sterling function for businessmen and tourists with a different form of transport. The bar lounge with its low-beamed ceiling exudes a mellow welcome, the very place to enjoy a glass of one's fancy whilst studying a comprehensive à la carte restaurant menu. Splendid modern accommodation awaits overnight guests. *AA Two Rosettes.*

18 BEDROOMS, ALL WITH PRIVATE BATHROOMS; FREE HOUSE WITH REAL ALE; HISTORIC INTEREST; CHILDREN AND PETS WELCOME; BAR AND RESTAURANT MEALS; NON-SMOKING AREAS; LEICESTER 10 MILES; S££££, D££££.

THE EXETER ARMS
Wakerley, Oakham, Rutland LE15 8PA
Tel: 01572 747817 • Fax: 01572 747100

Welcome back Rutland (although we know you never went away!) and welcome also to this homely inn set in the picturesque Welland Valley with Rockingham Forest harbouring a host of interesting walks. Burghley House and Rockingham Castle are nearby as is Rutland Water, Europe's largest man-made lake which offers excellent fishing, sailing and bird watching. Good wholesome fare is available at prices that represent real value for money. A newly-renovated annexe provides attractive accommodation with all rooms having en suite facilities, colour television, tea/coffee-makers and central heating. This is a quiet and well-run hostelry ideal for a break that is just that little bit different. *CAMRA – Gold Award.*

5 BEDROOMS, ALL WITH PRIVATE BATHROOM; FREE HOUSE WITH REAL ALE; HISTORIC INTEREST; CHILDREN AND PETS WELCOME; BAR MEALS (NOT MON.); STAMFORD 7 MILES; S££, D£.

FHG PUBLICATIONS
publish a large range of well-known
accommodation guides.

We will be happy to send you details or you can use
the order form at the back of this book.

Lincolnshire

TALLY HO INN
Aswarby, Near Sleaford, Lincolnshire NG34 8SA
Tel: 01529 455205

It is well worth seeking out this unashamedly rural inn for its refreshingly individual selection of starters, main courses and puddings. Try Kromeskies (bacon rolls stuffed with turkey, ham, mushrooms and herbs, served with a chilli marie rose dip) followed by Lincolnshire Lamb Stew and Dumplings (with rosemary, cider and apples) and you'll certainly know you have had a meal! The bucolic theme is emphasised by the fact that the 17th century building lies in the middle of the Aswarby Estate and is surrounded by parkland on which sheep graze contentedly and that the handful of en suite bedrooms are set away from the house in a carefully converted dairy/cowshed. Friendly and informal, this is an unusually good port of call – a veritable collector's item. *AA QQQ*.

6 BEDROOMS, ALL WITH PRIVATE BATHROOM; FREE HOUSE WITH REAL ALE; HISTORIC INTEREST; CHILDREN WELCOME; BAR FOOD, RESTAURANT EVENINGS ONLY AND SUNDAY LUNCH; SLEAFORD 4 MILES; S£££, D££££.

BLACK HORSE INN
Main Road, Donnington-on-Bain, Lincolnshire LN11 9TJ
Tel & Fax: 01507 343640

Situated on the Viking Way, the long-distance footpath that runs from the Humber to Oakham, this attractively decorated hostelry attracts dedicated walkers as well as visitors intent on exploring the tranquil pleasures of the Lincolnshire Wolds. The excellent 'Black Horse' deserves special consideration by reason of its first-rate home cooking with choice made from either the à la carte menu or one of the daily 'blackboard specials'. Lighter fare is obtainable in the bar in company with traditional real ales. Children are understandingly catered for and, at the rear, is a secluded beer garden with swings. A rewarding place in which to stay, this recommended inn has spacious en suite bedrooms with colour television and tea and coffee-making facilities.

8 BEDROOMS, ALL WITH PRIVATE BATHROOM; FREE HOUSE WITH REAL ALE; HISTORIC INTEREST; CHILDREN WELCOME AND PETS BY ARRANGEMENT; BAR AND RESTAURANT MEALS; NON-SMOKING AREAS; SPALDING 9 MILES; S£, D£.

LEA GATE INN
Lea Gate Road, Coningsby, Lincolnshire LN4 4RS
Tel: 01526 342370 • Fax: 01526 345468 • e-mail: theleagateinn@breathe.net
website: www.leagateinn.co.uk

Dating from 1542 and with its ancient timbers, open fireplaces and secret recesses exuding an atmosphere absorbed through centuries of care and comfort for the weary traveller of the fens, this fine old inn is traditional personified. The treacherous bogs and marshes have been tamed and the gallows that used to cast its grim shadow at the front of the inn has not been employed for years. It is said that the 'Last Supper' engraving over the fireplace in the main lounge was where last rites were given to condemned souls; this same fireplace featuring a priests' hole where Roman Catholic priests hid from Cromwell and his Roundhead soldiers. But cast gloom aside, for today this historically fascinating hostelry extends the most cheerful of welcomes from hosts, Mark and Sharon Dennison. A new extension is now completed, comprising eight luxury en suite rooms, all individually designed; four-poster rooms and disabled facilities. One may still enjoy honest ale from the cask and the most appetising fare, including imaginative vegetarian dishes, which are served in a comfortable restaurant transformed some time ago from an old barn. Meals are served all week at lunchtimes and in the evenings and families are catered for. The inn stands in lovely gardens where children may play safely whilst their parents relax. A recommended wayside inn of great charm

8 BEDROOMS, ALL WITH PRIVATE BATHROOM; FREE HOUSE WITH REAL ALE; HISTORIC INTEREST; CHILDREN WELCOME; BAR MEALS, RESTAURANT EVENINGS ONLY; NON-SMOKING AREAS; WOODHALL SPA 4 MILES; S£££, D££.

THE MARQUIS OF GRANBY
High Street, Wellingore, Lincoln, Lincolnshire LN5 0HW
Tel: 01522 810442 • Fax: 01522 810740

Equidistant from Lincoln, Sleaford, Newark and Grantham, this friendly and go-ahead hostelry attracts a healthy business clientele as well as discerning tourists. In fact, this is a great place to stay; all rooms have private facilities, colour television and tea and coffee-makers and the reasonable terms include a full English breakfast. Also offering excellent value for money are the dishes featured on an expansive menu with daily 'specials' also available. Friday is very much 'fish day' with an appetising range of fresh produce on offer at lunchtime and in the evening. Traditional roasts served each Sunday lunchtime prove extremely popular.

7 BEDROOMS, ALL WITH PRIVATE BATHROOM; FREE HOUSE WITH REAL ALE; HISTORIC INTEREST; CHILDREN AND PETS WELCOME; BAR AND RESTAURANT MEALS; NON-SMOKING AREAS; LINCOLN 9 MILES; S£, D£

THE RED LION INN
Main Road, Partney, Spilsby, Lincolnshire PE23 4PG
Tel: 01790 752271 • Fax: 01790 753360 • e-mail: redlionpartney@onetel.net.uk

The Red Lion Partney has been owned and run by Derek and Lorna Gamblin for the past 12 years and is ideally situated on the edge of the Lincolnshire Wolds, an area of great natural beauty. Centrally situated for the historic city of Lincoln with its cathedral, castle and old streets, Horncastle - the centre for antiques, Grimsby with its National Heritage Centre and the renowned coastal resort of Skegness. Great for walking and sightseeing and there is a leisure centre nearby which has an indoor swimming pool and gymnasium. Award winning home-made food, with over 20 dishes to choose from, including vegetarian selection. En suite rooms with radio, colour TV and beverage making facilities. *AA. See also Colour Advertisement on page 7.*

3 BEDROOMS, ALL WITH PRIVATE BATHROOM; FREE HOUSE WITH REAL ALE; CHILDREN AND PETS WELCOME; BAR MEALS WED.-SUN; SPILSBY 2 MILES; S££, D£.

FINCH HATTON ARMS HOTEL
43 Main Street, Ewerby, Sleaford, Lincolnshire NG34 9PH
Tel: 01529 460363 • Fax: 01529 461703

This is something of a surprise – a fully equipped small hotel of some distinction in a picturesque little village, if not in the middle of nowhere, then precious near to it! Its success is due, in no small part, to its attractive Tudor-style bar and restaurant where traditional ales and an imaginative menu draw custom from nearby Sleaford and even Newark, Grantham, Boston and Lincoln to prove the proposition that value for money is a sure winner. The hotel wing provides first-class overnight accommodation, each room having a bath/shower en suite, remote-control colour television, direct-dial telephone and tea and coffee-making facilities and there is the promise of a hearty English breakfast in the morning. *Tourist Board Listed.*

8 BEDROOMS, ALL WITH PRIVATE BATHROOM; FREE HOUSE WITH REAL ALE; HISTORIC INTEREST; CHILDREN WELCOME, PETS BY ARRANGEMENT; BAR AND RESTAURANT MEALS; NON-SMOKING AREAS; SLEAFORD 4 MILES; S£££, D££

PENNY FARTHING INN
Station Road, Timberland, Lincolnshire LN4 3SA
Tel & Fax: 01526 378359

Set in the pretty village of Timberland, this ivy-clad inn with roses round the door offers that trinity of virtues – good food, good rest and good cheer – for which the English pub is renowned. An extensive blackboard menu caters for bar meals and the à la carte restaurant is open in the evenings, both using fresh local produce served at reasonable prices. Guest rooms with private facilities are delightfully furnished in country pine, and there is also a four-poster suite. The famous Woodhall Spa Golf Club is nearby; tennis, fishing, bowling, boating and horse riding are all readily available in the area. *Les Routiers.*

6 BEDROOMS, ALL WITH PRIVATE BATHROOM; FREE HOUSE WITH REAL ALE; BAR AND RESTAURANT MEALS; WOODHALL SPA 6 MILES.

Merseyside

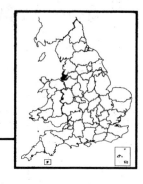

THE SHIP HOTEL
Parkgate, Merseyside
Tel & Fax: 0151 336 3931 • e-mail: shiphotel@pgen.net
website: www.the-shiphotel.co.uk

A character pub serving real ales, guest beers, lagers, fine wines and spirits in our refurbished bar with panoramic views across the Dee to North Wales. The finest food is served in the bar at lunchtimes and early evenings while our restaurant is open every night and serves a traditional lunch on Sundays. En suite accommodation is available at modest prices to suit most pockets. *ETC* ★★

23 BEDROOMS, ALL WITH PRIVATE BATHROOM; FREE HOUSE WITH REAL ALE; HISTORIC INTEREST; CHILDREN WELCOME; BAR AND RESTAURANT MEALS; NON-SMOKING AREAS; S£/££, D££.

FOR THE MUTUAL GUIDANCE OF GUEST AND HOST

Every year literally thousands of holidays, short breaks and overnight stops are arranged through our guides, the vast majority without any problems at all. In a handful of cases, however, difficulties do arise about bookings, which often could have been prevented from the outset.

It is important to remember that when accommodation has been booked, both parties – guests and hosts – have entered into a form of contract. We hope that the following points will provide helpful guidance.

GUESTS: When enquiring about accommodation, be as precise as possible. Give exact dates, numbers in your party and the ages of any children. State the number and type of rooms wanted and also what catering you require – bed and breakfast, full board etc. Make sure that the position about evening meals is clear – and about pets, reductions for children or any other special points.

Read our reviews carefully to ensure that the proprietors you are going to contact can supply what you want. Ask for a letter confirming all arrangements, if possible.

If you have to cancel, do so as soon as possible. Proprietors do have the right to retain deposits and under certain circumstances to charge for cancelled holidays if adequate notice is not given and they cannot re-let the accommodation.

HOSTS: Give details about your facilities and about any special conditions. Explain your deposit system clearly and arrangements for cancellations, charges etc. and whether or not your terms include VAT.

If for any reason you are unable to fulfil an agreed booking without adequate notice, you may be under an obligation to arrange suitable alternative accommodation or to make some form of compensation.

While every effort is made to ensure accuracy, we regret that FHG Publications cannot accept responsibility for errors, omissions or misrepresentations in our entries or any consequences thereof.
Prices in particular should be checked because we go to press early. We will follow up complaints but cannot act as arbiters or agents for either party.

Norfolk

SPREAD EAGLE COUNTRY INN
Church Road, Barton Bendish, King's Lynn, Norfolk PE33 9DP
Tel: 01366 347295 • Fax: 01366 347995 • mobile: 07808 906201
e-mail: seagle.barton@virgin.net • website: http//:freespace.virgin.net/seagle.barton/

This true country inn, run personally by the Gransden family for the past seven years, stands in the centre of a quiet, picturesque, old village, in a large, well-stocked garden with customer seating. Barton Bendish lies south of RAF Marham off the A1122, with Swaffham and Downham just six miles away. There is a mainline station at Downham, with Cambridge half-an-hour by train. King's Lynn and beyond, Sandringham and the unspoilt Norfolk coast are a 30 minute drive away. Bedrooms (double en suite and twins with bathroom close by) are well-furnished with television, tea-making facilities, etc. The two restaurants, one non-smoking, serve excellent home-cooked food; real ales and other drinks are available in the bar, which has a log fire. Open all year.

4 BEDROOMS, 1 WITH PRIVATE BATHROOM; FREE HOUSE WITH REAL ALE; BAR AND RESTAURANT MEALS; NON-SMOKING AREAS; SWAFFHAM 5 MILES; S£, D£.

GEORGE AND DRAGON HOTEL
High Street, Cley-next-the-Sea, Near Holt, Norfolk NR25 7RN
Tel: 01263 740652 • Fax: 01263 741275

Built in classic Edwardian style on the site of a former inn, the George and Dragon looks out over the famous North Norfolk salt marshes, so beloved of birdwatchers. Numerous rare birds are protected through the aegis of the Norfolk Naturalists Trust which was actually formed at the hotel. The inn dominates the white-washed cottages and cobbled courtyards that surround it. Gentle breezes sigh through the grasses of this haunting landscape, lamenting the withdrawal of the sea but no wistful spirits exist in this comradely and cosy place where traditional real ales and super fare attracts dyed-in-the-wool inn enthusiasts. Warmly welcoming, this happy hostelry also provides splendid overnight accommodation. *ETC* ◆◆◆.

9 BEDROOMS; 6 WITH PRIVATE BATHROOM; FREE HOUSE WITH REAL ALE; HISTORIC INTEREST; CHILDREN AND PETS WELCOME; BAR AND RESTAURANT MEALS; NON-SMOKING AREAS; HOLT 4 MILES; S£££, D££.

FFOLKES ARMS HOTEL
Lynn Road, Hillington, King's Lynn, Norfolk PE31 6BJ
Tel: 01485 600210 • Fax: 01485 601196 • e-mail: ffolkespub@aol.com
website: www.ffolkes-arms-hotel.co.uk

Happily placed for Norfolk's peaceful pastoral scenery and only minutes from Sandringham and Castle Rising, this attractive free house was once a popular coaching stop on the main Midlands to Norwich mailing route. Less happy is the legend that the building is haunted by a young nursemaid who reputedly fell from one of the attic bedrooms in the late 19th century and was impaled on railings below. However, today the hotel extends a cheerful welcome to family parties, being justly proud of its bars, splendid carvery-style restaurant and landscaped gardens. The accommodation wing houses rooms with superb en suite facilities, colour television, direct-dial telephone, hairdryers and trouser press. and tea-makers amongst their thoughtful appointments. *ETC* ★★★, *AA* .

20 BEDROOMS, ALL WITH PRIVATE BATHROOM; FREE HOUSE WITH REAL ALE; HISTORIC INTEREST; CHILDREN WELCOME, PETS IN GARDEN ONLY; BAR AND RESTAURANT MEALS; NON-SMOKING AREAS; KING'S LYNN 7 MILES; S££, D£.

FEATHERS HOTEL
Manor Road, Dersingham, King's Lynn, Norfolk PE31 6LN
Tel & Fax: 01485 540207

In the gently undulating countryside of north-west Norfolk, this solid and welcoming stone-built inn stands on the fringe of Sandringham Estate, one of the Queen's favourite country homes. While not claiming to compete with that offered to Her Majesty, the Feathers provides comfortable and reasonably priced en suite accommodation with bedrooms simply furnished in the modern style and each having colour television. Real ale is served in the two popular bars, the Saddle Room and the Sandringham, and a right royal cuisine is provided with both à la carte and table d'hôte menus available. Well-tended gardens make a most pleasant setting for this attractive hostelry. *CAMRA*

5 BEDROOMS, ALL WITH PRIVATE BATHROOM; PUNCH TAVERNS HOUSE WITH REAL ALE; HISTORIC INTEREST; CHILDREN AND PETS WELCOME; BAR AND RESTAURANT MEALS; HUNSTANTON 7 MILES; S££, D££.

THE JOHN H. STRACEY
West End, Briston, Melton Constable Norfolk NR24 2JA
Tel: 01263 860891 • Fax: 01263 862984

Named after a famous boxer, this fine old inn, in fact, dates from the 16th century when it was a staging post on the Wells to Norwich road. We were captivated by the time-honoured ambience exuded by its low ceilings, oak beams and copper knick-knacks reflecting the glow of a welcoming log fire. The old hostelry used to be called the Three Horseshoes and synonymous with the change of name, the stables were converted into a splendid, well-patronised restaurant known for its wholesome, home-cooked fare. This is a place of infinite character in tranquil, rural Norfolk with the coast within easy reach. *Les Routiers.*

3 BEDROOMS, 1 WITH PRIVATE BATHROOM; FREE HOUSE WITH REAL ALE; HISTORIC INTEREST; CHILDREN WELCOME; BAR AND RESTAURANT MEALS; NON-SMOLING AREAS; HOLT 4 MILES; S£.

EAST NORWICH INN
Old Road, Acle, Norwich, Norfolk NR13 3QN
Tel: 01493 751112 • Fax: 01493 751109

Midway between Norwich and Great Yarmouth, we are ideally located for visiting all Heritage, National Trust and holiday attractions. The inn is sited on a quiet residential road and has a full "on" licence with a good local bar trade. All bedrooms are well away from the bar area and are en suite, have tea/coffee making facilities and colour televisions. Families welcome. Pets free of charge. Ample car parking. Meals available in bar or at local restaurants. Three night break prices available. Please telephone for brochure.

ALL BEDROOMS WITH PRIVATE BATHROOM; CHILDREN AND PETS WELCOME; BAR MEALS; GREAT YARMOUTH 8 MILES.

THE HALF MOON INN
Rushall, Near Diss, Norfolk IP21 4QD
Tel & Fax: 01379 740793

This 16th century coaching inn offers a warm welcome to business guests and holidaymakers alike. Seven bedrooms are in modern chalet-style accommodation, and the remainder are in the inn which has a wealth of exposed beams. Bedrooms have colour television, centreal heating and tea and coffee making facilities. An excellent selection of home-cooked meals are available and reservations may be made in the conservatory dining area. The bar offers a range of real ales and a good value wine list is available. The friendly atmosphere, reasonably priced accommodation and delightful rural location combine to make this an excellent base for visiting East Anglia. *South Norfolk Council Gold Award Winner 98/99/2000.*

10 BEDROOMS, 8 WITH PRIVATE BATHROOM; FREE HOUSE WITH REAL ALE; HISTORIC INTEREST; CHILDREN WELCOME; BAR AND RESTAURANT MEALS; NON-SMOKING AREAS; HARLESTON 3 MILES; S£, D££££.

The **£** symbol when appearing at the end of the italic section of an entry shows the anticipated price, during 2001, for full Bed and Breakfast.

Normal Bed & Breakfast rate per person (in single room)		Normal Bed & Breakfast rate per person (sharing double/twin room)	
PRICE RANGE	CATEGORY	PRICE RANGE	CATEGORY
Under £25	S£	**Under £25**	D£
£26-£35	S££	**£26-£35**	D££
£36-£45	S£££	**£36-£45**	D£££
Over £45	S££££	**Over £45**	D££££

This is meant as an indication only and does not show prices for Special Breaks, Weekends, etc. Guests are therefore advised to verify all prices on enquiring or booking.

THE LIFEBOAT INN,
Ship Lane, Thornham, Norfolk PE36 6LT
Tel: 01485 512236 • Fax: 01485 512323 • wesite: www.lifeboatinn.co.uk

A lovely sixteenth century traditional English inn, the Lifeboat, once the haunt of smugglers, is today some little way from the sea but the briny is still within sight in the distance. The bar with its low ceiling, pillars and uneven floor conjured up visions of the unhurried life of years gone by as we sampled an excellent pint of real ale and tucked into our fisherman's pie. Daily specials increase the already excellent choice of freshly prepared dishes available in the bar; alternatively one may dine in the restaurant, where a frequently changing menu makes the best of local seasonal produce. All the comfortable bedrooms have en suite bathrooms and most enjoy views over the harbour to the sea. *See also Colour Advertisement on page 7.*

12 BEDROOMS, ALL WITH PRIVATE BATHROOM; FREE HOUSE WITH REAL ALE; HISTORIC INTEREST; CHILDREN AND PETS WELCOME; BAR MEALS, RESTAURANT EVENINGS ONLY; HUNSTANTON 4 MILES; ££££.

THREE HORSESHOES
Bridge Street, Warham All Saints, Wells-next-the-Sea, Norfolk NR23 1NL
Tel: 01328 710547

Well worth finding, this is a real old Norfolk pub with no carpet and gas lighting, an integral part of a peaceful village of flint cottages. The secret here is the wonderful home cooking; real country fare (no chips!) with local seafood a speciality. In fine weather meals can be enjoyed in the garden. The A149 coast road between Wells next-the-Sea and Stiffkey is just under a mile away, beyond which stretch the famous saltings, haunt of rare birds. In this rare and tranquil backwater, comfortable accommodation is available next door to the inn at Old Post Office Cottage, a lovely old Grade II Listed building with exposed beams and many other period features.

4 BEDROOMS, 1 WITH PRIVATE BATHROOM; FREE HOUSE WITH REAL ALE; HISTORIC INTEREST; CHILDREN AND PETS WELCOME; BAR MEALS; NON-SMOKING AREAS; WELLS 2 MILES; S£, D££.

SARACEN'S HEAD INN WITH ROOMS
Wolterton, Near Erpingham, Norfolk NR11 7LX
Tel: 01263 768909

A free house with a delightful courtyard and walled garden, the Saracen's Head is well recommended for its delicious and reasonably-priced food, made even more enjoyable by the casual atmosphere in which it may be appreciated – no piped music, no fruit machines! During the year a series of gourmet feasts is organised in the long tabled Upper Room. The ideal place for a quiet fun night out, the inn and its increasingly popular Eating House is within half-an-hour's drive from Norwich. It is a trifle difficult to find but well worth the effort. Erpingham lies a mile or so to the west of the A140 Aylsham-Cromer road and is signposted. From there a further sign points to Wolterton (not marked on most maps). *Good Pub Guide, Which? Hotel Guide, Which? Pub Guide, Michelin Pub Guide.*

4 BEDROOMS, ALL WITH PRIVATE BATHROOM; FREE HOUSE WITH REAL ALE; HISTORIC INTEREST; CHILDREN WELCOME, PETS BY ARRANGEMENT; BAR AND RESTAURANT MEALS LUNCHTIMES ONLY; NORWICH 9 MILES; S£££, D££.

Northumberland

THE FAMOUS SCHOONER HOTEL
Northumberland Street, Alnmouth, Northumberland NE66 2RS
Tel: 01665 830216 • Fax: 01665 830287 • e-mail: ghost@schooner.sagehost.co.uk
website: www.schooner.sagehost.co.uk

The Famous Schooner Hotel is a Listed 17th century coaching inn situated in the heart of Alnmouth alongside miles and miles of golden beaches and within close proximity to Northumbria's famous castles, historic sites and golf courses. Each of our 32 superbly appointed en suite rooms is furnished to a high standard. The hotel has two well stocked bars renowned for a superb selection of real ales. Enjoy the freshest fish and the finest game in the fine dining Seahunters Restaurant. Along with Harry's Restaurant, two conservatories where bar meals are served throughout the day and car parking, the Schooner offers a traditional welcome, typical of this rural area. *RAC* ★★★. *See also Colour Advertisement on page 7.*

32 BEDROOMS ALL WITH PRIVATE BATHROOM; FREE HOUSE WITH REAL ALE; HISTORIC INTEREST; BAR AND RESTAURANT MEALS; ALNWICK 4 MILES.

THE COTTAGE INN
Dunstan Village, Craster, Alnwick, Northumberland NE66 3SZ
Tel: 01665 576658 • Fax: 01665 576788

Unspoiled Northumberland has something for everyone, whether your idea of a good holiday is strolling along an uncrowded sandy beach, visiting historic castles, or enjoying a wide range of leisure activities such as golf, watersports, fishing or even parachute jumping. And if your idea of relaxation is to do absolutely nothing, then this is the ideal place to do it! Just a few minutes from the coast, the Cottage Inn offers a friendly welcome and comfortable accommodation, all bedrooms having bath and shower, television, tea and coffee tray, and telephone. The fully licensed Harry Hotspur Restaurant provides first-rate food in a most delightful setting, with meals also available in the beamed bar and in the airy conservatory. *ETB* ◆◆◆, *AA, Les Routiers.*

10 BEDROOMS, ALL WITH PRIVATE BATHROOM; FREE HOUSE WITH REAL ALE; CHILDREN WELCOME; BAR MEALS, RESTAURANT EVENINGS ONLY PLUS SUN. LUNCH; NON-SMOKING AREAS; ALNWICK 4 MILES; S££, D££.

THE HOTSPUR HOTEL
Bondgate Without, Alnwick, Northumberland NE66 1PR
Tel: 01665 510101 • Fax: 01665 605033

Originally a coaching inn, the Hostspur is located in the town centre, within walking distance of Alnwick Castle, the seat of the Duke of Northumberland. Set between sandy beaches and rolling moorland, it is surrounded by numerous places of interest, including many fine golf courses. The hotel offers a friendly welcome, comfortable en suite bedrooms, a high standard of food, and fine ales. Non-smoking accommodation available. Children welcome, reductions when sharing with adults. Please telephone for brochure. *AA/RAC* ★★, *Les Routiers.*

30 BEDROOMS, ALL WITH PRIVATE BATHROOM; REAL ALES; CHILDREN WELCOME; MORPETH 17 MILES.

THE PHEASANT INN
Stannersburn, Falstone, Hexham, Northumberland NE48 1DD
Tel & Fax: 01434 240382 • e-mail: thepheasantinn@kielderwater.demon.co.uk

Set in the Northumberland National Park, the Pheasant Inn is everything a country inn should be. Originally a farm, it is nearly four centuries old, with stone walls and low beams. It became a staging post for mail and tax collection, but has since developed into a welcome and homely oasis to accommodate tourists and locals alike. The Barn and Hemmel now house eight delightfully appointed bedrooms, all of which have en suite facilities. There are two bars serving meals at lunchtime and in the evenings, and the restaurant is open at night. Traditional, freshly prepared food. Please write or telephone for full colour brochure. *ETC/AA* ◆◆◆◆. *See also Colour Advertisement on page 7.*

8 BEDROOMS, ALL WITH PRIVATE BATHROOM; CHILDREN WELCOME; BAR MEALS, RESTAURANT EVENINGS ONLY; NON-SMOKING AREAS; BELLINGHAM 8 MILES; S£££, D££.

SPOTTED COW INN
Castle Hill, Haltwhistle, Northumberland NE49 0EN
Tel: 01434 320327

Hadrian's Wall with its Roman remains at Housesteads, Vindolanda, Birdoswald and Carvoran Roman Army Museum is a fascinating place to explore. At its very heart, this traditional beamed inn is an excellent base, convenient for touring options to the Scottish Border Country, Edinburgh and Glasgow in one direction and the Lake District in the other. Cosy and convivial, the hostelry supplies all refreshment needs signally well: the restaurant presents both a bar meal menu and a good à la carte selection. Fresh produce is used whenever available and all meals are cooked to order. Three well-appointed en suite bedrooms with colour television and tea and coffee-making facilities await guests wishing to stay overnight.

3 BEDROOMS, ALL WITH PRIVATE BATHROOM; SCOTTISH AND NEWCASTLE HOUSE; HISTORIC INTEREST; CHILDREN WELCOME, PETS BY ARRANGEMENT; BAR AND RESTAURANT MEALS; NON-SMOKING AREAS; HEXHAM 14 MILES; S£, D£.

TANKERVILLE ARMS HOTEL
Cottage Road, Wooler, Northumberland NE71 6AD
Tel: 01668 281581 • Fax: 01668 281387 • e-mail: enquiries@tankervillehotel.co.uk
website: www.tankervillehotel.co.uk

The Tankerville Arms is a charming 17th century coaching inn with a relaxing and cosy atmosphere, situated in the heart the of Northumbrian countryside. It is an ideal base for the unspoilt attractions of Bamburgh, Holy Island, The Cheviots and Scottish Borders. Fine food, excellent service, quality bedrooms are combined with a strong desire to make your stay both enjoyable and memorable. The Tankerville Arms Hotel is situated just off the A697. *ETC/ AA/ RAC* ★★.

16 BEDROOMS, ALL WITH PRIVATE BATHROOM; FREE HOUSE WITH REAL ALE; HISTORIC INTEREST; CHILDREN AND PETS WELCOME; BAR AND RESTAURANT MEALS; NON-SMOKING AREAS; ALNWICK 15 MILES; S£££, D£££.

For details of Tourist Board Gradings in England, Scotland and Wales see page 17

Oxfordshire

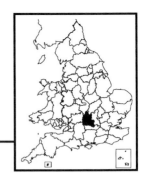

THE LAMB AT BUCKLAND
Buckland, Faringdon, Oxfordshire SN7 8QN
Tel: 01367 870484 • Fax: 01367 870675

When one thinks of the Lamb, one automatically thinks of food for its tempting range of bar meals and dinners are worth coming a long way to marvel at and enjoy. Owners, Peta and Paul Barnard, are so engrossed in the culinary arts that they have started their own outside catering business. In a peaceful village on the edge of the Cotswolds, the 18th century Lamb is a welcoming port of call with a convivial bar serving real ale and a pleasant garden where refreshment may be taken in good weather. Rest assured, the food served in the restaurant and bar is calculated to suit all palates and purses. Excellent overnight en suite accommodation is available, also at moderate rates. *AA Rosette, Egon Ronay*

7 BEDROOMS, ALL WITH PRIVATE BATHROOM; FREE HOUSE WITH REAL ALE; HISTORIC INTEREST; CHILDREN WELCOME; BAR AND RESTAURANT MEALS; NON-SMOKING AREAS; FARINGDON 4 MILES; S£££, D£££.

GEORGE HOTEL
High Street, Dorchester-on-Thames, Oxfordshire OX10 7HH
Tel: 01865 340404• Fax: 01865 341620

The antiques, heavy oaken beams, stone-flagged floor and fine old fireplaces well stacked with aromatic logs add to the plentiful charms of this 15th century coaching inn, particularly in the charismatic Potboys Bar. Unlike the time-hallowed atmosphere, however, facilities are thoroughly up-to-date, all the en suite guest rooms are decorated in individual style and have colour television, telephone, radio alarm and tea and coffee tray. The dining room is a lovely setting worthy of the fine cuisine. Menus change every day with the chef providing a wide variety of original and exciting dishes. Excellent amenities for conferences exist in the superb, self-contained Stable Suite. *AA Two Rosettes.*

17 BEDROOMS, ALL WITH PRIVATE BATHROOM; FREE HOUSE WITH REAL ALE; HISTORIC INTEREST; CHILDREN AND PETS WELCOME; BAR AND RESTAURANT MEALS; NON-SMOKING AREAS; WALLINGFORD 4 MILES; S£££££, D£££££.

SHEPHERDS HALL INN
Witney Road, Freeland, Oxfordshire OX8 8HQ
Tel: 01993 881256 • Fax: 01993 883455

One of the finest houses for miles, the welcoming Shepherds Hall stands on the A4095 Woodstock to Witney road, in an area famed for its sheep rearing, hence its name. Rooms are now modernised, with colour television, direct-dial telephones and tea/coffee making facilities, yet retain the atmosphere of a true country inn, and proprietors Liz and David Fyson present a comprehensive selection of appetising meals and snacks in the bar every day. This is a good place to bring the family (perhaps after visiting Woodstock and Blenheim Palace) for there is an attractive beer garden and children's play area. Wholesome accommodation is available at reasonable rates and this includes a full English breakfast. *ETC* ◆◆◆

5 BEDROOMS, ALL WITH PRIVATE BATH OR SHOWER AND TOILET; FREE HOUSE WITH REAL ALE; CHILDREN WELCOME; BAR FOOD; OXFORD 12 MILES, WITNEY 4, WOODSTOCK 4; S££, D££.

PEAR TREE INN
Scotland End, Hook Norton, Banbury, Oxfordshire OX15 5NU
Tel: 01608 737482

This attractive, old-world pub has the distinction (and undoubted advantage!) of being just about 300 yards from its parent (Hook Norton) brewery. A real village inn with few ideas above its station, this is a friendly port of call and very much one for the collector. Apart from the well-known ale, a surprisingly comprehensive range of home cooked dishes is on offer in the bar with the menu varied enough to suit most tastes. For a quiet break in idyllic and unsophisticated surroundings, the little inn has accommodation available with en suite shower and wc, colour television and tea/coffee making facilities. The ideal 'away from it all' location. *ETC* ◆◆◆

3 BEDROOMS, ALL WITH PRIVATE BATHROOM; HOOK NORTON HOUSE WITH REAL ALE; HISTORIC INTEREST; CHILDREN AND PETS WELCOME; BAR MEALS (NOT SUN. EVENING); NON-SMOKING AREAS; CHIPPING NORTON 5 MILES; S££, D££££.

THE KING'S HEAD INN AND RESTAURANT
Bledington, Near Kingham, Oxfordshire OX7 6XQ
Tel: 01608 658365 • Fax: 01608 658902 • e-mail: kingshead@orr-ewing.com

Facing Bledington's village green with its brook and ducks stands the 15th century King's Head Inn, an establishment which has echoed with the sounds of convivial hospitality for over four centuries. Bledington nestles in the heart of the Cotswolds and is within easy reach of all top tourist attractions. The charming accommodation is in keeping with the atmosphere, all bedrooms (en suite) having television, telephone and hot drinks facilities. High quality and inventive bar fare is served, with full à la carte and table d'hôte menus in the award-winning restaurant in the evenings. A selection of real ales and interesting whiskies is served in the bar which has original old beams and an inglenook fireplace. *AA* ◆◆◆◆, *Egon Ronay* ★, *Good Pub Guide Dining County Pub of the Year, Logis.*

12 BEDROOMS, ALL WITH PRIVATE BATHROOM; FREE HOUSE WITH REAL ALE; HISTORIC INTEREST; CHILDREN WELCOME; BAR FOOD, RESTAURANT EVENINGS ONLY; NON-SMOKING AREAS; STOW-ON-THE-WOLD 4 MILES; S£££, D£££.

KILLINGWORTH CASTLE INN

Glympton Road, Wootton, Woodstock, Oxfordshire 0X20 1EJ
Tel & Fax: 01993 811401 • e-mail: kil.cast@btinternet.com
website: www.oxlink.co.uk/woodstock/kilcastle

Built in 1637, this one-time coaching halt on the Worcester to London run stands on the edge of a picturesque village just outside Woodstock. Now run by Paul and Maureen Barrow, the inn retains much of its original character. Acknowledged for the quality of its cask-conditioned ales, the inn is also known for its extensive à la carte meal selection available seven days a week in the bar area. A small separate dining area caters for non-smokers and family parties. Adjoining is a games room, and a pleasant lawned garden, safe for children, includes 'Aunt Sally', the traditional Oxfordshire game. Close to Blenheim Palace and the Cotswolds, this fine hostelry offers spacious, tastefully decorated, en suite accommodation. *Cask Marque.*

4 BEDROOMS, ALL WITH PRIVATE BATHROOM; MORLAND HOUSE WITH REAL ALE; HISTORIC INTEREST; CHILDREN WELCOME; BAR AND RESTAURANT MEALS; NON-SMOKING AREAS; WOODSTOCK 2 MILES; S£££, D££.

Shropshire

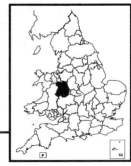

THE BULLS HEAD INN
Chelmarsh, Bridgnorth, Shropshire WV16 6BA
Tel: 01746 861469 • Fax: 01746 862646 • e-mail: bullshead@virtual-shropshire.co.uk
e-mail: dave@bulls-head-fsnet.co.uk • website: www.virtual-shropshire.co.uk

Excellent accommodation and a traditional welcome in the heart of Shropshire. Relax and enjoy your break in the warm, friendly atmosphere of a traditional country inn. Set amidst Shropshire's rolling hills, The Bulls Head Inn is a splendid base for exploring Wenlock Edge, Ironbridge Gorge and the glorious Severn valley. All bedrooms (one with four-poster bed) are luxuriously appointed with en suite bathrooms, full central heating, colour television and tea/coffee making facilities. There are ground level rooms with access and facilities for people with disabilities. Fishermen's storage facilities available. Choose from our comprehensive menus, served in our bar or one of our dining rooms. Self-catering accommodation also available (3 Stars). Mastercard and Visa accepted. *ETC* ◆◆◆◆ *See also Colour Advertisement on page 8.*

10 BEDROOMS, ALL EN SUITE; FREE HOUSE WITH REAL ALE; CHILDREN WELCOME; BAR AND RESTAURANT MEALS; NON-SMOKING AREAS; BRIDGNORTH 4 MILES; S££, D££.

BOARS HEAD HOTEL
Church Street, Bishops Castle, Shropshire SY9 5AE
Tel: 01588 638521 • Fax: 01588 630126

Close to the medieval towns of Ludlow and Shrewsbury and slumbering amidst delightful, unspoilt countryside, Bishops Castle is the perfect location for a quiet, relaxing break away from the hustle and bustle of urban life. The Boars Head, with its wealth of exposed beams and welcoming log fire, is just the place to choose as a base for such an escapade. It comfortably meets the challenge of contemporary times by providing excellent en suite accommodation, the rooms having colour television, telephone and tea and coffee making facilities. In the matter of refreshment, an extensive choice ranges from lunchtime bar meals to a full à la carte evening selection with a traditional roast on Sundays. Places of interest within easy reach include the towns of Newtown and Welshpool across the Welsh border and Ironbridge Gorge. *ETC* ◆◆◆, *AA*.

4 BEDROOMS, ALL WITH PRIVATE BATHROOM; FREE HOUSE WITH REAL ALE; CHILDREN WELCOME, PETS IN BEDROOMS ONLY; BAR AND RESTAURANT MEALS; NON-SMOKING AREAS; CRAVEN ARMS 8 MILES; S£££, D££.

THE ROEBUCK INN
Brimfield, Ludlow, Shropshire SY8 4NE
Tel: 01584 711230 • Fax: 01584 711654 • e-mail: dave@roebuckinn.demon.co.uk
website: www.roebuckinn.demon.co.uk

In a pretty village between Ludlow and Leominster, the Roebuck is widely renowned for its superb dining room which serves imaginative and interesting dishes based on the finest fresh local ingredients. This is an ideal venue for a rewarding break in tranquil surroundings, and excellent en suite accommodation is available in comfortable and cosy bedrooms. Three bars offer a choice of venues for relaxation and convivial conversation. Ludlow is a picturesque market town steeped in history with an impressive Norman castle, whilst Leominster, with its origins in the wool trade, has numerous antique shops. *AA* ◆◆◆.

3 BEDROOMS, ALL WITH PRIVATE BATHROOM; FREE HOUSE WITH REAL ALE; CHILDREN AND PETS WELCOME; BAR AND RESTAURANT MEALS; NON-SMOKING AREAS; LUDLOW 4 MILES, LEOMINSTER 7 MILES; S£££, D££.

OLD MILL INN
Candy, Near Trefonen, Shropshire SY10 9AZ
Tel: 01691 657058 • Fax: 01691 680918 • e-mail: theoldmill.inn@virgin.net

The Candy Valley sounds like every child's dream, a place where they can gorge themselves on their favourite food. Alas, the dream fades but the connection with food remains very much to the point. The Candy Valley in question is indeed an idyllic spot set between the Welsh mountains and the pleasant old market town of Oswestry and is the location of this homely inn where food is its very 'raison d'etre'.. Under the watchful eye of the gifted David Atkinson, an intriguing and ever-changing menu has been recognised by the thrice-repeated award of the AA's much coveted Red Rosette. A popular Hog Roast is organised every Friday night during the summer (rain or shine!) and food can be eaten outside in the delightful covered area. A selection of real ales provide a good accompaniment at all times. The inn is beautifully sited over an old watermill in its own 12 acres of fields and woodland with the River Morda and the famous Offa's Dyke both running right through the grounds. An enclosed garden boasts an imaginative 'Pirates' play area for children which can be watched by parents in the comfort of the conservatory whilst having dinner. There is a beer garden and ample space in the grounds for campers for whom all the facilities of the hotel are available. The less adventurous wishing to dally longer in this enchanting place will find a choice of double, twin and single bedrooms at their disposal at very reasonable rates – call David or Sharon who also organise a series of outdoor activities. *AA Rosette.*

5 BEDROOMS; FREE HOUSE WITH REAL ALE; HISTORIC INTEREST; CHILDREN AND PETS WELCOME; BAR AND RESTAURANT MEALS; NON-SMOKING AREAS; SHREWSBURY 16 MILES; S£, D££.

THE GROVE (incorporating the Fat Frog Restaurant)
10 Wellington Road, Coalbrookdale, Telford, Shropshire TF8 7DX
Tel & Fax: 01952 433269 • e-mail: frog@fat-frog.co.uk
website: www.fat-frog.co.uk

Ironbridge had a significant role to play in the Industrial Revolution and situated next to the Coalbrookdale Museum, The Grove was the first commercial hotel to cater for visitors to the Ironbridge Gorge. A coaching inn with its origins in the 18th century, the hostelry is a fascinating place to call upon. The Lily Pad Bar is themed around the gorge with hand-painted designs on the bar and furniture; this is a popular rendezvous before or after dining memorably in the Fat Frog Restaurant below. The beautiful and unspoilt county of Shropshire has much to offer sightseers, and excellent overnight accommodation is provided in rooms with baths/showers en suite and colour television; residents have their own private lounge. *ETC* ◆◆◆, *AA.*

4 BEDROOMS, ALL WITH PRIVATE BATHROOM; FREE HOUSE WITH REAL ALE; HISTORIC INTEREST; CHILDREN AND PETS WELCOME; BAR MEALS, RESTAURANT EVENINGS ONLY; NON-SMOKING AREAS; DAWLEY 2 MILES; S££, D££.

Please mention *Recommended Wayside & Country Inns*
when enquiring about accommodation featured in these pages.

STOKESAY CASTLE COACHING INN
School Road, Craven Arms, Shropshire SY7 9PE
Tel: 01588 672304 • Fax: 01588 673877

Shropshire has a special magic which, once experienced, casts a lasting spell. Rich in undulating farmland and dotted with quiet market towns, the county has, in the past, taken a leading role in often violent struggles across its border with Wales typified by Stokesay Castle, a perfectly preserved 13th century fortified manor house from which this little gem of an hotel takes its name. The present owners lost no time in enhancing the inn's reputation for excellent, well presented food with a positive flair for traditional home cooking by bringing in first class, well-trained staff with a special gift of making visitors feel welcome. To discover the secret allure of the area, acquaintance with this friendly retreat is strongly recommended. First-rate accommodation is available in rooms with en suite facilities, satellite television and tea and coffee-makers. *AA* ★★★★

12 BEDROOMS, ALL WITH PRIVATE BATHROOM; FREE HOUSE WITH REAL ALE; HISTORIC INTEREST; CHILDREN AND PETS WELCOME; BAR AND RESTAURANT MEALS; NON-SMOKING AREAS; LUDLOW 7 MILES; S££, D££/££££.

THE CROWN INN
Hopton Wafers, Near Cleobury Mortimer, Shropshire DY14 0NB
Tel: 01299 270372 • Fax: 01299 271127 • e-mail: desk@crownathopton.co.uk
website: www.crownathopton.co.uk

It is difficult to decide whether to concentrate on cuisine, accommodation or indeed the surroundings of this lovely old 16th century coaching inn – for all are appealing enough in themselves. Open fires add warmth and atmosphere throughout The Crown, in bar, lounge and restaurant; guest bedrooms have received the same loving attention to detail as public rooms, being furnished and decorated in a delightful country-cottage style and equipped with all practical necessities. Sandwiches, steaks and everything in between can be found on the excellent bar menu, and the light airy AA Rosette restaurant provides such delights as Beef Wellington, Chicken en Croute and Lobster Thermidor, prepared and presented with flair and imagination. *ETC/AA* ◆◆◆◆, *AA Rosettte.*

7 BEDROOMS, ALL WITH PRIVATE BATHROOM; FREE HOUSE WITH REAL ALE; HISTORIC INTEREST; CHILDREN WELCOME; BAR AND RESTAURANT MEALS; NON-SMOKING AREAS; CLEOBURY MORTIMER 2 MILES; S£££, D£££.

THE CHURCH INN
Buttercross, Ludlow, Shropshire SY8 1AW
Tel: 01584 872174 • Fax: 01584 877146

This historic inn has undergone several changes of name over the centuries – it was originally called the "Cross Keys" – but retains the fine old-fashioned traditions of good ale and good food which have ensured its lasting popularity through the ages. Nine cosy en suite bedrooms provide first-rate overnight accommodation, and a full range of catering, from freshly cut sandwiches to succulent steaks, ensures that appetites large and small will be amply satisfied. Regularly changing guest beers supplement the already extensive range of wines, spirits and ales on offer. The ancient town of Ludlow is an ideal base for exploring the Border counties and the Welsh Marches, and is conveniently located for road and rail links to the Midlands. *ETC/AA/RAC* ◆◆◆, *CAMRA, Egon Ronay.*

9 BEDROOMS, ALL WITH PRIVATE BATHROOM; FREE HOUSE WITH REAL ALE; HISTORIC INTEREST; CHILDREN WELCOME; BAR LUNCHES, RESTAURANT EVENINGS ONLY; NON-SMOKING AREAS; SHREWSBURY 24 MILES; S££, D££.

TALBOT INN
High Street, Much Wenlock, Shropshire TF13 6AA
Tel: 01952 727077 • Fax: 01952 728436

Once part of Wenlock Abbey, this charming 13th century inn is entered through an archway which opens into a quiet courtyard garden; inside the exposed beams, open log fires and fresh flowers create a mood of relaxed contentment. Guest rooms with private facilities are in a converted malthouse in the courtyard, which also houses a comfortable residents' lounge and breakfast room; all are attractively furnished. A good choice of home-cooked dishes is available lunchtime and in the evening and even those on the strictest of diets should give in for once and sample the famous Bread and Butter Pudding, a speciality of the house.

6 BEDROOMS, ALL WITH PRIVATE BATHROOM; FREE HOUSE WITH REAL ALE; HISTORIC INTEREST; CHILDREN WELCOME; BAR AND RESTAURANT MEALS; NON-SMOKING AREAS; SHREWSBURY 11 MILES, BRIDGNORTH 9; S££££, D££££

GASKELL ARMS HOTEL
Much Wenlock, Shropshire TF13 6AQ
Tel: 01952 727212 • Fax: 01952 728505 • e-mail: maxine@gaskellarms.co.uk
website: www.SmoothHound.co.uk/hotels/gaskell.html

A fascinating little town in the beautiful Shropshire countryside, Much Wenlock is steeped in history with many of its buildings dating back to the 15th century. The mellow Gaskell Arms did not take its place until the 17th century but it is now one of the features of the town. Warm, traditional hospitality is the order of the day at this typically English wayside inn. An interesting and varied selection of hot and cold food is always available in the cosy lounge with a full à la carte menu on offer in the oak-beamed restaurant. Overnight accommodation is provided in delightfully decorated guest rooms appointed with television, telephone and tea and coffee-making facilities. Additional superior Coach House Suite, sleeps four. *ETC/AA* ◆◆◆◆ *See also Colour Advertisement on page 8.*

11 BEDROOMS, 6 WITH PRIVATE BATHROOM; FREE HOUSE WITH REAL ALE; HISTORIC INTEREST; CHILDREN WELCOME; BAR AND RESTAURANT MEALS; NON-SMOKING AREAS; BRIDGNORTH 8 MILES; S£££, D££.

ARLESTON INN HOTEL AND RESTAURANT
Arleston Lane, Wellington, Telford, Shropshire TF1 2LA
Tel: 01952 501881 • Fax: 01952 506429

Peacefully located but conveniently close to Telford town centre, this attractively furnished inn has a popular restaurant renowned for its fine food and service. The bar has traditional appeal and is brightly decorated. Built in Tudor style, the hostelry also has a spacious lounge and conservatory with picture windows overlooking the garden and a number of handsomely furnished guest rooms, each one appointed with en suite facilities, colour television, direct-dial telephone, beverage-makers and central heating. Excellent arrangements are made for functions and business meetings. *ETC/AA* ◆◆.

7 BEDROOMS, ALL WITH PRIVATE BATHROOM, FREE HOUSE WITH REAL ALE; HISTORIC INTEREST; CHILDREN WELCOME; BAR AND RESTAURANT MEALS; NON-SMOKING AREAS; SHREWSBURY 11 MILES; S£££, D£.

Stokesay Castle, Shropshire

Somerset

THE KINGS ARMS
Litton, Near Bath, Somerset BA3 4PW
Tel: 01761 241301

It was a glorious sunny day and the popularity of this charming hostelry was easy to see for the lovely garden was crowded with visitors enjoying an appetising selection of hot and cold dishes as well as well-kept ales tapped from the cask. Thought to have been converted from two cottages, the inn dates from the 15th century and is as pretty as a picture, with its pantiled roof and windows topped by gently curved oak beams. Children are welcome here and the swings and slides in the garden will amuse them whilst parents relax. Tucked away down the B3114 between West Harptree and Chewton Mendip, this little gem is a real find.

NO ACCOMMODATION; FREE HOUSE WITH REAL ALE; CHILDREN AND PETS WELCOME; BAR MEALS; WELLS 6 MILES.

LION HOTEL
Bank Square, Dulverton, Somerset TA22 9BU
Tel: 01398 323444 • Fax: 01398 323980

The perfect headquarters for exploring the magic land of heather-clad moors, leafy lanes, nature trails, red deer and wild ponies of Exmoor, the attractive and comfortable Lion Hotel is set in the heart of the delightful little town of Dulverton, on Exmoor's southern fringe. Warm and friendly, the hotel takes great pride in the delicious home-cooked cuisine on offer in the charming restaurant. Alternatively, there is an extensive selection of meals available in the lounge bar. Full of character, guest rooms are fully en suite and have colour television, direct-dial telephone and beverage makers. Sporting activities available locally include riding, river and reservoir fishing, and golf. *AA* ★★

13 BEDROOMS, ALL WITH PRIVATE BATHROOM; FREE HOUSE WITH REAL ALE; HISTORIC INTEREST;
CHILDREN AND PETS WELCOME; BAR AND RESTAURANT MEALS; NON-SMOKING AREAS; TIVERTON 10 MILES; S££, D££.

HELYAR ARMS COUNTRY INN, HOTEL & RESTAURANT
Moor Lane, East Coker, Near Yeovil, Somerset BA22 9JR
Tel: 01935 862332 • Fax: 01935 864129 • e-mail: info@helyar-arms.co.uk
website: www.helyar-arms.co.uk

At the heart of a beautiful village on the Dorset/Somerset border, this lovely old inn has a welcoming traditional bar, its time-hallowed atmosphere fostered by many features dating back to Elizabethan days. In a charming restaurant created from the former apple loft, one will be rewarded by excellent food, drink and company. An intriguing menu ranges from local specialities to international favourites. The excellent accommodation available is equipped to the highest standards; all rooms have en suite facilities and such modern practicalities as remote-control colour television, direct-dial telephone, computer modem points and tea and coffeemakers amongst their thoughtful appointments. There is a large beer garden and a skittle alley. *AA* ◆◆◆.

6 BEDROOMS, ALL WITH PRIVATE BATHROOM; FREE HOUSE WITH REAL ALE; HISTORIC INTEREST; CHILDREN WELCOME; BAR AND RESTAURANT MEALS; NON-SMOKING AREAS; YEOVIL 3 MILES; S££££, D££.

THE PECKING MILL INN
Evercreech, Near Shepton Mallet, Somerset BA4 6PG
Tel: 01749 830336/830006 • Fax: 01749 831316
e-mail: peckingmill@peckingmill.freeserve.co.uk

History, legend and breathtaking scenery combine in the Mendip area of Somerset to make it the perfect setting for a short break or longer stay, and at the Pecking Mill you will find added to these attractions warm hospitality and a friendly welcome for all. Bedrooms have everything one could wish for to make one's stay comfortable, including private bathrooms, colour television, direct-dial telephone, hairdryer and trouser press; the most attractive room rate includes a full English breakfast. The bar and restaurant retain the traditional atmosphere of the inn's 16th century origins and offer an excellent choice of good food, well kept ales and other refreshments. *ETC/RAC* ◆◆◆

6 BEDROOMS, ALL WITH PRIVATE BATHROOMS; FREE HOUSE WITH REAL ALE; CHILDREN WELCOME; BAR AND RESTAURANT MEALS; NON-SMOKING AREAS; SHEPTON MALLET 4 MILES; S££, D£.

THE HOOD ARMS
Kilve, Somerset TA5 1EA
Tel: 01278 741210 • Fax: 01278 741477

The Hood Arms nestles in the heart of the Quantocks in an area which is totally unspoilt. A traditional black and white 17th century coaching inn owned by Barry and Vanessa Eason, it is set in landscaped lawns, with a spacious walled garden. The comfortable bars have distinct character created by old beams, large fireplaces with roaring log fires in season, and candlelight for evening dining. The extensive and varied menus will satisfy the heartiest of appetites, with a comprehensive wine list to complement your meal. The five double bedrooms are fully en suite, with television, trouser press, hairdryer and hospitality tray. One cottage adjacent to the Inn is available for weekend or longer breaks and is ideal for families. Resident managers Matthew Haggett and Brian Pook look forward to welcoming you. *AA* ◆◆◆◆ *See also Colour Advertisement on page 8.*

5 BEDROOMS, ALL WITH PRIVATE BATHROOM; FREE HOUSE WITH REAL ALE; HISTORIC INTEREST; CHILDREN AND PETS WELCOME; BAR MEALS, RESTAURANT FRI/SAT; NON-SMOKING AREAS; WILLITON 5 MILES; S£££, D££.

OLD POUND INN
Aller, Langport, Somerset TA10 0RA
Tel & Fax: 01458 250469

With all the credentials of a classic wayside inn, the 'Old Pound' changed its name from the 'White Lion' as recently as 1980 as it stands on the site of the old village pound. Starting life as a cider house in 1571, it has pursued its purpose of providing sustenance to the inhabitants of an idyllic Somerset village ever since, quite unmoved by the ravages of the Civil War which raged nearby. Peace reigns today with standards of refreshment and accommodation upgraded to a level somewhat higher than the surrounding fen-like countryside – a rich land of imposing sunsets. Two resident chefs hold sway over a splendid à la carte restaurant and the excellent accommodation comprises rooms with en suite facilities, colour television and tea and coffee-makers. *ETC* ◆◆◆, *Winner of JPC National Award for Best Pub of the Year 1999 and 2000.*

6 BEDROOMS, FREE HOUSE WITH REAL ALE; HISTORIC INTEREST; CHILDREN AND PETS WELCOME; BAR AND RESTAURANT MEALS; NON-SMOKING AREAS; LANGPORT 2 MILES; S££, D£££.

THE DRAGON HOUSE HOTEL & RESTAURANT
Bilbrook, Near Minehead, Somerset TA24 6HQ
Tel: 01984 640215 • Fax: 01984 641340 • e-mail: info@dragonhouse.co.uk

This charming, family-run 1700's country house is located in three acres of natural beauty between Exmoor and the Somerset coast, an ideal base to explore many renowned beauty spots. All bedrooms encompass the requirements of the modern traveller, with telephone, television and en suite facilities, each room retaining its individuality. The oak-panelled restaurant is the perfect setting to enjoy an evening of fine classical and West Country cuisine, accompanied by an impressive wine list. Simpler light meals, bar snacks, drinks and refreshments are available throughout the day in the comfortable bar, conservatory, colonnaded courtyard or underneath the largest Black Poplar in England. *See also Colour Advertisement on page 10.*

9 BEDROOMS, ALL WITH PRIVATE BATHROOM; FREE HOUSE; HISTORIC INTEREST; BAR AND RESTAURANT MEALS; NON-SMOKING AREAS; DUNSTER 3 MILES; S£££, D££.

THE WHEELWRIGHTS ARMS
Monkton Combe, Near Bath, Somerset BA2 7HD
Tel: 01225 722287 • Fax: 01225 723029

With excellent accommodation housed in the converted barn and stables, this is a lovely base from which to visit the numerous houses, gardens and places of interest which lie within a few miles, including of course the city of Bath itself. The hostelry stands in the peace and quiet of the lovely Midford valley. A large selection of home cooked food is served, with the addition of a grill menu in the evening. In addition there is a choice of three real ales. The bedrooms (mostly beamed) are equipped with shower, toilet, washbasin, colour television, central heating, tea and coffee making facilities, direct-dial telephones and hairdryers. The inn is also a lovely base for walking, fishing, riding or just relaxing. In the summer guests are free to use the pleasant garden and patio, and in winter cosy log fires warm the bar. *ETC* ◆◆.

8 BEDROOMS, ALL WITH PRIVATE BATHROOM; FREE HOUSE WITH REAL ALE; HISTORIC INTEREST; BAR LUNCHES, RESTAURANT EVENINGS ONLY; BATH 2 MILES; S£££, D££.

THE CATASH INN
North Cadbury, Near Yeovil, Somerset BA22 7DH
Tel & Fax: 01963 440248 • e-mail: Sandra&Clive@catash.demon.co.uk
website: www.catash.demon.co.uk

200 year old Village Inn, half a mile north of A303. Ideally situated for Yeovilton and Sparkford Motor museums; excellent location for tourists, walkers and cyclists. Restaurant and bar snacks served seven days a week. Clive and Sandra Robinson assure you of a warm welcome, where good food, fine wine and traditional beers complement the happy, friendly atmosphere of this village inn.

3 BEDROOMS, ALL WITH PRIVATE BATHROOM; REAL ALE; HISTORIC INTEREST; CHILDREN WELCOME; BAR AND RESTAURANT MEALS; NON-SMOKING AREAS; WINCANTON 5 MILES; S££, D££.

The Manor Arms, North Perrott.

MANOR ARMS
North Perrott, Somerset TA18 7SG
Tel: 01460 72901

A focal point in a village of lovely hamstone cottages, this handsome 16th century Grade II Listed building displays abundant character through its exposed stonework, inglenook fireplace and original oak beams, the bar warmed by a log fire in cool weather. Lovingly restored and having acquired a reputation for its superb (and reasonably-priced) English fare, this typical wayside inn overlooks the green. This is a tranquil area of picture-book villages and verdant, undulating countryside with the Dorset coast within 20 minutes' drive and a number of historic houses close at hand. Bed and breakfast accommodation is available in both the Inn and in the Coach House situated in the gardens in a quiet setting behind the inn. All guest rooms have en suite shower rooms and are comfortably furnished, the ideal venue for a quiet and rewarding break. *ETC/AA* ◆◆◆.

8 BEDROOMS, ALL WITH PRIVATE BATHROOM; FREE HOUSE WITH REAL ALE; HISTORIC INTEREST; CHILDREN WELCOME; BAR AND RESTAURANT MEALS; NON-SMOKING AREAS; CREWKERNE 2 MILES; S£££, D£.

THE CASTLE HOTEL
Porlock, Somerset TA24 8PY
Tel & Fax: 01643 862504

The Castle Hotel is a small, fully licensed family-run hotel in the centre of the lovely Exmoor village of Porlock. It is an ideal holiday location for those who wish to enjoy the grandeur of Exmoor on foot or by car. The beautiful villages of Selsworthy and Dunster with its castle are only a short distance away. There are 13 en suite bedrooms, all fully heated, with colour television and tea/coffee making facilities. The Castle Hotel has a well-stocked bar with real ale, draught Guinness and cider. A full range of bar meals are available at lunchtimes and evenings or dine in our restaurant. Children and pets are most welcome. Family room available, cots available on request. Pools, darts and skittles all available. *See also Colour Advertisement on page 9.*

13 BEDROOMS, ALL WITH PRIVATE BATHROOM; REAL ALE; CHILDREN AND PETS WELCOME; BAR AND RESTAURANT MEALS; MINEHEAD 5 MILES.

THE OLD RED LION, N. BREWHAM

OLD RED LION
North Brewham, Near Bruton, Somerset BA10 0JL
Tel: 01749 850287

Deep in cider country and a noted dispenser of that delectable tipple, this attractive free house has a cellar bar with beams, flagstone floor, open fire and a timeless atmosphere. Good real ales are served and each day's 'specials' are featured on the blackboard menu, whilst the dining room is a pleasant setting for an imaginative selection of freshly-prepared meals. Tom and Anne O'Toole supervise the well-being of visitors and are to be congratulated on what they have achieved in this tranquil retreat. The gardens and meadow give fine views across the Brue Valley. Why not stay for a few days? Relaxation was never so easily acquired and there is a choice of comfortable en suite double-bedded rooms.

2 BEDROOMS, BOTH WITH PRIVATE BATHROOM; FREE HOUSE WITH REAL ALE; CHILDREN WELCOME; BAR AND RESTAURANT MEALS; NON-SMOKING AREAS; BRUTON 3 MILES; S£, D£££.

GREYHOUND INN
Staple Fitzpaine, Taunton, Somerset TA3 5SP
Tel: 01823 480227 • Fax: 01823 481117

In the shadow of the Blackdown Hills and in an area of outstanding rural beauty, this is a true wayside inn with all the traditional values of good company, good contemporary accommodation and very, very good fare. In the latter cause, guests are invited to indulge themselves with a smoked salmon and champagne breakfast as a suitable start to the day and later to a visit to a warm and welcoming bar which offers home-cooked country fare. The actively inclined may while away the hours in gentle exploration of an area where time seems to stand still and return to the promise of a splendid à la carte meal in the 54-cover restaurant and, at the close of the day, to sound repose in a delightful en suite bedroom. *AA* ◆◆◆◆.

4 BEDROOMS, ALL WITH PRIVATE BATHROOM; LIONHEART HOUSE WITH REAL ALE; HISTORIC INTEREST; CHILDREN AND PETS WELCOME; BAR AND RESTAURANT MEALS; NON-SMOKING AREAS; TAUNTON 5 MILES; S££, D££.

LETHBRIDGE ARMS
Gore Square, Bishops Lydeard, Taunton, Somerset TA4 3BW
Tel: 01823 432234 • Fax: 01823 433982

Visitors are drawn to this traditional, 16th century former coaching inn by its first-rate food and beer, plus good service and the warmest of welcomes. Particularly impressive is the wide choice of real ales and home-made dishes on offer. There is a large beer garden, children's play area, a skittle alley and a convivial bar where various pub games may invoke a challenge or two, but beware – the locals are playing 'at home'! This is a fine centre from which to explore the nearby Quantocks, Exmoor and the Somerset and Devon coasts and for this purpose very comfortable Bed and Breakfast accommodation is available. Some of the cosy bedrooms are en suite, and all have colour television, and tea/coffee making facilities. *ETC* ◆◆◆.

8 BEDROOMS, 2 WITH PRIVATE BATHROOM; WHITBREAD HOUSE WITH REAL ALE; HISTORIC INTEREST; CHILDREN AND PETS WELCOME; BAR AND RESTAURANT MEALS; TAUNTON 5 MILES; S£, D£££.

THE BULL TERRIER
Croscombe, Wells, Somerset BA5 3QJ
Tel: 01749 343658

Good food and plenty of choice – that is very much the order of the day at this friendly country inn where menus range from freshly cut sandwiches to generous helpings of home-made traditional dishes – and don't forget to leave space for one of the wickedly tempting desserts! A choice of vegetarian meals is available. The three cosy bars serve a good range of refreshments including well-kept real ales, lager and cider. Should overnight accommodation be required, there are two prettily decorated en suite double bedrooms, comfortably furnished and complete with colour television and tea/coffee making facilities. There are many lovely walks in the area and the village itself has a fine church with Jacobean carvings.

2 BEDROOMS, BOTH WITH PRIVATE BATHROOM; FREE HOUSE WITH REAL ALE; HISTORIC INTEREST; BAR AND RESTAURANT MEALS; NON-SMOKING AREAS; WELLS 3 MILES; £/££.

CROSSWAYS INN
West Huntspill, Near Highbridge, Somerset TA9 3RA
Tel: 01278 783756 • Fax: 01278 781899 • e-mail: crossways.inn@virgin.net

Conveniently located on the A38 (Exits 22 and 23 from the M5), this spacious 17th century inn is very popular with families, whether on a day out or staying overnight. Children sharing a room with their parents are accommodated free and there is a special family room for meals and refreshments. In fine weather meals can be taken on picnic tables under the trees in the spacious garden. A good range of real ales is available, including a weekly-changing guest beer, and service is cheerful and efficient. The Crossways is ideally situated for exploring the West Country and is just a short drive from the lively holiday resort of Weston-super-Mare. *AA, Which? Guide to Country Pubs.*

3 BEDROOMS; ALL WITH PRIVATE BATHROOM; FREE HOUSE WITH REAL ALE; HISTORIC INTEREST; CHILDREN AND PETS WELCOME; BAR AND RESTAURANT MEALS; NON-SMOKING AREAS; BURNHAM-ON-SEA 2 MILES; S£, D££.

The **FHG**
GOLF GUIDE
Where to Play
Where to Stay
2001

Available from most bookshops, the 2001 edition of **THE GOLF GUIDE** covers details of every UK golf course – well over 2500 entries – for holiday or business golf. Hundreds of hotel entries offer convenient accommodation, accompanying details of the courses – the 'pro', par score, length etc.

In association with 'Golf Monthly' and including the Ryder Cup Report as well as Holiday Golf in Ireland, France, Portugal, Spain, The USA, South Africa and Thailand .

£9.99 from bookshops or £10.50 including postage (UK only) from FHG Publications, Abbey Mill Business Centre, Paisley PA1 1TJ

ROYAL OAK INN
Withypool, Somerset TA24 7QP
Tel: 01643 831506/7 • Fax: 01643 831659

As an inspiration to lovers of fine food, comfort and old-world grace, this lovely old hostelry has a character that is locked in time, its appeal also inspiring author, R.D.Blackmore to write his famous novel *'Lorna Doone'* whilst staying here in 1866. In a delightful little village on the River Barle and surrounded by the breathtaking and tranquil beauty of Exmoor, this is a wonderful place in which to relax and forget one's cares whilst appreciating the worthwhile things of life: the Rod Room and residents' bars with their beamed ceilings and log fires foster the mood. Bedrooms with individual furnishings are handsomely appointed, all having colour television, radio, telephone, hairdryer and tea and coffee-making facilities. *AA Rosette, RAC Restaurant and Comfort Awards.*

8 BEDROOMS, 7 WITH PRIVATE BATHROOM; FREE HOUSE WITH REAL ALE; HISTORIC INTEREST;
CHILDREN AND PETS WELCOME; BAR MEALS, RESTAURANT EVENINGS ONLY; EXFORD 2 MILES; S£££££, D£££££.

SPARKFORD INN
Sparkford, Yeovil, Somerset BA22 7JN
Tel: 01963 440218 • Fax: 01963 440358

Handy for the A303, the Sparkford Inn is a homely and welcoming old coaching inn with en suite accommodation, a rambling series of beamed bars and carvery restaurant, all with a mix of antique furniture and interesting old prints and photographs. No pool table, juke box or darts. There is a log fire in the lounge bar and restaurant. The inn has a large car park, beer garden and children's adventure play area. At the Sunday luncheon with speciality choice of roasts, the two-course carvery is very reasonably priced; there is also a specials board in the bars. Every evening including Sunday there are à la carte and chalkboard specialities. Evening meals are served from 7 to 10 pm. The pub is a free house and there are always five real ales available. Children are welcome in the restaurant and in some areas in the bar. *ETC* ◆◆◆. *See also Colour Advertisement on page 9.*

10 BEDROOMS, ALL WITH PRIVATE BATHROOM; FREE HOUSE WITH REAL ALE; HISTORIC INTEREST; CHILDREN WELCOME,
DOGS ALLOWED IN BAR ON LEADS; BAR AND RESTAURANT MEALS; NON-SMOKING AREAS; CASTLE CARY 4 MILES; S££/D£££.

Staffordshire

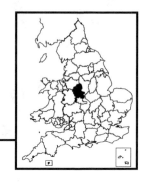

THREE HORSESHOES INN & RESTAURANT
Blackshaw Moor, Leek, Staffordshire ST13 8TW
Tel: 01538 300296 • Fax: 01538 300320 • website: www.threeshoesinn.co.uk

This family-run inn is situated on the A53, approximately seven miles from Buxton, with breathtaking views of the Staffordshire Moorlands and the bizarre stone formation of The Roaches. Stone walls, oak beams and log fires give an olde worlde atmosphere. Fine traditional foods are served in the Carvery, while the restaurant offers à la carte and candlelit menus using fresh vegetables and local beef, poultry, game and cheeses, accompanied by a fine wine list. At weekends a well-attended dinner dance offers a fine choice of food, wine, music and dancing into the early hours. Accommodation is available in six cottage-style bedrooms, with showers, telephone, television and tea-making facilities. For relaxation in fine weather there are large gardens with patios, terraces and a children's play area. *ETC* ★★, *Johansens, AA Rosette.*

6 BEDROOMS, ALL WITH PRIVATE SHOWER; FREE HOUSE WITH REAL ALE; CHILDREN WELCOME; BAR AND RESTAURANT MEALS; NON-SMOKING AREAS; DERBY 28 MILES, STAFFORD 24, STOKE-ON-TRENT 11, S£££, D££.

THE OLDE CORNER HOUSE HOTEL
Walsall Road, Muckley Corner, Lichfield, Staffordshire WS14 0BG
Tel: 01543 372182 • Fax: 01543 372211

An interesting old coaching inn, parts of which date back to 1683, gave way to a new inn in 1891 with the extended buildings converted into cottages. In 1984, Brian and Pamela Higgins purchased the hostelry, then known as 'Muckley Corner Hotel' and proceeded to bring the cottages back to hotel use. This long, laborious and loving task has resulted in the excellent establishment we see today, where two separate restaurants have already acquired a reputation for outstanding food and where efficient service from a friendly staff is assured. Also contributing to the convivial mood is the adjoining pub, whilst the carefully planned accommodation now offers en suite bedrooms of individual style, appointed to the highest standards. *AA* ★★.

23 BEDROOMS, ALL WITH PRIVATE BATHROOM; FREE HOUSE WITH REAL ALE; HISTORIC INTEREST; CHILDREN WELCOME; BAR AND RESTAURANT MEALS; NON-SMOKING AREAS; BIRMINGHAM 15 MILES; S£££, D££.

Suffolk

CROWN HOTEL
High Street, Bildeston, Suffolk IP7 7EB
Tel & Fax: 01449 740510

Built in 1495 and probably a wealthy merchant's house for some time after, there is later proof of the Crown's existence as an inn in the mid-17th century because tokens were issued here to overcome the almost total absence of small change. Over the past 20 years or so this former coaching inn has been restored to former glory. The timbered facade and a wealth of old beams in the bar still take the eye although first-rate modern amenities have been introduced. The restaurant boasts an extensive à la carte menu featuring some intriguing speciality dishes and an extensive range of lighter meals and snacks may be enjoyed in the bar. Bedrooms are individually decorated in romantic style and all have private facilities and colour television. A four-poster and some king-sized beds are available. All rooms have tea-making facilities. This fascinating and relatively unexplored part of East Anglia has much to recommend it both architecturally and historically, this splendid hostelry in particular. Sheltered gardens to the rear provide a tranquil setting for relaxation and for the more energetic, there are opportunities for tennis, golf and swimming nearby. Two and three-day breaks are organised, terms for Bed, Breakfast and Evening Meal representing excellent value. *AA.*

12 BEDROOMS, ALL WITH PRIVATE BATHROOM; FREE HOUSE WITH REAL ALE; HISTORIC INTEREST; CHILDREN AND PETS WELCOME; BAR AND RESTAURANT MEALS; NON-SMOKING AREAS; HADLEIGH 5 MILES; S£££, D££££.

The **£** symbol when appearing at the end of the italic section of an entry shows the anticipated price, during 2001, for full Bed and Breakfast.

Normal Bed & Breakfast rate per person
(in single room)

Normal Bed & Breakfast rate per person
(sharing double/twin room)

PRICE RANGE	CATEGORY	PRICE RANGE	CATEGORY
Under £25	*S£*	**Under £25**	*D£*
£26-£35	*S££*	**£26-£35**	*D££*
£36-£45	*S£££*	**£36-£45**	*D£££*
Over £45	*S££££*	**Over £45**	*D££££*

This is meant as an indication only and does not show prices for Special Breaks, Weekends, etc. Guests are therefore advised to verify all prices on enquiring or booking.

PEACOCK INN
37 The Street, Chelsworth, Near Lavenham, Suffolk IP7 7HU
Tel: 01449 740758

Amidst the colour-washed cottages of the idyllic village of Chelsworth, the welcoming 'Peacock' dates from 1870 and is full of character. Only a few miles from the picturesque wool town of Lavenham with its Tudor and timber and plaster houses, this is a recommended port of call with genuine oak beams, an impressive inglenook fireplace and a beer garden for warmer weather. Cask-conditioned ales and excellent wines make the perfect complement for the fine food served every lunchtime and evening. A most rewarding place in which to stay, the inn has three comfortable bedrooms full of beams, nooks and crannies. In fact, there is not a level floor or straight wall in the pub! *AA*.

3 BEDROOMS; FREE HOUSE WITH REAL ALE; HISTORIC INTEREST; CHILDREN AND PETS WELCOME; BAR AND RESTAURANT MEALS; NON-SMOKING AREAS; HADLEIGH 4 MILES; S££, D£.

THE OLD BULL HOTEL
Church Street, Sudbury, Suffolk CO10 6BL
Tel: 01787 374120 • Fax: 01787 379044

Originally a 16th century beamed coaching inn, now lovingly converted and restored into a guest house and restaurant, the Old Bull Hotel retains that olde worlde charm with a relaxed atmosphere. Each bedroom has a unique character and charm and offers colour television, satellite, telephone and tea and coffee facilities; most are fully en suite. It is situated in the ancient market town of Sudbury, birthplace of Gainsborough, and is surrounded by many places of interest. Ideal centre for touring the area. Most credit cards accepted. *AA and RAC Listed*.

10 BEDROOMS, ALL WITH PRIVATE BATHROOM OR SHOWER; HISTORIC INTEREST; CHILDREN WELCOME; CAMBRIDGE 23 MILES, IPSWICH 16, COLCHESTER 13; S£££, D££££.

TUDDENHAM MILL COUNTRY INN AND RESTAURANT
Tuddenham St Mary, Near Bury St Edmunds, Suffolk 1P28 6FQ
Tel: 01638 713552 • website: www.ravenwoodhall.co.uk

Only three or four miles north of the busy A45 Ipswich to Cambridge road, this exquisite retreat could be on another planet. An 18th century working water mill, it stands encompassed by lovely gardens, the epitome of picturesque tranquillity. In a magnificent riverside setting, it is worth coming a long way not only to see but to partake of the excellent real ales and intriguing selection of 'blackboard specials', changed daily; first-rate fare supported by an extensive wine list. The atmosphere is relaxed, friendly and informal and it is no surprise to learn that this idyllic place is a favourite with discerning racegoers en route with high hopes to nearby Newmarket or returning later triumphant or crestfallen – but what a consolation!

NO ACCOMMODATION; FREE HOUSE; HISTORIC INTEREST; CHILDREN AND PETS WELCOME; BAR AND RESTAURANT MEALS; NON-SMOKING AREAS; IPSWICH 3 MILES.

For details of Tourist Board Gradings in England, Scotland and Wales see page 17

Surrey

CHASE LODGE HOTEL
10 Park Road, Hampton Wick, Kingston-upon-Thames, Surrey KT1 4AS
Tel: 0208 943 1862 • Fax: 0208 943 9363 • website: www.chaselodgehotel.com

An award-winning hotel with style and elegance set in tranquil surroundings at affordable prices. Quality en suite bedrooms. Full English breakfast and à la carte menu. Licensed bar. Wedding receptions catered for; honeymoon suite available. Easy access to Kingston town centre and all major transport links; 20 minutes from Heathrow Airport. All major credit cards accepted. *London Tourist Board/AA* ★★★, *RAC Highly Acclaimed, Les Routiers, AA Two Rosette Restaurant.*

13 BEDROOMS, ALL WITH PRIVATE BATHROOM; FREE HOUSE WITH REAL ALE; HISTORIC INTEREST; CHILDREN AND PETS WELCOME; BAR AND RESTAURANT MEALS; NON-SMOKING AREAS; LONDON 10 MILES; S££££, D£££.

THE RUNNING HORSES
Old London Road, Mickleham, Surrey RH5 6DU
Tel: 01372 372279 • Fax: 01372 363004 • e-mail: enqs@therunninghorses.totalserve.com
website: www.therunninghorses.totalserve.co.uk

Set amidst beautiful National Trust countryside with the vantage point of Box Hill a mere half-a-mile away, this lovely 400-year-old inn has welcomed a wide spectrum of society over the years. The main bar, even today, features a highwayman's hideaway and a cosy bar with an impressive inglenook fireplace. Owners, Josie and Steve Slayford, dispense good cheer and the present day visitor will find a restaurant offering a high standard of cuisine and accommodation facilities that would do credit to many a multi-starred establishment; en suite bedrooms, named after local racecourses, are appointed with colour television, direct-dial telephone and tea and coffee-makers. A function room is available for meetings and private parties. *Les Routiers Gold Key Award 2000, CAMRA, AA.*

5 BEDROOMS, ALL WITH PRIVATE BATHROOM; REAL ALE; HISTORIC INTEREST; DOGS IN BAR ONLY ON LEAD; BAR AND RESTAURANT MEALS; LEATHERHEAD 2 MILES; S££££, D£££££.

East Sussex

BULL HOTEL
2 High Street, Ditchling, East Sussex BN6 8TA
Tel: 01273 843147 • Fax: 01273 857787 • e-mail: ditchlingbull@aol.com

An attractive old black-and-white hostelry on the corner of the High Street of an attractive downland village, the Bull dates from the 16th century and retains much of its original character, a virtue of which the present licensee is obviously enthusiastically aware, as witness the splendid main bar with its open fireplace, beams and pillars. In good weather, refreshment may be enjoyed outside, either on the terrace or at bench tables on the spacious lawns. An ideal base for a country holiday with the sea within easy driving distance, the hotel has single and double en suite bedrooms at most reasonable rates.

4 BEDROOMS, ALL WITH PRIVATE BATHROOM; FREE HOUSE WITH REAL ALE; HISTORIC INTEREST; CHILDREN AND PETS WELCOME; BAR AND RESTAURANT MEALS; NON-SMOKING AREAS; BURGESS HILL 3 MILES; S££, D££.

West Sussex

THE ANGEL HOTEL
North Street, Midhurst, West Sussex GU29 9DN
Tel: 01730 812421 • Fax: 01730 815928 • e-mail: angel@hshotels.co.uk
website: www.hshotels.co.uk

In the heart of the lush and leafy West Sussex countryside, this 16th century coaching inn extends a high standard of traditional English hospitality in a lovely English setting. Centrally situated in a historic market town, the Angel invites guests to drink, dine and dally awhile. The informal Brasserie features fresh seafoods and hearty roasts in its daily-changing menu, and the elegant Court Room restaurant has won many accolades for its high standards of presentation and service, its imaginative menus supported by an intriguing and unusual wine list. Popular for meetings and social functions, the hotel has individually furnished bedrooms, some with four-posters, all with bathrooms en suite, colour television and direct-dial telephone. *ETC* ★★★.

28 BEDROOMS, ALL WITH PRIVATE BATHROOM; FREE HOUSE WITH REAL ALE; HISTORIC INTEREST; CHILDREN WELCOME, PETS IN BAR ONLY; BAR LUNCHES, RESTAURANT MEALS; NON-SMOKING AREAS; CHICHESTER 11 MILES; S££££, D££££.

Warwickshire

THE BELL
Alderminster, Near Stratford-upon-Avon, Warwickshire CV37 8NY
Tel: 01789 450414 • Fax: 01789 450998 • e-mail: thebellald@aol.com
website: www.thebellald.co.uk

A refreshing sight on the A3400 Oxford to Stratford-upon-Avon road, this attractive wayside hostelry backs on to lovely, secluded gardens. In this tranquil and delightful situation, a programme of special events is organised by go-ahead hosts, Keith and Vanessa Brewer, and the restaurant is a popular rendezvous. Good facilities also exist for social functions. A recommended touring base, the inn has four handsomely furnished and decorated bedrooms with double or twin beds; each one has colour television and tea and coffee-makers. A typically English breakfast is served in the conservatory overlooking the Stour Valley and hills beyond. *ETC* ◆◆◆◆, *AA*.

5 BEDROOMS, 3 WITH PRIVATE BATHROOM; FREE HOUSE WITH REAL ALE; CHILDREN WELCOME, PETS ONLY IN BAR AND GARDEN; BAR AND RESTAURANT MEALS; NON-SMOKING AREAS; STRATFORD-UPON-AVON 4 MILES; S££, D£.

Wiltshire

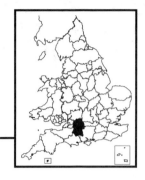

THE QUEEN'S HEAD HOTEL
North Street, Broad Chalke, Salisbury, Wiltshire SP5 5EN
Tel & Fax: 01722 780344

There are four double rooms, with own bathroom and colour TV, central heating, tea/coffee making facilities and telephone. Self-contained, motel-style, so that you are free to come and go as you wish. Relax in comfort in the friendly atmosphere of the low-beamed bars with part of the lounge area reserved for non-smokers. Well-behaved children are welcome in the lounge area. Your hosts, Michael and Norma Craggs, invite you to enjoy the superb menu available every lunchtime and evening, prepared from the finest and freshest food. There is also an excellent selection of real ales. *ETC* ◆◆◆◆ . *See also Colour Advertisement on page 10.*

4 BEDROOMS, ALL WITH PRIVATE BATHROOM; FREE HOUSE WITH REAL ALE; HISTORIC INTEREST; CHILDREN WELCOME; BAR AND RESTAURANT MEALS; NON-SMOKING AREAS; BOURNEMOUTH 30 MILES, SALISBURY 7; S££, D££.

CASTLE INN
Castle Combe, Chippenham, Wiltshire SN14 7HN
Tel: 01249 783030 • Fax: 01249 782315 • e-mail: res@castle-inn.co.uk
website: www.castle-inn.co.uk

Standing proudly in the market place of what is regarded by many as England's prettiest village, the Castle Inn typifies all that is finest in the hallowed traditions of English inn-keeping. Under the expert guidance of a talented and imaginative chef, it has gained an enviable reputation for its fine English cooking based on the freshest of ingredients, meals being taken in the elegant conservatory restaurant or in the informal surroundings of the bar. Needless to say, the range of refreshments on offer includes some excellent real ales, plus a good selection of lagers, spirits and wines. Accommodation is of the same superb standard, five of the eleven tastefully furnished bedrooms featuring whirlpool baths, and all having a full range of modern conveniences. *AA* ★★★ *and Rosette.*

11 BEDROOMS, ALL WITH PRIVATE BATHROOM; FREE HOUSE WITH REAL ALE; HISTORIC INTEREST; CHILDREN WELCOME; BAR AND RESTAURANT MEALS; NON-SMOKING AREAS; BATH 12 MILES; S££££, D££££.

VALE INN AND RESTAURANT
32 High Street, Cricklade, Wiltshire SN6 6AY
Tel & Fax: 01793 750223 • e-mail: valehotel@btinternet. com

On the A419 midway between Cirencester and Swindon, this small private hotel attracts its fair share of business types and tourists seeking a high standard of refreshment – and at the most reasonable prices, too! Dine informally in the bar or in a no-smoking restaurant, choosing from an interesting selection of à la carte dishes. Bar snacks are available at lunchtime. Dispensing hospitality to travellers since the 16th century, this Grade II listed building is an ideal stopover venue for Thames Path walkers and Cotswold explorers; just four miles away is the Cotswold Water Park. The hotel has well-appointed accommodation, rooms of various sizes having either a bath or shower en suite, colour television and tea and coffee-makers. *Les Routiers Good Food Awards 2000.*

8 BEDROOMS, ALL WITH PRIVATE BATHROOM; FREE HOUSE WITH REAL ALE; HISTORIC INTEREST; CHILDREN AND PETS WELCOME; BAR LUNCHES, RESTAURANT EVENINGS ONLY; NON-SMOKING AREAS; SWINDON 7 MILES; S£££, D£.

BLACK SWAN HOTEL
Market Place, Devizes, Wiltshire SN10 1JQ
Tel: 01380 723259 • Fax: 01380 729966 • e-mail: lugg@blackswanhotel.fsnet.co.uk
website: www.blackswanhotel.co.uk

Overlooking the picturesque Market Place, this 18th century former coaching inn has traditional appeal in its spruce bar where visitors may enjoy excellent Wadworth ales as well as a range of tempting snacks; meals of high quality are served in a restaurant with seating for 25 diners. The service is friendly and helpful, the atmosphere relaxing and the cuisine varied and imaginative. Whether on holiday or on business, this is a rewarding place in which to stay; cosy, well-appointed rooms all have en suite bathroom/shower, colour television and beverage making facilities. Conferences and banquets are expertly catered for. *ETC* ★★.

10 BEDROOMS, ALL WITH PRIVATE BATHROOM; WADWORTH HOUSE WITH REAL ALE; HISTORIC INTEREST; CHILDREN WELCOME; BAR AND RESTAURANT MEALS; NON-SMOKING AREAS; CHIPPENHAM 10 MILES; S££££, D£££.

THE INN AT HIGH POST
High Post, Salisbury, Wiltshire SP4 6AT
Tel: 01722 782592 • Fax: 01722 782630
e-mail: theinnsalisbury@highpost.freeserve.co.uk

This remarkable broad-fronted inn just north of Salisbury, eschews the image of the traditional wayside inn: it is ultra-modern and proud of it. A long, sprucely furnished bar dispenses a wide choice of liquid and solid refreshment and the restaurant caters for tastes ranging from standard favourites to the exotic, with vegetarians and informal business lunches well catered for. Accommodation is superbly appointed in best contemporary style, each room having full en suite facilities, colour television with satellite channels, direct-dial telephone, trouser press and tea and coffee-makers. For the duration of their stay, guests have the use of the hotel's superb Leisure Club, a beautiful complex with a heated indoor swimming pool, fully-equipped gymnasium, jacuzzi and sauna. *ETC* ★★, *Les Routiers 2000 Silver Key.*

30 BEDROOMS, ALL WITH PRIVATE BATHROOM; FREE HOUSE WITH REAL ALE; CHILDREN WELCOME, PETS RESTRICTED; BAR AND RESTAURANT MEALS; NON-SMOKING AREAS; SOUTHAMPTON 21 MILES; S££££, D£££.

THE OLD CROWN
Ogbourne St George, Marlborough, Wiltshire SN8 1SQ
Tel: 01672 841445 • Fax: 01672 841506 • e-mail: info@theinnwiththewell.com

This homely old country free house has seen service as a village local for over 300 years and the present incumbent personally tastes each guest beer before unleashing it on his customers. You will find no pool table and no jukebox and, as a place to eat, the inn is highly recommended, a traditional menu of home-made dishes being specially prepared by chef, Jason Gaughran. When entering the (non-smoking) restaurant, look down and you will see you are stepping over a well, separated by a glass partition – not recommended after over-indulgence! Proprietors, Michael and Megan Shaw, warmly welcome all visitors to this tranquil retreat amidst the rolling Marlborough Downs and provide excellent overnight accommodation in en suite twin rooms and newly-built chalet units.

4 BEDROOMS, ALL WITH PRIVATE BATHROOM; FREE HOUSE WITH REAL ALE; HISTORIC INTEREST; CHILDREN AND PETS WELCOME; BAR AND RESTAURANT MEALS; NON-SMOKING AREAS; SWINDON 10 MILES; S££, D£££.

THE LAMB AT HINDON
Hindon, Near Salisbury, Wiltshire SP3 6DP
Tel: 01747 820573 • Fax: 01747 820605

The fascinating history of this ancient inn is related in its brochure, which reveals among other intriguing facts that it was once the headquarters of a notorious smuggler. No such unlawful goings-on today – just good old-fashioned hospitality in the finest traditions of English inn-keeping. Charmingly furnished single, double and four-poster bedrooms provide overnight guests with cosy country-style accommodation, and the needs of the inner man (or woman!) will be amply satisfied by the varied, good quality meals served in the bar and restaurant. Real ales can be enjoyed in the friendly bar, where crackling log fires bestow charm and atmosphere as well as warmth. *AA* ★★ *and Courtesy & Care Award, RAC* ★★.

13 BEDROOMS, ALL WITH PRIVATE BATHROOM; FREE HOUSE WITH REAL ALE; HISTORIC INTEREST; CHILDREN AND PETS WELCOME; BAR AND RESTAURANT MEALS; BATH 28 MILES, SALISBURY 16; ££.

Worcestershire

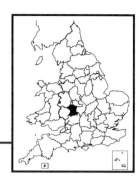

MALVERN HILLS HOTEL
Wynds Point, Malvern, Worcestershire WR13 6DW
Tel: 01684 540690 • Fax: 01684 540327 • e-mail: malhilhotl@aol.com
website: www.malvernhillshotel.com

Nestling some 800 feet up the majestic western slopes of the Malverns, a hostelry for travellers has stood here for more than 500 years. This privately owned and run hotel is the ideal place for walking and enjoying the breathtaking views ('one of the goodliest vistas in England') from British Camp, the Iron Age hillfort and ancient earthworks which stand opposite the hotel. An oak-panelled lounge bar with open log fire offers excellent bar food and a fine selection of real ales. Nightingales Restaurant provides traditional rustic English cuisine complemented by a comprehensive wine list to suit all tastes. Open all year. *ETC/AA/RAC* ★★

15 BEDROOMS, ALL EN SUITE; FREE HOUSE WITH REAL ALE; HISTORIC INTEREST; CHILDREN AND PETS WELCOME; BAR AND RESTAURANT MEALS; NON-SMOKING AREAS; GREAT MALVERN 4 MILES; S£££, D£££.

FHG PUBLICATIONS

publish a large range of well-known
accommodation guides.

We will be happy to send you details or you can use
the order form at the back of this book.

East Yorkshire

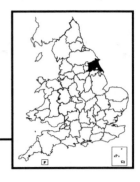

THE WOLDS INN
Driffield Road, Huggate, East Yorkshire YO42 1YH
Tel: 01377 288217 • e-mail: huggate@woldsinn.freeserve.co.uk

A peaceful country inn in farming country high in the Wolds, the hostelry exudes an atmosphere well in keeping with its 16th century origins. Panelling, brassware and crackling fires all contribute to a mood of contentment, well supported in practical terms by splendid food served either in the convivial bar or the award-winning restaurant where choice may be made from a mouth-watering à la carte menu. Huggate lies on the Wolds Way and the inn is justly popular with walkers, whilst historic York and Beverley and their racecourses and the resorts of Bridlington, Hornsea and Scarborough are within easy reach. First-rate overnight accommodation is available, all rooms having en suite facilities, central heating, colour television and tea and coffee tray. *AA, CAMRA.*

3 BEDROOMS, ALL WITH PRIVATE BATHROOM; FREE HOUSE WITH REAL ALE; HISTORIC INTEREST; CHILDREN AND PETS WELCOME; BAR MEALS, RESTAURANT TUESDAY — SUNDAY EVENINGS ONLY; POCKLINGTON 6 MILES; S£, D£.

WHITE HORSE INN
Main Street, Hutton Cranswick, Driffield, East Yorkshire Y025 9QN
Tel & Fax: 01377 270383

Amidst the rolling Yorkshire Wolds, peaceful, remote even, this friendly hostelry is happily placed for rural pleasures and pursuits, yet is within easy reach of the seaside attractions of Bridlington and the more sedate appeal of Hornsea. Surprisingly well organised and appointed for a traditional village inn, there is a genuine desire to please as the Bed and Breakfast facilities bear witness. Guest rooms are equipped to a high degree of comfort and convenience, all having fully fitted furniture, shower and toilet en suite, remote-control colour television, radio alarm, hairdryer, trouser press and tea and coffee-makers. There are ironing facilities and a laundry service is available. *ETC/AA/RAC* ◆◆◆.

8 BEDROOMS, ALL WITH PRIVATE BATHROOM; FREE HOUSE WITH REAL ALE; CHILDREN AND PETS WELCOME; BAR MEALS EVENINGS ONLY; NON-SMOKING AREAS; DRIFFIELD 4 MILES; S££, D£.

THE STAR INN
Warter Road, North Dalton, East Yorkshire YO25 9UX
Tel: 01377 217688 • Fax: 01377 217791

Set in the heart of the Yorkshire Wolds and nestling beside the village pond, this Georgian inn enjoys an idyllic setting. Located within easy reach of York, Beverley and the East Coast, it makes the ideal base. Whether your interests are history, nature or just relaxing in front of a nice log fire, this is the place for you. The inn has seven en suite rooms, all with remote-control colour television, tea and coffee making facilities and direct-dial telephone. Meals are available in the cosy, open-fired bar and in the award-winning à la carte restaurant. Special rates are available. For a brochure just call and ask for Keith or Jo. 👑👑👑👑. *See also Colour Advertisement on page 11*

7 BEDROOMS, ALL WITH PRIVATE BATHROOM; REAL ALE; WELL-BEHAVED DOGS AND CHILDREN WELCOME; BAR AND RESTAURANT MEALS; DRIFFIELD 6 MILES.

North Yorkshire

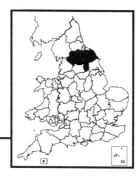

FOX AND HOUNDS INN
Ainthorpe, Danby, Whitby, North Yorkshire Y021 2LD
Tel & Fax: 01287 660218 • e-mail: ajbfox@globalnet.co.uk

With the unspoilt delights of the North York Moors beckoning wild and free, this attractive and welcoming hostelry is highly recommended as a base from which to commune with nature in all her glory, revivifying both body and soul. Whether making a casual visit or planning a longer stay, refreshment of the highest order is the reward with good ale complementing the tempting range of 'blackboard specials', whilst an excellent à la carte selection is available every lunchtime and evening. Comforts, excellent fare and beautiful surroundings all conspire to make this a difficult place to leave; splendidly appointed guest rooms await and terms in all respects are moderate indeed. *ETC* ◆◆◆.

7 BEDROOMS, ALL WITH PRIVATE BATHROOM; FREE HOUSE WITH REAL ALE; HISTORIC INTEREST;
CHILDREN AND PETS WELCOME; BAR AND RESTAURANT MEALS; WHITBY 12 MILES: S££,D££.

GEORGE AND DRAGON INN
Aysgarth, Leyburn, North Yorkshire DL8 3AD
Tel: 01969 663358 • Fax: 01969 663773

Surrounded by the stunning scenery of Upper Wensleydale, this attractive and well-tended inn has supplied travellers with rest and refreshment for nigh on 300 years. Today, tourists in the know flock here to relax in a cosy, beamed bar bedecked by interesting antiques and warmed by an open fire. True Dales hospitality is provided by proprietors, Neil and Alison Vaughan, and the accommodation is splendidly appointed. Locally brewed Black Sheep and Theakston's prove popular tipples amongst the cask-conditioned ales on offer, and lunch and dinner menus cover a wide spectrum of appetising dishes. Visitors to this lovely area are spoilt for sightseeing choice with picturesque falls, rivers, moorland, caves and castles to thrill the senses. *ETC* ★★, *AA*.

7 BEDROOMS, ALL WITH PRIVATE BATHROOM; FREE HOUSE WITH REAL ALE; HISTORIC INTEREST;
CHILDREN AND PETS WELCOME; BAR AND RESTAURANT MEALS; NON-SMOKING AREAS; RICHMOND 8 MILES; S££, D££.

ROSE & CROWN HOTEL
Bainbridge, Wensleydale DL8 3EE
Tel: 01969 650225 • Fax: 01969 650735
e-mail: stay@rose-and-crown.freeserve.co.uk

15th century coaching inn which has an enviable reputation as the 'Pride of Wensleydale'. 12 bedrooms, all en suite and some with four-poster beds; all have remote-control colour TV, radio, tea and coffee makers and hairdryers. The restaurant is open to non-residents, and lunch and evening bar meals are served in the lounge snug and popular locals bar which has games facilities. A moderately priced wine list and traditional beers will complement your meal. Cosy residents' lounge and small conference room. Children are catered for and dogs are welcome.

12 BEDROOMS, ALL WITH PRIVATE BATHROOM; REAL ALE; HISTORIC INTEREST; CHILDREN AND PETS WELCOME;
BAR AND RESTAURANT MEALS; HAWES 4 MILES.

THE BUCK INN
Thornton Watlass, Near Bedale, Ripon, North Yorkshire HG4 4AH
Tel: 01677 422461 • Fax: 01677 422447

Friendly country inn overlooking the delightful cricket green in a peaceful village just five minutes away from the A1. Newly refurbished bedrooms, most with en suite facilities, ensure that a stay at The Buck is both comfortable and relaxing. Delicious freshly cooked meals are served lunchtimes and evenings in the cosy bar and dining area. On Sundays a traditional roast with Yorkshire pudding is on the menu. Excellent hand-pulled Theakstons, John Smiths, Black Sheep and Tetley cask beer is available, as is a regular guest ale. This is an ideal centre for exploring Herriot country. There is a children's playground in the secluded beer garden where quoits are also played. Private fly fishing available on River Ure and six golf courses within 20 minutes' drive. *ETC/AA* ★, *CAMRA Good Beer Guide, Room at the Inn.* **See also Colour Advertisement on page 10.**

7 BEDROOMS, 5 WITH PRIVATE FACILITIES; FREE HOUSE WITH REAL ALE; CHILDREN WELCOME; BAR FOOD AND DINING AREA; NON-SMOKING AREAS; RIPON 11 MILES, NORTHALLERTON 9; S£££, D££.

THE FLEECE INN
47 Main Street, Bishop Wilton, Near York, North Yorkshire YO42 1RU
Tel: 01759 368251

Set in the picturesque and unspoilt village of Bishop Wilton on the edge of the Yorkshire Wolds, the Fleece Inn is a fine touring base, with much to see locally including the City of York and the East Coast. And after a long day's walk on the moors, what could be more relaxing than to return to a satisfying, freshly prepared meal and a glass of good traditional hand-pulled beer? The Fleece has a wide range of good beers and fine wines to be enjoyed on their own or with your bar meal – served at lunchtimes and in the evenings – or your dinner in the dining room. Overnight accommodation is available in cheerful and spotlessly clean bedrooms, to be followed by a hearty breakfast to set you up for the next day.

4 BEDROOMS, ALL WITH PRIVATE BATHROOM; FREE HOUSE WITH REAL ALE; CHILDREN WELCOME; BAR LUNCHES AND RESTAURANT MEALS; NON-SMOKING AREAS; YORK 13 MILES; S££, D£££.

FERRY INN
2 King Street, Cawood, Near Selby, North Yorkshire YO8 3TL
Tel: 01757 268515 • Fax: 0870 1656161 • e-mail: deelynn.phil@virginnet.co.uk
website: ferryinn.f9.co.uk

Cawood has an interesting history very much bound up in this hostelry which stands on the banks of the River Ouse next to a small swing bridge, successor to the one-time ferry. Nearby is the site of a castle where Cardinal Wolsey was domiciled after falling out of favour with King Henry VIII. Local legend has it that there was an underground passage extending from the castle to the inn and Wolsey was found by the King's men in the outbuildings. Today's visitor will find excellent sustenance – the menu is extremely varied and the bar stocks several fine real ales. There is a large riverside beer garden and very comfortable overnight accommodation is available.

3 BEDROOMS, 1 WITH PRIVATE BATHROOM; FREE HOUSE WITH REAL ALE; HISTORIC INTEREST; CHILDREN AND PETS WELCOME; BAR FOOD; SELBY 4 MILES; S££, D£.

PUBLISHER'S NOTE

While every effort is made to ensure accuracy, we regret that FHG Publications cannot accept responsibility for errors, omissions or misrepresentations in our entries or any consequences thereof. Prices in particular should be checked because we go to press early. We will follow up complaints but cannot act as arbiters or agents for either party.

FLYING HORSESHOE HOTEL
Clapham, North Yorkshire LA2 8ES
Tel & Fax: 015242 51229 • e-mail: alan@laughing-gravy.co.uk
website: www.laughing-gravy.co.uk

Between the unspoilt and diverse scenery of the Forest of Bowland and the Yorkshire Dales, this convivial and well regarded retreat also seeks variety in its location as it lies within walking distance of the Lancashire border. In the shadow of lofty Ingleborough (2373ft), with Whernside and Pen-y-Ghent one of the famous 'Three Peaks', and near the spectacular Clapham Cave, just one of several caverns in the area, a more beautiful setting would be hard to imagine; also nearby are five miles of free trout fishing and several breathtaking waterfalls. Standing in over three acres of its own grounds, the hotel is the ideal sightseeing base, among its salient attractions being fine cuisine, bar meals which offer great value, real ales and excellent en suite accommodation, including family rooms with their own private lounges, and a romantic suite with a four-poster bed and optional champagne service. Dining arrangements are calculated to suit all tastes and range from a constantly changing bar menu, children's meals at children's prices, to the full restaurant selection. Specially requested dishes can be catered for by prior agreement. There is a small camping and caravan site at the rear of the hotel recommended for those who like to waken to birdsong and panoramic views. Live music entertainment is provided most Friday and Saturday evenings. *ETC* ★★.

10 BEDROOMS, ALL WITH PRIVATE BATHROOM; FREE HOUSE WITH REAL ALE; HISTORIC INTEREST; CHILDREN WELCOME; BAR MEALS EVENINGS ONLY PLUS WEEKEND LUNCHTIMES, RESTAURANT; NON-SMOKING AREAS; SETTLE 6 MILES; S££, D£.

DUKE OF WELLINGTON INN
West Lane, Danby, Near Whitby, North Yorkshire YO21 2LY
Tel: 01287 660351 • e-mail: landlord@dukeofwellington.freeserve.co.uk
website: www.dukeofwellington.co.uk

An ivy-clad 18th century traditional inn located in the tranquil village of Danby in the heart of the North York Moors. Sample our CAMRA Award winning ales, interesting wines and range of malt whiskies whilst seated by the open fire in our friendly locals bar. Our home cooked meals are available in both bars and in the recently refurbished restaurant. The eight centrally heated en suite guest bedrooms are each equipped with colour television and tea/coffee making facilities. Danby and The Duke of Wellington Inn are conveniently located for exploring both the North York Moors, Whitby and the coast. Dogs welcome. *ETC* ◆◆◆.

8 BEDROOMS, ALL EN SUITE; FREE HOUSE WITH REAL ALE; HISTORIC INTEREST; CHILDREN AND PETS WELCOME; BAR LUNCHES, RESTAURANT EVENINGS ONLY; NON-SMOKING AREAS; WHITBY 12 MILES; S££, D££.

TENNANT ARMS
Kilnsey, Near Grassington, North Yorkshire BD23 5PS
Tel: 01756 752301

Friendly 17th century country inn hotel nestling under the famous Kilnsey Crag in the heart of Wharfedale, between the picturesque villages of Grassington and Kettlewell. All ten bedrooms are en suite. The cosy bars with log fires and beams serve delicious, individually prepared bar meals and hand-pulled ales; or dine in the beautiful pine-panelled non-smoking dining room and choose from our extensive à la carte menu. Ideal for exploring the Dales. Proprietors, Mr and Mrs N. Dean will give you a warm welcome. *ETC* ★★.

10 BEDROOMS, ALL WITH PRIVATE BATHROOM; FREE HOUSE WITH REAL ALE; HISTORIC INTEREST; CHILDREN WELCOME; BAR AND RESTAURANT MEALS; GRASSINGTON 3 MILES; S££, D£.

COCKETT'S HOTEL
Market Place, Hawes, North Yorkshire DL8 3RD
Tel: 01969 667312 • Fax: 01969 667162 • e-mail: cocketts@hawes50.freeserve.co.uk

Surrounded by the spectacular scenery of Upper Wensleydale, the delightful village of Hawes is the setting for this lovely, stone-built hostelry. Dating from the 17th century, it combines the relaxed ambience of days long gone with the fine modern amenities that have been introduced. En suite guest rooms, including two with four-poster beds, cater for overnight guests who are recommended to make this homely venue their base for touring the Dales. All rooms have central heating, colour television, shaver point, trouser press and tea-making facilities. The first-class catering is exemplified by worthy English and French fare with interesting wines provided at reasonable cost. Excellent value all round. *ETC* ◆◆◆◆, *AA* ★★.

8 BEDROOMS, ALL WITH PRIVATE BATHROOM; FREE HOUSE; HISTORIC INTEREST; CHILDREN OVER 10 WELCOME; RESTAURANT EVENINGS ONLY; NON-SMOKING AREAS; KIRKBY STEVEN 14 MILES; D££.

GEORGE AND DRAGON HOTEL
17 Market Place, Kirkbymoorside, North Yorkshire YO62 6AA
Tel: 01751 433334 • Fax: 01751 432933

Since the 17th century, this lovely old coaching inn has graced the centre of the picturesque little town of Kirkbymoorside. True, comforts and facilities have improved immeasurably over the years in line with contemporary demand but the time-honoured ambience remains unsullied. Acquaintance with the cosy, beamed bar confirms the warmth of hospitality. Enjoy a pint of one of the hand-pulled real ales or a choice malt or cognac and relax and wonder at the collection of sporting memorabilia that adorns the walls; no juke boxes or fruit machines disturb the reverie. Activated appetites will soon demand inspection of a mouth-watering list of 'blackboard specials' or maybe, in the evening, experience the chef's creative skills in a lovely candlelit restaurant. Fresh fish from Whitby, locally reared game and beef and home produce vie for attention amongst the stylishly presented dishes with an impressive selection of wines in attendance. Parting from such perfection is such sweet sorrow, so anticipate pleasures to come by booking accommodation at this multi-favoured hotel beforehand. Guest rooms are housed in a beautifully converted corn mill and rectory at the rear of the old inn. Superbly appointed with a tutored eye for elegance and harmonious colour co-ordinates, each delightful room has fine en suite facilities, remote-control colour television, clock radio, telephone and hospitality tray. Come and be spoilt! *ETC* ★★.

18 BEDROOMS, ALL WITH PRIVATE BATHROOM; FREE HOUSE WITH REAL ALE; HISTORIC INTEREST; CHILDREN AND PETS WELCOME; BAR LUNCHES AND RESTAURANT MEALS; NON-SMOKING AREAS; PICKERING 7 MILES; S££££, D£££.

Please mention *Recommended Wayside & Country Inns* when enquiring about accommodation featured in these pages.

THE WHITE ROSE HOTEL
Bedale Road, Leeming Bar, Northallerton, North Yorkshire DL7 9AY
Tel: 01677 424941/422707 • Fax: 01677 425123

Ideally situated between two National Parks, from where you can explore the Yorkshire Dales, the resorts of the East Coast, or even visit the Lake District. Both Herriot Country in the heart of North Yorkshire and the spectacular scenery of Heartbeat Country in the North Yorks Moors are just a short drive away. All our rooms have private bathroom, colour television, radio, tea/coffee making facilities, hairdryer, trouser press and private telephone. Spend an enjoyable time using our own friendly hotel as your base. *ETC/RAC* ★★.

18 BEDROOMS, ALL WITH PRIVATE BATHROOM; FREE HOUSE; CHILDREN AND PETS WELCOME;
RESTAURANT AND BAR MEALS; NON-SMOKING AREAS; NORTHALLERTON 6 MILES, BEDALE 2; S£££, D£.

THE QUEENS ARMS INN
Litton, Skipton, North Yorkshire BD23 5QJ
Tel: 01756 770208 • website: www.yorkshiredales.net/stayat/queens/

Traditional 17th century country inn situated in the parish of Litton, lying in the heart of the Yorkshire Dales National Park with beautiful views over to Fountains Fell which rises above the River Skirfare. Comfortable en suite accommodation is provided in double, twin or single rooms. The Queens Arms is renowned for its good food and extensive menu which includes local pheasant, rabbit and game, and there is a large choice of seafood. Cheerful atmosphere, blazing fire, oak beams and real ale served over a wooden bar.

BEDROOMS WITH PRIVATE BATHROOM; REAL ALE; HISTORIC INTEREST; BAR MEALS; ARNCLIFFE 2 MILES.

THE STIDDY
Lythe, Whitby, North Yorkshire YO21 3RT
Tel: 01947 893300 • Fax: 01947 893177

Just north of the historic fishing port of Whitby and only a mile from the beach at Sandsend, this little 17th century coaching inn extends its unpretentious favours to all who appreciate good food and drink as well as handsomely appointed Bed & Breakfast accommodation. With rewarding clifftop and woodland walks in the vicinity, this is a fine place in which to take a relaxing break. Under the hospitable auspices of hosts, John and Gill Wood, there are several well-known ales to be savoured and the bar meal menu will delight any appetite. Guest rooms are furnished to a high standard, all having a private bathroom with shower, remote-control colour television, radio alarm, hairdryer and tea and coffee-making facilities.

3 BEDROOMS, ALL WITH PRIVATE BATHROOM; FREE HOUSE WITH REAL ALE; CHILDREN AND PETS WELCOME; BAR FOOD;
WHITBY 4 MILES; S££, D£.

  For details of Tourist Board Gradings in England, Scotland and Wales see page 17

KING'S HEAD HOTEL
Market Place, Richmond, North Yorkshire DL10 4HS
Tel: 01748 850220 • Fax: 01748 850635 • e-mail: info@kingsheadrichmond.co.uk
website: www.kingsheadrichmond.co.uk

Enveloped in the mellow aura of a much-loved, former coaching inn, the King's Head overlooks the cobbled square of historic Richmond, capital of picturesque Swaledale. Gracious Georgian architecture blends perfectly with subtly introduced modern refinements, guest rooms being equipped with fine en suite facilities, satellite television, direct-dial telephone, radio, baby-listening device and hospitality tray; for a romantic break a four-poster room is available. An interesting feature is the Clock Lounge with no less than thirteen timepieces on view (silenced at night!). Reasonably-priced meals and drinks are obtainable in the popular Zetland Bar. On the first-floor is the splendid restaurant where, each evening, traditional à la carte and table d'hôte fare is served accompanied by well-chosen wines. *ETC/AA* ★★.

30 BEDROOMS, ALL WITH PRIVATE BATHROOMS,FREE HOUSE WITH REAL ALE; HISTORIC INTEREST; CHILDREN AND PETS WELCOME; BAR MEALS, RESTAURANT EVENINGS AND SUNDAY LUNCH ONLY; DARLINGTON 11 MILES; S££££, D£££.

MILBURN ARMS HOTEL
Rosedale Abbey, Pickering, North Yorkshire YO18 8RA
Tel & Fax: 01751 417312 • e-mail: info@milburnarms.com
website: www.milburnarms.com

Performing a dual function as country hotel and village pub, the charming Milburn Arms is a haven of comfort in the tranquil heart of the North Yorkshire Moors, amidst rambling footpaths and beautiful scenery. Particular pride is taken in the excellent cuisine, with the emphasis on British cooking presented with flair and imagination the skilled head chef and his team. In the convivial bar one may enjoy good ale (and perhaps a bar meal or snack), a chat with the locals and maybe a game of darts or dominoes .The hotel is attractively furnished throughout, en suite guest rooms being appointed with colour television, telephone, beverage making facilities and complimentary toiletries. *ETC* ★★, *AA Two Rosettes.*

11 BEDROOMS, ALL WITH PRIVATE BATHROOM; FREE HOUSE WITH REAL ALE; HISTORIC INTEREST; CHILDREN AND PETS WELCOME; BAR MEALS, RESTAURANT EVENINGS ONLY; NON-SMOKING AREAS; PICKERING 10 MILES; S£££, D££.

THE GANTON GREYHOUND
Ganton, Near Scarborough, North Yorkshire YO12 4NX
Tel: 01944 710116 • Fax: 01944 710705 • e-mail: gantongreyhound@supanet.com

Hosts, Terry and Margaret Bennett, are deservedly proud of their excellent reputation for providing good hospitality, good food, and a warm, friendly atmosphere. En suite bedrooms (double, twin, family and disabled) are tastefully furnished, with tea/coffee facilities and colour television, and there is a lounge for the exclusive use of guests. Drinks and meals can be enjoyed in the pleasant bar, where large open fireplaces and oak beams add to the welcoming ambience; meals are also available in the light and airy conservatory restaurant. Its location on the main A64 York to Scarborough road is ideal for exploring this scenic area; the North Yorkshire moors and several golf courses, including Ganton Championship Course, are within easy reach.

18 BEDROOMS, 16 WITH PRIVATE BATHROOM; FREE HOUSE WITH REAL ALE; CHILDREN WELCOME; BAR AND RESTAURANT MEALS; NON-SMOKING AREAS; FILEY 8 MILES; S£, D£.

PLEASE MENTION THIS GUIDE WHEN YOU WRITE OR PHONE TO ENQUIRE ABOUT ACCOMMODATION

IF YOU ARE WRITING, A STAMPED, ADDRESSED ENVELOPE IS ALWAYS APPRECIATED

GOLDEN LION HOTEL
Duke Street, Settle, North Yorkshire BD24 9DU
Tel: 01729 822203 • Fax: 01729 824103 • e-mail: bookings@goldenlion.yorks.net
website: www.yorkshirenet.co.uk/stayat/goldenlion

Surrounded by a dramatic countryside of peaks and dales, caverns and castles, this traditional 17th century coaching inn lies in the market place of the homely little Ribblesdale town of Settle. A popular eating house for locals and visitors alike, the hostelry proffers a variety of appetising dishes, meals being taken either in the 70-seater restaurant or before an open log fire in the bar lounge. Virtually on the doorstep is the famous Settle-Carlisle railway and with the scenic delights of the Yorkshire Dales National Park close at hand, the hotel is a recommended place in which to take an extended break. Bedrooms in a variety of sizes await those acting upon this advice. Special deals for groups of ramblers. *ETC* ◆◆◆, *AA, RAC.*

13 BEDROOMS, 5 WITH PRIVATE BATHROOM; THWAITES OF BLACKBURN HOUSE WITH REAL ALE; HISTORIC INTEREST; CHILDREN WELCOME, PETS BY ARRANGEMENT; BAR AND RESTAURANT MEALS; SKIPTON 13 MILES; S££, D££.

THE FOX AND HOUNDS COUNTRY INN
Main Street, Sinnington, North Yorkshire YO62 6SQ
Tel: 01751 431577 • Fax: 01751 432791 • e-mail: foxhoundsinn@easynet.co.uk

This beautiful village just off the A170 is the setting for a country inn with a difference. Renowned for our warm welcome, good wine and quality food served in the olde worlde bar or the non-smoking restaurant, with a residents' lounge to relax in at any time of the day. The visitor can stroll through the peaceful village, along the pretty riverside, or the more energetic can venture through the woodland to the moors beyond. There are golf courses within easy reach, riding stables in the village and fishing. This is Heartbeat Country with York, Scarborough and Castle Howard all within easy reach. *ETC* ◆◆◆◆, *AA Rosette.*

10 BEDROOMS, ALL WITH PRIVATE BATHROOM; FREE HOUSE; HISTORIC INTEREST; CHILDREN AND PETS WELCOME; BAR AND RESTAURANT MEALS; NON-SMOKING AREAS; PICKERING 4 MILES; S£££, D££.

MAYPOLE INN
The Green, Long Preston, Skipton, North Yorkshire BD23 4PH
Tel: 01729 840219 • Fax: 01729 840456 • e-mail: landlord@maypole.co.uk
website: www.maypole.co.uk

With a menu to suit all tastes and pockets, from freshly cut sandwiches, salads and filled baked potatoes to traditional favourites such as fish, lasagne and steaks, this friendly inn is understandably popular at lunchtimes and in the evenings. It has been providing hospitality and good cheer for over 300 years, and prides itself on maintaining the high standards which has gained it such a fine reputation over the centuries. Hand-pulled traditional ales are a speciality here, and can be enjoyed beside a crackling open fire, or outside overlooking the village green in finer weather. Spick-and-span bedrooms of varying sizes offer overnight accommodation at extremely attractive rates. *ETC* ◆◆◆.

6 BEDROOMS, ALL WITH PRIVATE BATHROOM; WHITBREAD HOUSE WITH REAL ALE; HISTORIC INTEREST; CHILDREN AND PETS WELCOME; BAR AND RESTAURANT MEALS; NON-SMOKING AREAS; BRADFORD 16 MILES; S££, D£.

CASTLE ARMS INN
Snape, Near Bedale, North Yorkshire DL8 2TB
Tel: 01677 470270 • Fax: 01677 470837 • e-mail: castlearms@aol.com

The sleepy village of Snape is the perfect location for an 'away from it all' break, of particular interest to those wishing to experience the scenic splendour of the Yorkshire Dales and North York Moors and also attractive to racing enthusiasts, for five of the principal Yorkshire racecourses (Ripon, Thirsk, Wetherby, Catterick and York) are within easy reach. Visitors to the area could do no better than base themselves at this neat and tidy inn, a Grade II Listed building which dates from the 14th century. Handsomely appointed bedrooms all have bath or shower rooms en suite, central heating, colour television and tea and coffee-making facilities. Lunches and dinners are served daily in a cosy restaurant where the emphasis is on traditional home cooking. *ETC/AA* ◆◆◆◆.

9 BEDROOMS, ALL WITH PRIVATE BATHROOM; FREE HOUSE WITH REAL ALE; HISTORIC INTEREST; CHILDREN WELCOME, PETS BY ARRANGEMENT; BAR AND RESTAURANT MEALS; NON-SMOKING AREAS; BEDALE 2 MILES; S£££, D££.

GOLDEN FLEECE HOTEL
Market Place, Thirsk, North Yorkshire YO7 1LL
Tel: 01845 523108 • Fax: 01845 523996

Set in the heart of Herriot Country, the Golden Fleece Hotel is a 400-year-old coaching inn. This season's special "Mini Break" will provide you with local information on what to see and where to go around this delightful part of North Yorkshire. The Break is a dinner, bed and breakfast package and further information and current prices can be obtained by contacting the reception team at the hotel. *ETC/AA* ★★ *Silver Award*.

18 BEDROOMS, ALL WITH PRIVATE BATHROOM; FREE HOUSE WITH REAL ALE; HISTORIC INTEREST; CHILDREN WELCOME, PETS BY ARRANGEMENT; BAR AND RESTAURANT MEALS; NON-SMOKING AREA; YORK 20 MILES, NORTHALLERTON 8; S££££, D££££.

LONG ASHES INN
Threshfield, Near Skipton, North Yorkshire BD23 5PN
Tel: 01756 752434 • Fax: 01756 752937 • website: www.longashesinn.co.uk

You will receive a warm welcome and personal attention in this charming traditional old Dales inn, set in picturesque Wharfedale in the Yorkshire Dales National Park. A tranquil retreat in an idyllic setting, perfect for relaxing or as a base from which to enjoy everything the Yorkshire Dales have to offer at any time of the year. The de luxe accommodation includes en suite bathrooms, central heating, tea/coffee making facilities and television, and there is also a honeymoon suite. There is a wide range of hand-pulled ales and freshly prepared food served in the restaurant and in the bar, as well as a heated indoor pool, sauna, squash court etc. adjacent, which are available for use by residents. Children's play area. *ETC/AA* ◆◆◆. *See also Colour Advertisement on page 10*

5 BEDROOMS, ALL WITH PRIVATE BATHROOM; REAL ALE; CHILDREN WELCOME; BAR AND RESTAURANT MEALS; NON-SMOKING AREAS; SKIPTON 9 MILES, GRASSINGTON 3; S££££, D£££.

THE NEW INN MOTEL
Main Street, Huby, York, North Yorkshire YO6 1HQ
Tel: 01347 810219

Nine miles north of York in the village of Huby in the Vale of York, the Motel is an ideal base for a couple of nights away to visit York (15 minutes to the nearest long-stay car park), or a longer stay to visit the East Coast of Yorkshire, the Dales, the Yorkshire Moors, Herriot Country, Harrogate and Ripon. The Motel is situated behind the New Inn (a separate business) which, contrary to its name, is a 500-year old hostelry, originally an old coaching inn, and full of character. All rooms are en suite (singles, doubles, twin and family rooms), and have colour television and tea-making facilities. Good home cooking is served, including vegetarian meals, and a full English breakfast is a speciality. PETS ARE WELCOME. The accommodation is suitable for the disabled. Special three-day breaks always available. Telephone for brochure. *AA* ◆◆◆.

8 ROOMS, ALL EN SUITE, WITH SHOWER; RESTAURANT MEALS; CHILDREN WELCOME; NON-SMOKING AREAS; YORK 9 MILES; S££, D£.

West Yorkshire

THREE ACRES INN AND RESTAURANT
Roydhouse, Shelley, Near Huddersfield, West Yorkshire HD8 8LR
Tel: 01484 602606 • Fax: 01484 608411 • e-mail: 3acres@globalnet.co.uk

Good cooking is the very heartbeat of this remarkable inn, the innovative menus combining the best of traditional English cooking with exotic and sophisticated dishes from all over the world. It is little surprise, therefore, to learn that the hostelry was designated as the 'Best Dining Pub in Britain - 2000' by a fellow publication. Set in the rolling Pennine foothills, this is a rewarding place to visit whilst exploring 'Last of the Summer Wine' country – Holmfirth is just down the road – for the neatly appointed bedrooms all have en suite facilities, television and telephone; ten of these are situated in the adjacent 'Cottages' annexe, all of which have their own gardens. *ETC* ◆◆, *Les Routiers*.

20 BEDROOMS, ALL WITH PRIVATE BATHROOM; FREE HOUSE WITH REAL ALE; CHILDREN WELCOME; BAR AND RESTAURANT MEALS; HUDDERSFIELD 5 MILES; S££££, D£££.

THE DUKE OF YORK INN
West Street, Shelf, Halifax, West Yorkshire HX3 7LN
Tel: 01422 202056 • Fax: 01422 206618 • website: www.dukeofyork.co.uk

If you are planning to walk the Calderdale Way or visit the unspoiled moors and dales, then make a note of this 17th century former coaching inn, which is the perfect place to stop for rest and refreshment. An above average choice of real ales, plus a comprehensive selection of beers, wines and spirits guarantees that thirsts will be fully quenched, while a glance at the menu is sure to bring a gleam to the eye of the hungry traveller. From sandwiches to steaks, all appetites are catered for, including an intriguing selection of home-made Indian dishes which will delight more exotic palates. Neat bedrooms offer en suite bathrooms and colour television should overnight accommodation be required. *ETC* ◆◆◆.

7 BEDROOMS, ALL WITH PRIVATE BATHROOM; WHITBREAD HOUSE WITH REAL ALE; HISTORIC INTEREST; CHILDREN WELCOME; BAR AND RESTAURANT MEALS; NON-SMOKING AREAS; BRADFORD 7 MILES; S££, D£££/££££.

MEWS HOTEL
77 Dale Street, Ossett, Wakefield, West Yorkshire WF5 9HN
Tel: 01924 273982 • Fax: 01924 279389 • e-mail: paul@mews-hotel.co.uk
website: www.mews-hotel.co.uk

Much of the charm and character of this friendly, country-style hotel lies in its rich and varied history. The courtyard wing was originally a warehouse and the many windows which now overlook the lawns were necessary in those days to give sufficient natural light to enable the wives of the local textile workers to carry out their skilled work, mixing the best of old rags and woollen clothing to make shoddy, which in turn was used to manufacture cloth for the uniforms of Queen Victoria's armies in Europe. This family-run free house features a popular bar where residents and regulars mix happily enjoying their own favourite tipples from the hand-pulled draught ales, lagers, malt whiskies and wines on offer. The hotel has an excellent restaurant which presents a superb choice of chef-inspired, freshly cooked dishes from its standard menu plus a 'specials' blackboard which is changed daily. Tastefully refurbished bedrooms ensure relaxation and rewarding rest; all are appointed to a high standard of comfort and convenience and incorporate en suite facilities, colour television, direct-dial telephone and tea and coffee-makers. A full English breakfast is included in the reasonable terms. The hotel is handily situated a mere five minutes from Wakefield and ten minutes from Leeds. Private parties and functions are expertly catered for. *AA* QQQQ

14 BEDROOMS, ALL WITH PRIVATE BATHROOM; FREE HOUSE WITH REAL ALE; HISTORIC INTEREST; CHILDREN WELCOME; PETS BY ARRANGEMENT; BAR AND RESTAURANT MEALS; WAKEFIELD 3 MILES; S££££, D££££.

The **£** symbol when appearing at the end of the italic section of an entry shows the anticipated price, during 2001, for full Bed and Breakfast.

Normal Bed & Breakfast rate per person (in single room)		Normal Bed & Breakfast rate per person (sharing double/twin room)	
PRICE RANGE	CATEGORY	PRICE RANGE	CATEGORY
Under £25	*S£*	**Under £25**	*D£*
£26-£35	*S££*	**£26-£35**	*D££*
£36-£45	*S£££*	**£36-£45**	*D£££*
Over £45	*S££££*	**Over £45**	*D££££*

This is meant as an indication only and does not show prices for Special Breaks, Weekends, etc. Guests are therefore advised to verify all prices on enquiring or booking.

PLEASE MENTION THIS GUIDE WHEN YOU WRITE
OR PHONE TO ENQUIRE ABOUT ACCOMMODATION.
IF YOU ARE WRITING, A STAMPED,
ADDRESSED ENVELOPE IS ALWAYS APPRECIATED.

Recommended
Wayside &
Country Inns 2001
Scotland

THE FHG
DIPLOMA

HELP IMPROVE
BRITISH TOURIST STANDARDS

You are choosing holiday accommodation from our very popular FHG Publications.
Whether it be a hotel, guest house, farmhouse or self-catering accommodation, we think you will find it hospitable, comfortable and clean, and your host and hostess friendly and helpful.

Why not write and tell us about it?

As a recognition of the generally well-run and excellent holiday accommodation reviewed in our publications, we at FHG Publications Ltd. present a diploma to proprietors who receive the highest recommendation from their guests who are also readers of our Guides. If you care to write to us praising the holiday you have booked through FHG Publications Ltd. – whether this be board, self-catering accommodation, a sporting or a caravan holiday, what you say will be evaluated and the proprietors who reach our final list will be contacted.

The winning proprietor will receive an attractive framed diploma to display on his premises as recognition of a high standard of comfort, amenity and hospitality. FHG Publications Ltd. offer this diploma as a contribution towards the improvement of standards in tourist accommodation in Britain. Help your excellent host or hostess to win it!

FHG DIPLOMA

We nominate ....

....

Because

Name   ....

Address..

....

Telephone No...

FHG

Aberdeenshire, Banff & Moray

INVER HOTEL
Crathie, By Balmoral, Aberdeenshire AB35 5UL
Tel: 013397 42345 • Fax: 013397 42009

It is hardly surprising that walkers, climbers,skiers – in fact outdoor types of all persuasions – find their way to this delightful little inn, set as it is amid the hills of the Upper Deeside Valley, just a short drive from two of the main ski centres. Those of a less active inclination are drawn here too by the breathtaking scenery, the area's royal associations, and, perhaps, by the attractions of Scotland's national drink (Royal Lochnagar distillery is a mere two miles away). Completely renovated and with all modern amenities, the inn nevertheless retains its traditional character and offers all that is finest in food and comfort, featuring the best local produce and genuine personal service.

9 BEDROOMS, ALL FULLY EN SUITE; FREE HOUSE; HISTORIC INTEREST; CHILDREN AND PETS WELCOME; BAR AND RESTAURANT MEALS; NON-SMOKING AREAS; BALLATER 9 MILES, BRAEMAR 5; S££, D£.

MINMORE HOUSE HOTEL
Glenlivet, Ballindalloch, Banffshire AB37 9DB
Tel: 01807 590378 • Fax: 01807 590472
website: www.SmoothHound.co.uk/hotels/minmore.html

In the lee of the magnificent Cairngorms and sheltered by four acres of gardens, this hospitable hotel was once the home of George Smith, founder of Glenlivet whisky. It is only fitting, therefore, that there should be such an impressive array of single malt whiskies displayed in the oak-panelled bar. After a hearty breakfast, days may be filled with a wide spectrum of activities: walking, fishing, bird watching, playing golf, horse riding; visiting art galleries, museums, historic castles or setting out on the famous Whisky Trail. 'At home' moments may be spent playing tennis or croquet in the grounds or swimming in the outdoor pool. Always there is the promise of a sumptuous five-course dinner to round off a perfect day. *STB* ★★★ *Hotel, Taste of Scotland.*

10 BEDROOMS, ALL WITH PRIVATE BATHROOM; FREE HOUSE WITH REAL ALE; HISTORIC INTEREST; CHILDREN AND PETS WELCOME; BAR LUNCHES AND RESTAURANT MEALS; NON-SMOKING AREAS; TOMINTOUL 6 MILES; S£££, D£££.

Argyll & Bute

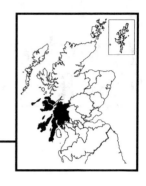

CAIRNDOW STAGECOACH INN
Cairndow, Argyll PA26 8BN
Tel: 01499 600286 • Fax: 01499 600220

Amidst the beautiful scenery which characterises the upper reaches of Loch Fyne, this historic stagecoach inn enjoys a spectacular sheltered position. In the delightful restaurant one may dine well by candlelight from the table d'hôte and à la carte menus; bar meals are served all day. There is also a new functions bar and games room. Bedrooms are centrally heated, with radio, television, direct-dial telephone, baby listening, and tea-making facilities. There are two de luxe rooms with two-person spa baths, king-size beds and 20" television! This is an ideal spot for touring Oban, the Western Highlands, Glencoe, the Trossachs, the Cowal Peninsula, Kintyre and Campbeltown. The inn is under the personal supervision of hosts Mr and Mrs Douglas Fraser, and the area offers opportunities for many outdoor pursuits and visits. Lochside beer garden, exercise room, sauna and solarium. *STB* ★★★ *Inn. See also Colour Advertisement on page 11.*

12 BEDROOMS, ALL EN SUITE; FREE HOUSE WITH REAL ALE; HISTORIC INTEREST; CHILDREN WELCOME; BAR AND RESTAURANT MEALS; NON-SMOKING AREAS; ARROCHAR 12 MILES, INVERARAY 10; S££, D££.

LOCHNELL ARMS HOTEL
North Connel, Argyll PA37 1RP
Tel: 01631 710408 • e-mail: lochnellarms@aol.com

A family concern, the warmth of the welcome at the Lochnell is as much part of its charm as the magnificent view, clean and comfortable guest rooms (all with en suite shower and wc), and varied and interesting cuisine. Meals and snacks can be taken both lunchtime and evening in the lounge bar with conservatory, and the extensive menu features homemade chilli, fish and steaks. Well kept gardens roll down to the beach. Children are warmly welcomed, and a play area will keep them occupied while parents relax. Nearby attractions include the busy and picturesque town of Oban, Sea Life Centre, Rare Breeds Park, and a wide selection of leisure facilities including sailing, loch cruises and fishing.

9 BEDROOMS, ALL WITH PRIVATE SHOWER; SCOTTISH BREWERS HOUSE WITH REAL ALE; HISTORIC INTEREST; CHILDREN WELCOME; BAR AND RESTAURANT MEALS; NON-SMOKING AREAS; DUNBEG 2 MILES, D£/££.

INSHAIG PARK HOTEL
Easdale, Seil Island, By Oban, Argyll PA34 4RF
Tel and Fax: 01852 300256

The famous eighteenth century "Bridge over the Atlantic" takes one onto Seil Island and Easdale where you will find this comfortable Victorian hotel, set in its own grounds overlooking the sea and the scattered islands of the Inner Hebrides. This family-run hotel has six comfortable bedrooms, all with central heating, colour television and tea-making facilities. Meals can be taken either in Slaters Bar and Bistro (over 40 malt whiskies to sample) or in the Victorian dining room overlooking the sea. Fresh local seafood is a speciality. An ideal place to stay for an "away from it all" holiday. Open all year. *STB* ★★★ *Hotel, Les Routiers Casserole Award 1997 and Silver Key Award 1998. See also Colour Advertisement on p11.*

6 BEDROOMS, ALL WITH PRIVATE BATHROOM; FREE HOUSE; BAR AND RESTAURANT MEALS; NON-SMOKING AREAS; OBAN 16 MILES; S£££, D££.

Ayrshire & The Island of Arran

FINLAYSON ARMS HOTEL
24 Hillhead, Coylton, Ayr, Ayrshire KA6 6JT
Tel: 01292 570298 • Fax: 01292 570298

Of special appeal to golfers, this fine hotel stands almost in the centre of a county famous for its courses, all 32 of them, including the championship courses of Troon and Turnberry. But even if a gentle round of putting is the limit of your activity, you will find much of interest here – Coylton itself lies in the heart of Burns Country, the county town of Ayr with its excellent leisure and shopping facilities is just four miles away and its popular racecourse stages numerous meetings throughout the year. Food at the Finlayson Arms is good and plentiful, served either in the restaurant or a bar which boasts a selection of malt whiskies. Neat bedrooms are all en suite and the hearty Scottish breakfast is guaranteed to start the day off well.

8 BEDROOMS, ALL WITH PRIVATE BATHROOM; FREE HOUSE; HISTORIC INTEREST; CHILDREN WELCOME; BAR AND RESTAURANT MEALS; NON-SMOKING AREAS; AYR 6 MILES; S££, D£.

The **£** symbol when appearing at the end of the italic section of an entry shows the anticipated price, during 2001, for full Bed and Breakfast.

Normal Bed & Breakfast rate per person (in single room)		Normal Bed & Breakfast rate per person (sharing double/twin room)	
PRICE RANGE	CATEGORY	PRICE RANGE	CATEGORY
Under £25	S£	**Under £25**	D£
£26-£35	S££	**£26-£35**	D££
£36-£45	S£££	**£36-£45**	D£££
Over £45	S££££	**Over £45**	D££££

This is meant as an indication only and does not show prices for Special Breaks, Weekends, etc. Guests are therefore advised to verify all prices on enquiring or booking.

Borders

TRAQUAIR ARMS
Traquair Road, Innerleithen, Peeblesshire EH44 6PD
Tel: 01896 830229 • Fax: 01896 830260

A solidly constructed traditional 19th century Scottish inn, just 40 minutes from Edinburgh and 10 minutes from Peebles, in a delightful Borders valley. Gig and Dianne Johnston run it as a relaxing, friendly, family-run hotel with genuine concern for the comfort of their guests. Imaginative menus utilise the best local produce, and in appropriate weather can be enjoyed beside a blazing log fire in the dining room or al fresco in the secluded garden. The bar prides itself on its real ales. Egon Ronay's Good Pub Guide says "Bed and breakfast is recommended, particularly the handsome Scottish meal complete with superb kippers". *STB ★★★ Inn, AA ◆◆◆, Taste of Scotland, CAMRA, Best Breakfast in Britain 1990, "In Britain" Scottish Finalist 1993, 'Best Bar Food' Winner 1997.* **See also Colour Advertisement on page 11.**

10 BEDROOMS, ALL WITH PRIVATE BATHROOM; FREE HOUSE WITH REAL ALE; CHILDREN AND PETS WELCOME; BAR AND RESTAURANT MEALS; NON-SMOKING AREAS; PEEBLES 6 MILES; S£££. D££.

THE CROOK INN
Tweedsmuir, Peeblesshire ML12 6QN
Tel: 01899 880272 • Fax: 01899 880294 • e-mail: thecrookinn@btinternet.com
website: www.crookinn.co.uk

Robert Burns wrote his poem *Willie Wastle's Wife* in the kitchen of this inspiring hostelry, which has played host to Covenanter and cattle reiver as well as poet in its four-hundred-year history. Situated in attractive gardens in the upper Tweed Valley, this comfortable, family-run hotel caters for those who would stay to savour the peace of this once-violent countryside. All rooms have en suite facilities and a full Scottish breakfast is included in the accommodation charge. Bar meals are always available, along with the Dining Room menu in the evenings. Reputed to be the oldest licensed coaching inn in Scotland, the hotel has many interesting features, not least the original Art Deco from the 1936 refurbishment.

7 BEDROOMS, ALL WITH PRIVATE BATHROOM; FREE HOUSE WITH REAL ALE; HISTORIC INTEREST; CHILDREN AND PETS WELCOME; BAR MEALS; NON-SMOKING AREAS; EDINBURGH 37 MILES; S£££, D££.

PLEASE MENTION THIS GUIDE WHEN YOU WRITE

OR PHONE TO ENQUIRE ABOUT ACCOMMODATION

IF YOU ARE WRITING, A STAMPED, ADDRESSED

ENVELOPE IS ALWAYS APPRECIATED

TIBBIE SHIELS INN
St Mary's Loch, Selkirk, Selkirkshire TD7 5LH
Tel: 01750 42231

Named after a remarkable woman who moved into what was then known as St.Mary's Cottage in 1823, this famous inn has grown out of her initiative. Widowed with six bairns to support, Isabella (Tibbie) Shiel began taking in gentlemen lodgers. The business flourished, and the inn, as it was now recognised, acquired considerable notoriety. Until her death in 1878, Tibbie played hostess to many famous men, Robert Louis Stevenson, William Gladstone and James Hogg (The Ettrick Shepherd) amongst them. Low ceilinged, cosy, full of character and hidden away in a place of incredible beauty, the spirit of the inn remains unchanged and offers first-class food, drink and accommodation. *AA, CAMRA.*

5 BEDROOMS, ALL WITH PRIVATE BATHROOM; FREE HOUSE; HISTORIC INTEREST; CHILDREN WELCOME; BAR AND RESTAURANT MEALS; NON-SMOKING AREAS; SELKIRK 13 MILES; S££, D£.

Dumfries & Galloway

THE POWFOOT HOTEL
Powfoot, Near Annan, Dumfriesshire DG12 5PN
Tel: 01461 700254 • Fax: 01461 700288 • e-mail: info@powfoothotel.co.uk
website: www.powfoothotel. co.uk

This family-owned and managed Edwardian hotel is uniquely situated on the shoreline of the Solway Firth. Accommodation is available in 18 en suite bedrooms, most with sea and golf links views, and families and pets are most welcome. Local produce is very much in evidence in the delicious meals served here, with an emphasis on dishes featuring freshly caught seafood. The hotel is just one hour's drive from North East England and one-and-a-half hours from Yorkshire, and with Gretna Green only ten miles away, it is ideal for 'one stop' Scottish weddings. Special Short Breaks feature activities such as golf, salmon and sea trout fishing, birdwatching, watercolour painting for beginners, and wildfowling (private shoreline available). Further details are available on request. *STB ★★ Hotel, AA ★★ 70%, Minotels..*

18 BEDROOMS, ALL WITH PRIVATE BATHROOM; FREE HOUSE; HISTORIC INTEREST; CHILDREN AND PETS WELCOME; BAR AND RESTAURANT MEALS; ANNAN 3 MILES; S££££, D£££.

BLACK BULL HOTEL
Churchgate, Moffat, Dumfriesshire DG10 9EG
Tel: 01683 220206 • Fax: 01683 220483 • e-mail: hotel@blackbullmoffat.co.uk
website: www.blackbullmoffat.co.uk

Much care has been taken to preserve the authentic atmosphere of this famous, 16th century inn. Many colourful characters have sat within these hospitable walls taking food and drink amongst convivial company, most notably, one Rabbie Burns, a regular patron, who complemented his mood by writing the famous 'Epigram to a Scrimpit Nature' here and possibly other whimsies. The warm welcome is still there with good real ale and a selection of bar snacks available, whilst the Mail Coach Restaurant is renowned for its top quality food and friendly service. Excellent fishing and golf may be enjoyed locally, further reasons for taking advantage of the high standard of modern accommodation. *STB ★★★ Hotel.*

7 BEDROOMS, 5 WITH PRIVATE BATHROOM; FREE HOUSE WITH REAL ALE; HISTORIC INTEREST; CHILDREN WELCOME;
BAR AND RESTAURANT MEALS; NON-SMOKING AREAS; DUMFRIES 19 MILES; S££, D££.

Dundee & Angus

FISHERMAN'S TAVERN HOTEL
Fort Street, Broughty Ferry, Dundee DD5 2AD
Tel: 01382 775941 • Fax: 01382 477466
website: www.fishermans-tavern-hotel.co.uk

A "must" for real ale aficionados who find themselves in this traditional little resort just on the edge of Dundee, the Fisherman's Tavern boasts of having been elected "Best in UK" by CAMRA. But whatever your tipple, this comfortably rambling inn is a pleasant spot for relaxation and good conversation, and in addition offers a good bar food menu which ranges from sandwiches and burgers to more substantial dishes such as steak pie and lasagne. The usual menu is supplemented by a choice of daily specials which are well worth looking out for. Centrally heated bedrooms provide cosy accommodation, and the very reasonable room rate includes a full Scottish breakfast. *STB ★ Hotel, AA.*

13 BEDROOMS, 7 WITH PRIVATE BATHROOM; FREE HOUSE WITH REAL ALE; HISTORIC INTEREST; CHILDREN AND PETS WELCOME; BAR MEALS, RESTAURANT IF PRE-BOOKED; NON-SMOKING AREAS; DUNDEE 4 MILES; S£/£££, D£££/££££.

Edinburgh & Lothians

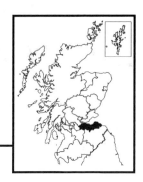

LAIRD AND DOG HOTEL
5 High Street, Lasswade, Near Edinburgh, Midlothian EH18 1NA
Tel & Fax: 0131-663 9219

Almost 300 years old, this historic village inn once brewed its own beer, and the old well which supplied the brewery is now incorporated into the newly refurbished lounge bar. "The Olde Worlde Bar" is the popular haunt of locals and offers a wide range of real ales, malt whiskies and wines. A full menu is on offer serving the best of Scottish beef, lamb and local produce in the beautifully furnished conservatory restaurant. Conveniently placed for the many delights of Edinburgh, with the benefit of a large car park and excellent bus service, this recommended hotel offers first class accommodation for those seeking adventure in sightseeing, hillwalking, horse riding, cycling, fishing, golfing or skiing at Hillend ski slope. *CAMRA.*

9 BEDROOMS, ALL WITH PRIVATE BATHROOM; FREE HOUSE WITH REAL ALE; HISTORIC INTEREST; CHILDREN AND PETS WELCOME; BAR MEALS, RESTAURANT EVENINGS ONLY; NON-SMOKING AREAS; EDINBURGH 6 MILES; S££, D££.

YE OLDE ORIGINAL ROSLIN INN
Main Street, Roslin, Midlothian EH25 9LE
Tel: 0131-440 2384 • Fax: 0131-440 2514

The 'Old Original' was in former times a temperance hotel but those seeking refreshment today may be assured that all four bars are well stocked with good beers, spirits and an interesting selection of fine wines. Substantial lunches are served in the comfortable lounge bar and the à la carte dinner menu attracts locals as well as tourists to a dining room graced by an absorbing collection of antiques; here one may dine memorably by candlelight. Six centrally heated, en suite bedrooms are available for letting, including two honeymoon suites; all have pleasing decor, television and tea and coffee-making facilities. Edinburgh is only seven miles away and there is a new leisure centre with a swimming pool nearby in Loanhead. *AA, Les Routiers.* **See also Colour Advertisement on page 12.**

6 BEDROOMS, ALL WITH PRIVATE BATHROOM; FREE HOUSE; HISTORIC INTEREST; CHILDREN AND PETS WELCOME; BAR MEALS, RESTAURANT EVENINGS ONLY; NON-SMOKING AREAS; EDINBURGH 7 MILES; S£££, D££.

Highlands

APPLECROSS HOTEL
Applecross, Wester Ross, Ross-shire 1V54 8LR
Tel: 01520 744262 • Fax: 01520 744400

The very remoteness of the Applecross Peninsula is one of its attractions but, on a practical note, this fine hostelry commands immediate attention. With magnificent views overlooking the Inner Sound and the island of Raasay with the Cuillin Hills of Skye forming a dramatic backdrop, this is a naturalist's paradise beckoning, in particular, the hill-walker, angler and ornithologist, whilst the ski resort of Aviemore is just over two hours' drive away. The inn-cum-hotel specialises in an exciting variety of fresh, locally caught seafood as well as steaks and local venison. Bar meals are available all day. A note to would-be escapees: the Bed and Breakfast accommodation is reasonable in price but in great demand. *AA, Good Pub Guide, "Which?" Guide, Egon Ronay.*

5 BEDROOMS; FREE HOUSE; CHILDREN AND PETS WELCOME; BAR MEALS, RESTAURANT EVENINGS ONLY; NON-SMOKING AREAS; SHIELDAIG 18 MILES; S£, D£.

The **£** symbol when appearing at the end of the italic section of an entry shows the anticipated price, during 2001, for full Bed and Breakfast.

Normal Bed & Breakfast rate per person (in single room)		Normal Bed & Breakfast rate per person (sharing double/twin room)	
PRICE RANGE	CATEGORY	PRICE RANGE	CATEGORY
Under £25	S£	**Under £25**	D£
£26-£35	S££	**£26-£35**	D££
£36-£45	S£££	**£36-£45**	D£££
Over £45	S££££	**Over £45**	D££££

This is meant as an indication only and does not show prices for Special Breaks, Weekends, etc. Guests are therefore advised to verify all prices on enquiring or booking.

DUNBEATH HOTEL
Dunbeath, Caithness KW6 6EG
Tel: 01593 731208 • Fax: 01593 731242

Dunbeath Hotel is situated with views to the sea and is ideally placed for touring the north of Scotland or visiting the Orkney Islands. All rooms are en suite and our restaurant menu includes salmon, venison, seafood and a fine selection of fine wines. Sporting activities nearby include fishing and pony trekking. Special Break rates available on request. *Welcome Host, Les Routiers recommended.*

BEDROOMS WITH PRIVATE BATHROOMS; RESTAURANT MEALS; WICK 18 MILES.

NETHER LOCHABER HOTEL
Onich, Fort William, Inverness-shire PH33 6SE
Tel: 01855 821235 • Fax: 01855 821545

An ideal centre from which to explore Lochaber, the Ardnamurchan Peninsula and Glencoe. Traditional home cooking goes hand in hand with homely service, comfortable accommodation and private facilities. The inn stands on the shores of beautiful Loch Linnhe at Corran Ferry. ***See also Colour Advertisement on page 12.***

5 BEDROOMS; FREE HOUSE; HISTORIC INTEREST; BAR AND RESTAURANT MEALS; NON-SMOKING AREAS;
EDINBURGH 121 MILES, GLASGOW 91, OBAN 48, FORT WILLIAM 10; S££, D££.

For details of Tourist Board Gradings in England, Scotland and Wales see page 17

CASTLE ARMS HOTEL
Mey, By Thurso, Caithness KW14 8XH
Tel & Fax: 01847 851244 • e-mail: info@castlearms.co.uk
website: www.castle-armshotel.co.uk

This former 19th century coaching inn on the John O'Groats peninsula is set in six acres of parkland, close to the Queen Mother's Highland home, the Castle of Mey. Fully modernised, the hotel has eight centrally heated en suite bedrooms with colour television and tea making facilities; the spacious Pentland Suite offers a double and family room with en suite bathroom. Locally caught salmon, crab and other fine Highland produce feature on the varied table d'hôte and grill menus available in the Garden Room, while lighter meals and snacks can be enjoyed in the cosy Pentland Lounge. A warm Highland welcome awaits you. *STB ★★ Hotel.*

8 BEDROOMS, ALL WITH PRIVATE BATHROOM; FREE HOUSE; HISTORIC INTEREST; CHILDREN AND PETS WELCOME; BAR AND RESTAURANT MEALS; NON-SMOKING AREAS; JOHN O' GROATS 6 MILES; S£££, D££.

STRATHCARRON HOTEL
Strathcarron, Ross-shire IV54 8YR
Tel: 01520 722227 • Fax: 01520 722990 • e-mail: puzzell23@aol.com

Just 20 miles east of the Skye Bridge, this friendly inn welcomes lovers of mountain scenery and walkers, as the hotel fronts the footpath linking the Five Sisters and Dornie to Torridon via Attadale and Strathcarron. A traditional, cosy lounge bar features an open, log-burning fire and here one may sample good real ale and cider with hot, home-made snacks and basket meals. For dinner, there is an extensive range of Scottish dishes on offer, including, fresh local seafood and locally-smoked salmon. Accommodation comprises bedrooms with private bath or shower, colour television, and tea and coffee-making facilities.

9 BEDROOMS, ALL WITH PRIVATE BATHROOM; FREE HOUSE WITH REAL ALE; CHILDREN AND PETS WELCOME; BAR MEALS, RESTAURANT EVENINGS ONLY; NON-SMOKING AREAS; KYLE OF LOCHALSH 20 MILES; S££, D££.

Perth & Kinross

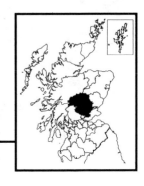

ALYTH HOTEL,
6-8 Commercial Street, Alyth, Perthshire PH11 8AF
Tel: 01828 632447 • Fax: 01828 632355

For hospitality in the good old Highland manner allied to contemporary amenities of the highest calibre, this brightly furnished former posting house merits serious consideration when seeking a break in an area famed for its rural beauty. The attractions here are many and diverse: enjoy good music or quiet conversation in the bar whilst, perhaps, sampling one of the many malt whiskies; savour a delicious Scottish High Tea or dine from a menu featuring fresh local fish, game from nearby estates and prime Aberdeen Angus beef; watch the wild trout and salmon in the burn that flows past the hotel. Rooms are delightfully appointed, so relax, you'll be glad you chose Alyth Hotel.

10 BEDROOMS, ALL WITH PRIVATE BATHROOM; FREE HOUSE; HISTORIC INTEREST; CHILDREN AND PETS WELCOME; BAR AND RESTAURANT MEALS; NON-SMOKING AREAS; BLAIRGOWRIE 5 MILES; S£££, D£££.

THE MUIRS INN KINROSS
49 Muirs, Kinross, Perth & Kinross KY13 8AU
Tel & Fax: 01577 862270 • e-mail: pch49m@aol.co.uk

Open all year round and listed as one of Scotland's best pubs, it is a traditional Scottish Country Inn – at its best. With all bedrooms en suite it is full of character and boasts its own award-nominated restaurant which serves home-cooked fresh country cuisine at sensible prices every day. Scottish real ales and malt whiskies are a speciality at this charming inn where you spend time and not a fortune. Historic Kinross is ideal for business or for pleasure and is a superb holiday centre with 130 golf courses and all major cities within driving distance. This Inn is simply something special. Details of special mid-week and weekend breaks sent on request. *AA* ◆◆◆, *Taste of Scotland*.

5 BEDROOMS, ALL WITH PRIVATE BATHROOM; FREE HOUSE WITH REAL ALE; HISTORIC INTEREST; CHILDREN WELCOME; BAR AND RESTAURANT MEALS; NON-SMOKING AREAS; DUNFERMLINE 9 MILES; S£££, D££.

THE STRATHARDLE INN
Kirkmichael, Perthshire PH10 7NS
Tel: 01250 881224 • Fax 01250 881373 • website: www.strathardleinn.co.uk

The Strathardle Inn is a country hotel set deep in the mountains of Highland Perthshire. The grounds of the inn include 700 feet of river bank with fishing rights, a beer garden and a hillside of mature Scottish oaks. The restaurant offers an à la carte menu of modern Scottish cooking together with an extensive wine list of classical European and New World wines. The atmosphere is relaxed, warm and welcoming as only a family-run hotel can be. The bar caters to an easy going mix of locals and visitors, serving a range of freshly cooked bar meals to the accompaniment of our resident classical pianist. Logs fires, a peaceful isolated location, and superb views over the Perthshire mountains ensure a stay to remember.

9 BEDROOMS, 8 WITH PRIVATE BATHROOM; FREE HOUSE WITH REAL ALE; CHILDREN AND PETS WELCOME; BAR AND RESTAURANT MEALS; NON-SMOKING AREAS; PITLOCHRY 9 MILES; S££, D£.

Recommended
Wayside &
Country Inns 2001
Wales

THE FHG
DIPLOMA

HELP IMPROVE
BRITISH TOURIST STANDARDS

You are choosing holiday accommodation from our very popular FHG Publications.
Whether it be a hotel, guest house, farmhouse or self-catering accommodation, we think you will find it hospitable, comfortable and clean, and your host and hostess friendly and helpful.

Why not write and tell us about it?

As a recognition of the generally well-run and excellent holiday accommodation reviewed in our publications, we at FHG Publications Ltd. present a diploma to proprietors who receive the highest recommendation from their guests who are also readers of our Guides. If you care to write to us praising the holiday you have booked through FHG Publications Ltd. – whether this be board, self-catering accommodation, a sporting or a caravan holiday, what you say will be evaluated and the proprietors who reach our final list will be contacted.

The winning proprietor will receive an attractive framed diploma to display on his premises as recognition of a high standard of comfort, amenity and hospitality. FHG Publications Ltd. offer this diploma as a contribution towards the improvement of standards in tourist accommodation in Britain. Help your excellent host or hostess to win it!

FHG DIPLOMA

We nominate ....

....

Because

Name ....

Address..

....

Telephone No..

FHG

North Wales

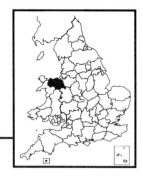

GOLDEN PHEASANT HOTEL
Glyn Ceiriog, Near Llangollen, North Wales LL20 7BB
Tel: 01691 718281 • Fax: 01691 718479

The Golden Pheasant has been described as a "home-from-home" – but that presupposes one's home enjoys the ultimate in comfort, breathtaking hill and valley views, and such facilities as whirlpool bath, four-poster bed and an attentive and willing staff! All guest accommodation is appointed to a high standard with tea and coffee facilities, colour television and bathroom en suite, and public rooms throughout combine charm and elegance with sumptuous comfort. The romantic split-level restaurant provides a lovely setting for the imaginative menus presented nightly. This scenic area offers many attractions and special rates for short breaks make an extended stay a particularly appealing prospect. *WTB ★★★ Hotel, AA ★★★*.

19 BEDROOMS, ALL WITH PRIVATE BATHROOM; FREE HOUSE; CHILDREN AND PETS WELCOME; BAR AND RESTAURANT MEALS; NON-SMOKING AREAS; LLANGOLLEN 3 MILES; S££, D££.

GALES HOTEL AND WINE BAR
18 Bridge Street, Llangollen, North Wales LL20 8PF
Tel: 01978 860089 • Fax: 01978 861313 • e-mail: rgale@galesofllangollen.co.uk
website: www.galesofllangollen.co.uk

With well over 100 wines and ports on offer and a reputation for outstanding food, this interesting establishment has gained rapidly in popularity since opening its doors in 1977. Situated within an 18th century town house, informal wine tastings are held regularly and there can be no better way to conclude the session than by staying overnight in one of the luxurious bedrooms, all of which have been sympathetically restored in keeping with the historic character of the premises: all have bathrooms en suite, colour televisions, direct-dial telephones, hairdryers and beverage-makers. Several non-smoking rooms and two superb executive suites are housed in a 17th century wing. *WTB ★★★ Restaurant with Rooms, Egon Ronay*.

15 BEDROOMS, ALL WITH PRIVATE BATHROOM; FREE HOUSE; CHILDREN WELCOME; RESTAURANT MEALS; NON-SMOKING AREAS; WREXHAM 9 MILES; S£££, D££.

Cardiganshire

GEORGE BORROW HOTEL
Ponterwyd, Aberystwyth, Cardiganshire SY23 3AD
Tel: 01970 890230 • Fax: 01970 890587 • e-mail: georgeborrow@clara.net
website: www.george-borrow.co.uk

Nestling in the foothills of the Cambrian Mountains, close to the source of the River Severn and the famous Devil's Bridge, this comfortable hostelry has two pleasant bars serving fine ale and home-cooked food whilst, for more formal dining, the 40-seater restaurant presents an interesting à la carte menu featuring local specialities and vegetarian meals. Antique furniture and log fires add to the homely ambience and for those wishing to extend their stay in an area of dramatic scenery, the hotel has a number of well-appointed bedrooms. Perched on the edge of the Rheidol Gorge, the hotel enjoys stunning views, emphasising that this is a splendid venue for walking, fishing and bird watching. *WTB/AA* ★★ *Hotel.*

9 BEDROOMS, ALL EN SUITE; FREE HOUSE WITH REAL ALE; HISTORIC INTEREST; CHILDREN WELCOME, PETS BY PRIOR ARRANGEMENT; BAR MEALS, RESTAURANT EVENINGS ONLY; DEVIL'S BRIDGE 3 MILES; S£, D£.

BLACK LION HOTEL
High Street, Cardigan, Cardiganshire SA43 1HJ
Tel: 01239 612532

Still retaining its classic 18th century frontage, this old hostelry has a long and colourful history. It was established on the site in 1105 as a one-roomed 'Grogge Shoppe' and is probably the oldest inn in Wales. In 1635, it was enlarged and improved and became the residence of a local squire. When Cardigan became an overnight stopover on the main route between North and South Wales, the 'Black Lion' became an important coaching inn. The mews entrance may still be seen leading off the High Street. Many interesting people have stayed here over the years: during Assize week, the judge would stay and the Assize banquet was held in the upstairs Long Room, popular with the local gentry for their meetings and balls in the 19th century. In the latter years of that century the hotel played host to a thriving cycling club – a new craze! Although still blessed with considerable old-world charm, the hotel has been brought gently into line with the requirements of the 20th and 21st century. Its historic bars thrum with the buzz of convivial conversation whilst serving Tomos Watkin Ltd's Welsh ales and the restaurant provides a selection of fine fare. Guest rooms now have en suite facilities, colour television, telephone and tea and coffee-makers and social events and functions are expertly catered for. For touring the Teifi Valley and the coast of West Wales, this is the ideal base.

14 BEDROOMS, ALL WITH PRIVATE BATHROOM; TOMOS WATKIN LTD HOUSE WITH REAL ALE; HISTORIC INTEREST; CHILDREN WELCOME; BAR LUNCHES, RESTAURANT EVENINGS ONLY; ABERYSTWYTH 34 MILES.

FHG PUBLICATIONS

publish a large range of well-known accommodation guides.
We will be happy to send you details or you can use
the order form at the back of this book.

Pembrokeshire

TREWERN ARMS HOTEL
Nevern, Newport, Pembrokeshire SA42 0NB
Tel: 01239 820395

Set deep in a forested and secluded valley on the banks of the River Nevern, this picturesque, 16th century hostelry has a warmth of welcome that is immediately apparent in the interestingly-shaped Brew House Bar with its original flagstone floors, stone walls, old settles and beams decorated with an accumulated collection of bric-a-brac. Bar meals are served here from a popular grill area. By contrast, the Lounge Bar is furnished on cottage lines and the fine restaurant has received many accolades from far and wide for its culinary delights. The tranquil village of Nevern is ideally placed for Pembrokeshire's historic sites and uncrowded, sandy beaches and the accommodation offered at this recommended retreat is in the multi-starred class. *WTB ★★★ Inn*

10 BEDROOMS, ALL WITH PRIVATE BATHROOM; FREE HOUSE WITH REAL ALE; CHILDREN WELCOME;
BAR MEALS, RESTAURANT THURS/FRI/SAT EVENINGS ONLY; NON-SMOKING AREAS; NEWPORT 2 MILES; S££, D£.

The **£** symbol when appearing at the end of the italic section of an entry shows the anticipated price, during 2001, for full Bed and Breakfast.

Normal Bed & Breakfast rate per person *(in single room)*		*Normal Bed & Breakfast rate per person* *(sharing double/twin room)*	
PRICE RANGE	CATEGORY	PRICE RANGE	CATEGORY
Under £25	*S£*	**Under £25**	*D£*
£26-£35	*S££*	**£26-£35**	*D££*
£36-£45	*S£££*	**£36-£45**	*D£££*
Over £45	*S££££*	**Over £45**	*D££££*

This is meant as an indication only and does not show prices for Special Breaks, Weekends, etc. Guests are therefore advised to verify all prices on enquiring or booking.

Powys

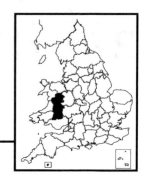

THE BLUE BELL INN
Llangurig, Powys SY18 6SG
Tel: 01686 440254 • Fax: 01686 440337

The Blue Bell Inn is situated on the main A44 road to Aberystwyth opposite the Llangurig village church behind which runs the River Wye whose source is just six miles away. The area is ideal for angling, walking, cycling, bird-watching and golf. The inn serves very good food - look out for Elsie's home-made specials on the blackboard. The menu also includes a good selection of vegetarian dishes. The inn is a free house and serves a variety of real ales and lagers. We currently have eight rooms providing accommodation. This family-run pub has a very good reputation for food and drink, and you'll always get a warm welcome from Gordon, Elsie, Neil, Andrea, Jimmy, Darryl and Fudge.

8 BEDROOMS; FREE HOUSE WITH REAL ALE; BAR MEALS; LLANIDLOES 4 MILES.

BLACK LION HOTEL
Llangurig, Powys SY18 6SG
Tel: 01686 440223 • Fax: 01686 440277 • e-mail: blacklion@llangurig.org.uk
website: http://llangurig.org.uk/

Originally a 16th century shooting lodge, this is a friendly little inn-cum-hotel on the upper reaches of the River Wye and in the heart of a lovely village, the highest in Wales. On the A44 Aberystwyth road and right in the centre of Wales, it is an ideal base for exploring Wales itself and for walking, fishing and bird watching in the locality. Refreshment is plentifully available in a cosy bar warmed by an open fire in cool weather, an extensive menu including many tempting home-made dishes served at lunchtime and in the evening. Fully centrally heated, the hotel has several well-appointed guest rooms and there is a large comfortable lounge with colour television.

8 BEDROOMS, 5 WITH PRIVATE BATHROOM; FREE HOUSE WITH REAL ALE; HISTORIC INTEREST; CHILDREN AND PETS WELCOME; BAR MEALS, RESTAURANT EVENINGS ONLY; NON-SMOKING AREAS; LLANIDLOES 4 MILES; S£,D£.

NEUADD ARMS HOTEL
Llanwrtyd Wells, Powys LD5 4RB
Tel: 01591 610236

Llanwrtyd Wells is the smallest town in Britain yet it can fairly claim to be the activity centre of mid-Wales with fabulous facilities for walking waymarked trails, pony trekking and riding, fishing, bird watching, mountain biking or just gentle sightseeing. As a recommended place to stay whilst indulging in these pastimes, the Red Dragon of Wales embellishing the facade of this fine hotel is a true symbol of its warmth of welcome. Its 19th century character is perpetuated in the bars where every night you can meet the townsfolk and listen to stories from the hills and valleys, some as broad as the fish that get away daily in the local River Irfon. Upstairs, comfortable and well-appointed bedrooms ensure sound repose after a day's activities; most of them have either a bath or shower room and colour television. Radios and shaver points are standard and there is a baby-listening intercom, ideal for parents relaxing in the bar, restaurant, games room or television lounge. Proprietors, Gordon and Di Green, hold benign sway over this purposely old-fashioned home from home and have fostered the hotel's excellent reputation for good food, a wide choice of meals being served in an attractive restaurant overlooking the square and surrounding hills. A whole raft of interesting 'special' events is organised throughout the year including the Man versus Horse Marathon and the World Bog Snorkelling Championships (held every August Bank Holiday Monday). *RAC* ★.

20 BEDROOMS, 15 WITH PRIVATE BATHROOM; FREE HOUSE WITH REAL ALE; HISTORIC INTEREST; CHILDREN AND PETS WELCOME; BAR MEALS, RESTAURANT EVENINGS ONLY; NON-SMOKING AREAS; LLANDOVERY 10 MILES; S££, D££.

SEVERN ARMS HOTEL
Penybont, Llandrindod Wells, Powys LD1 5UA
Tel: 01597 851224/851344 • Fax: 01597 851693

A handsome early Victorian coaching inn, the Severn Arms enjoys an enviable reputation for first-class service and hospitality at reasonable prices — a reputation which the friendly proprietors are determined to maintain. Olde worlde bars provide tasty and wholesome snacks and meals, while the à la carte restaurant is a most pleasant setting for the enjoyment of the fine cuisine offered there. Cosy bedrooms, all with private bathrooms and colour television, provide overnight accommodation, and the inn's position on the A44 makes it a perfect stop for travellers and tourists visiting the many attractions in the Welsh heartland. *WTB* ★★ *Hotel, Les Routiers, CAMRA, Egon Ronay.*

10 BEDROOMS, ALL WITH PRIVATE BATHROOM; FREE HOUSE WITH REAL ALE; HISTORIC INTEREST; CHILDREN AND PETS WELCOME; BAR MEALS, RESTAURANT EVENINGS ONLY PLUS SUNDAY LUNCH; LLANDRINDOD WELLS 4 MILES; S££, D££££.

For details of Tourist Board Gradings in England, Scotland and Wales see page 17

South Wales

YE OLDE CROWN INN
Old Hereford Road, Pant-y-Gelli, Abergavenny, Monmouthshire NP7 7HR
Tel & Fax: 01873 853314

A friendly welcome awaits all to our 15th century Coaching Inn situated on the lower slopes of the Sugar Loaf within the Brecon Beacons National Park. All bedrooms have television, tea and coffee facilities and enjoy magnificent views of the Holy Mountain. Sample our range of real ales (CAMRA Millennium Pub Guide) or try one of our numerous malts whilst browsing over our bar, special or restaurant menus featuring many tempting dishes created by our full time chef and team using local produce including game, lamb, pork and trout. Traditional dishes on our bar snack menu include the old favourites such as steak and ale, liver and onions, and faggots and peas. Our restaurant menu offers more exotic, international and traditional choices. There are many activities throughout the area and hosts Mel and Rosemary Mitchell will be only too happy to advise.

4 BEDROOMS, ALL WITH GUESTS' BATHROOM; FREE HOUSE WITH REAL ALE; CHILDREN AND PETS WELCOME; BAR AND RESTAURANT MEALS; NON-SMOKING AREAS; ABERGAVENNY 2 MILES.

THE ANGEL HOTEL
Cross Street, Abergavenny, South Wales NP7 5EN
Tel: 01873 857121 • Fax: 01873 858059

Nestling on the borders of the Brecon Beacons, The Angel, which has recently been refurbished, was once one of the great coaching inns on the busy London to Fishguard road. Of considerable architectural interest, the hostelry retains a haunting aura of the past whilst providing a high standard of modern comforts and conveniences. Dine in the new brasserie which serves English and Continental fare, or perhaps relax in the Foxhunter Bar with its enjoyable selection of snacks to complement the real ale. Guest rooms each have a private bathroom, satellite colour television, radio, direct-dial telephone and tea and coffee-making facilities. The Angel is an ideal base for a relaxing holiday and opportunities exist for a wide range of leisure and sporting activities. *AA* ★★★.

29 BEDROOMS, ALL WITH PRIVATE BATHROOM; OLD ENGLISH INNS HOUSE WITH REAL ALE; HISTORIC INTEREST; CHILDREN AND PETS WELCOME; BAR AND RESTAURANT MEALS; NON-SMOKING AREAS; PONTYPOOL 9 MILES; S£££££, D££.

CLYTHA ARMS
Near Abergavenny, South Wales NP7 9BW
Tel: 01873 840206 • e-mail: one.bev@lineone.net
website: http://website.lineone.net~one.bev/

A converted Dower House set in its own grounds alongside the old Abergavenny to Raglan road (B4598), the Clytha Arms is known primarily for its superb food; furthermore, it is very unpublike in its appearance and its facilities equate more to a distinguished country hotel. Indeed, the accommodation, limited though it may be, is of the highest calibre, the en suite rooms prettily decorated and sumptuously appointed. Nevertheless, this lovely retreat, in the hands of Andrew and Bev Canning, still maintains traditions of a wayside inn with six real ales and snacks available in the public bar. However, it is culinary art and expertise that is the big attraction here – imaginative fare, delightfully presented. *Egon Ronay, Taste of Wales.*

4 BEDROOMS, ALL WITH PRIVATE BATHROOM; FREE HOUSE WITH REAL ALE; CHILDREN WELCOME; BAR AND RESTAURANT MEALS; NON-SMOKING AREAS; USK 6 MILES; S£££, D£££.

LLANWENARTH ARMS RIVERSIDE HOTEL & RESTAURANT
Brecon Road, Abergavenny, South Wales NP8 1EP
Tel: 01873 810550 • Fax: 01873 811880

With delightful views of the River Usk and Sugarloaf Mountain, this renovated 16th century inn makes the most of its beautiful situation by offering good company and sustenance in its bars, including an interesting selection of real ales, whilst the restaurant is a popular venue for imaginative, home-cooked fare. Children are especially welcome and have their own menu. Golf, riding and hang-gliding are among the many sporting opportunities to be found locally and the hotel possesses two excellent stretches of salmon and trout water available to guests. Well-appointed double and twin-bedded rooms add further encouragement to stay in this lovely, peaceful area. *AA ★★ and Rosette.*

18 BEDROOMS, ALL WITH PRIVATE BATHROOM; FREE HOUSE WITH REAL ALE; CHILDREN WELCOME; BAR AND RESTAURANT MEALS; PONTYPOOL 9 MILES; S££££, D£££.

𝔉𝔥𝔊 𝔇iploma 𝔚inners 2000

Each year we award a small number of diplomas to holiday proprietors whose services have been specially commended by our readers. The following were our FHG Diploma Winners for 2000.

England

CUMBRIA

• Mr & Mrs Haskell, Borwick Lodge, Outgate, Hawkshead, Cumbria LA22 0PU (015394 36332).

• Mrs Val Sunter, Higher House Farm, Oxenholme Lane, Natland, Kendal, Cumbria LA9 7QH (015395 61177).

DEVON

• Jenny Fox, Highstead Farm, Bucks Cross, Bideford, Devon EX39 5DX (01237 431201).

DORSET

• Mr & Mrs Reynolds, The Vine Hotel, 22 Southern Rd, Southbourne, Bournemouth, Dorset BH6 3SR (01202 428309).

HAMPSHIRE

• Mrs Ellis, Efford Cottage Guest House, Milford Road, Everton, Lymington, Hampshire SO41 0JD (015906 42315).

KENT

• Pam & Arthur Mills, Cloverlea, Bethersden, Ashford, Kent TN26 3DU (01233 820353)

Wales

ANGLESEY & GWYNEDD

• Jim & Marion Billingham, Preswylfa, Aberdovey, Gwynedd LL35 0LE (01654 767239)

NORTH WALES

• Bob & Nesta Wivell, Pen-Y-Bont Fawr, Cynwyd, Near Corwen, North Wales LL21 0ET (01490 412663)

Scotland

ABERDEENSHIRE, BANFF & MORAY

• Garth Hotel, Grantown on Spey, Morayshire PH26 3HN (01479 872836)

PERTH & KINROSS

• The Windlestrae Hotel, The Muirs, Kinross, Tayside KY13 7AS (01577 863217)

HELP IMPROVE BRITISH TOURIST STANDARDS

Why not write and tell us about the holiday accommodation you have chosen from one of our popular publications?
Complete a nomination form (see back of book) giving details of why you think YOUR host or hostess should win one of our attractive framed diplomas.

FHG

The BETA Guide to Pet-Friendly Pubs

The  Guide to Pet-Friendly Pubs

Whenever you visit one of our public houses or hotels listed within the Beta Guide to Pet-Friendly Pubs you can be sure your four-legged friend will be more than welcome. He will find a fresh bowl of water, provided by the landlord to quench his thirst, and it's likely he will meet other canine visitors.

Beta Complete Dog Food
the best nutritional care at home and on holiday...

ENGLAND

BERKSHIRE

THE GREYHOUND (known locally as 'The Dog')
The Walk, Eton Wick, Berkshire (01753 863925).
Dogs allowed throughout the pub.
Pet Regulars: Harvey (Retriever), retrieves anything, including Beer mats. KIA - German Shepherd.

THE SWAN
9 Mill Lane, Clewer, Windsor, Berkshire (01753 862069).
Dogs allowed throughout the pub.
Pet Regulars: Ziggy and her family, Simba, Thumper and Cassy (Bichon Frise) – useful for keeping your lap warm; Taffy, who has a very waggy tail and who curls up and sleeps under a chair until closing time; Ben, a very friendly Alsatian who enjoys a drop or two of London Pride; Rupert, another Bichon, who calls in after his walks; Ben, the latest addition, a playful Springer Spaniel puppy.

THE TWO BREWERS
Park Street, Windsor, Berkshire (01753 855426).
Dogs allowed, public and saloon bars.
Pet Regulars: Harry (Pyrenean) and his mate Molly (Newfoundland) take up the whole bar, 'Bear' (Black Labrador), Tessa (Cocker Spaniel) and Charlie (Collie).

BUCKINGHAMSHIRE

WHITE HORSE
Village Lane, Hedgerley, Buckinghamshire SL2 3UY (01753 643225).
Dogs allowed at tables on pub frontage, beer garden (on leads), public bar.

CAMBRIDGESHIRE

YE OLD WHITE HART
Main Street, Ufford, Peterborough, Cambridgeshire (01780 740250).
Dogs allowed in non-food areas.

CHESHIRE

JACKSONS BOAT
Rifle Road, Sale, Cheshire (0161 973 8549).
Dogs allowed throughout on lead with the exception of the dining area.

CORNWALL

DRIFTWOOD SPARS HOTEL
Trevaunance Cove, St Agnes, Cornwall (01872 552428).
Dogs allowed everywhere except the restaurant.
Pet Regulars: Buster (Cornish Labrador cross) - devours anything.

JUBILEE INN
Pelynt, Near Looe, Cornwall PL13 2JZ (01503 220312).
Dogs allowed in all areas except restaurant; accommodation for guests with dogs.

THE MILL HOUSE INN
Trebarwith Strand, Tintagel, Cornwall PL34 0HD (01840 770200).
Pet Friendly.

THE MOLESWORTH ARMS HOTEL
Molesworth Street, Wadebridge, Cornwall PL27 7DP (01208 812055).
Dogs allowed in all public areas and in hotel rooms.
Pet Regulars: Thomson Cassidy (Black Lab), Ruby and Bertie (Golden Retriever).

THE WHITE HART
Chilsworthy, Near Gunnislake, Cornwall (01822 832307).
Dogs allowed in non-food bar, car park tables, beer garden.
Pet Regulars: Kai, Ben and Lawson (German Shepherds).

WELLINGTON HOTEL,
The Harbour, Boscastle, Cornwall (01840 250202).
Dogs allowed in bedrooms and on lead in pub.
Own private 10-acre woodland walk. Dogs welcome free of charge.

CUMBRIA

THE BRITANNIA INN
Elterwater, Ambleside, Cumbria LA22 9HP (015394 37210).
Dogs allowed in all areas except dining room.
Pet Regulars: Charlie (Collie cross), Annie (Retriever).

THE MORTAL MAN HOTEL
Troutbeck, Windermere, Cumbria LA23 lPL (015394 33193).
Dogs allowed throughout and in guest rooms.

STAG INN
Dufton, Appleby, Cumbria (017683 51608).
Dogs allowed in non-food bar, beer garden, village green plus B&B and cottage.
Pet Regulars: Toffee (cross between Saluki and Golden Setter); Willow (cross between Great Dane and an Old English Sheepdog); Kim (Weimaraner), best bitter drinker; Buster (Jack Russell), enjoys a quiet evening.

139

WATERMILL INN
School Lane, Ings, Near Staveley, Kendal, Cumbria (01539 821309).
Dogs allowed in beer garden, Wrynose bottom bar.
Pet Regulars: Smudge (sheepdog); Gowan (Westie) and Scruffy (mongrel). All enjoy a range of crisps and snacks. Scruffy regularly drinks Blacksheep special. Pub dogs Misty (Beardie). Owners cannot walk dogs past pub, without being dragged in! Biscuits and water provided.

DERBYSHIRE

JINGLERS/FOX & HOUNDS
(A517) Belper Road, Bradley, Ashbourne, Derbyshire (01335 370855).
Dogs allowed in non-food bars, beer garden, accommodation for guests with dogs.
Pet Regulars: Benson (Springer), Hamlet (Pointer/Lab) – pedigree drinkers and Walkers crisps crunchers.

THE GEORGE HOTEL
Commercial Road, Tideswell, Near Buxton, Derbyshire SK17 8NU (01298 871382).
Dogs allowed in snug and around the bar, water bowls provided.

DOG AND PARTRIDGE COUNTRY INN & MOTEL
Swinscoe, Ashbourne, Derbyshire (01335 343183).
Dogs allowed throughout, except restaurant.
Pet Regulars: Include Mitsy (57); Rusty (Cairn); Spider (Collie/GSD) and Rex (GSD).

DEVONSHIRE ARMS
Peak Forest, Near Buxton, Derbyshire SK17 8EJ (01298 23875)
Dogs allowed in bar.
Pet Regulars: Fergie (Collie-cross), known as "The Fireguard".

WHITE HART
Station Road, West Hallam, Derbyshire DE7 6GW (0115 932 6069).
Dogs allowed in all non-food areas.
Pet Regulars: Archie, Chester and Brewser. Three cats: Itsy, Bitsy and Jasper.

DEVON

THE SHIP INN
Axmouth, Devon EX12 4AF (01297 21838).
A predominantly catering pub, so dogs on a lead please.
Pet Regulars: Cassie, Charlie, Digby and Beamish. Also resident Tawny Owls.

BRENDON HOUSE HOTEL
Brendon, Lynton, North Devon EX35 6PS (01598 741206).
Dogs very welcome and allowed in tea gardens, guest bedrooms by arrangement.
Pet Regulars: Jasmine (cat), self appointed cream tea receptionist. Years of practice have perfected dirty looks at visiting dogs.

THE BULLERS ARMS
Chagford, Newton Abbot, Devon (01647 432348).
Dogs allowed throughout pub, except dining room/kitchen. "More than welcome".

CROWN AND SCEPTRE
2 Petitor Road, Torquay, Devon TQ1 4QA (01803 328290).
Dogs allowed in non-food bar, family room, lounge. All dogs welcome.
Pet Regulars: 4 Jack Russell's - Sprocket, Scrappy Doo, Mouse and Minnie Mouse.

THE DEVONSHIRE INN
Sticklepath, Near Okehampton, Devon EX20 2NW (01837 840626).
Dogs allowed in non-food bar, car park, beer garden, family room, guest rooms.
Pet Regulars: Bess (Labrador), 'minds' owner; Annie (Shihtzu), snoring a speciality; Daisy (Collie), accompanies folk singers.

THE JOURNEY'S END INN
Ringmore, Near Kingsbridge, South Devon TQ7 4HL (01548 810205).
Dogs allowed throughout the pub except in the dining room.

PALK ARMS INN
Hennock, Bovey Tracey, Devon TQ13 9QS (01626 836584).
Pets welcome.

THE ROYAL OAK INN
Dunsford, Near Exeter, Devon EX6 7DA (01647 252256).
Dogs allowed in bars, beer garden, accommodation for guests with dogs.
Pet Regulars: Cleo

THE SEA TROUT INN
Staverton, Near Totnes, Devon TQ9 6PA (01803 762274).
Dogs allowed in lounge and public bar, car park tables, beer garden, owners' rooms (but not on beds).
Pet Regulars: Billy (Labrador-cross), partial to drip trays; Curnow (Poodle), brings a blanket and Buster (Mongrel).

THE WHITE HART HOTEL
Moretonhampstead, Newton Abbot, Devon TQ13 8NF (01647 440406).
Dogs allowed throughout, except restaurant.
Pet Regulars: Daisy (Collie).

DORSET

THE ANVIL HOTEL
Sailsbury Road, Pimperne, Blandford, Dorset DT11 8UQ (01258 453431).
Pets allowed in bar, lounge and bedrooms.

DURHAM

MOORCOCK INN
Hill Top, Eggleston, Teesdale, County Durham DL12 9AU (01833 650395).
Pet Regulars: Thor, the in-house hound dog, and Raymond, the resident hack, welcome all equine travellers; Gem (Jack Russell); Arnie (Ginger Tom).

TAP AND SPILE
27 Front Street, Framwellgate Moor, Durham DH1 5EE (0191 386 5451).
Dogs allowed throughout the pub.

ESSEX

THE OLD SHIP
Heybridge Basin, Heybridge, Maldon, Essex (01621 854150).
Dogs allowed throughout pub.

GLOUCESTERSHIRE

THE CROWN INN

Frampton Mansell, Stroud, Gloucestershire GL6 8JG (01285 760601).
Well behaved pooches welcome in our comfortable hotel.
Pet Regulars: Petra (Labrador), collects logs.

THE OLD STOCKS HOTEL

The Square, Stow on the Wold, Gloucestershire GL54 1AF (01451 830666).
Dogs allowed in the beer garden, accommodation for dogs and their owners also available.
Pet Regulars: Ben (Labrador) enjoys bitter from the drip trays and Oscar (Doberman) often gets carried out as he refuses to leave.

GREATER LONDON

THE PHOENIX

28 Thames Street, Sunbury on Thames, Middlesex (01932 785358).
Dogs allowed in non-food bar, beer garden, family room. Capability 2 Grading.
Pet Regulars: "Olly" (57 variety), Dixie (German Shepherd) and Monster (Shihtzu).

THE TIDE END COTTAGE

Ferry Road, Teddington, Middlesex (0208 977 7762).
Dogs allowed throughout the pub.
Pet Regulars: Chester, Golder Retriever – eats anything.

HAMPSHIRE

HIGH CORNER INN

Linwood, Near Ringwood, Hampshire BH24 3QY (01425 473973).
Dogs, horses and even goats are catered for here.

THE CHEQUERS

Ridgeway Lane, Lower Pennington, Lymington, Hants (01590 673415).
Dogs allowed in non-food bar, outdoor barbecue area (away from food).
Pet Regulars: Otto (Hungarian Vizsla), eats beer-mats and paper napkins. Likes beer but not often indulged.

THE VICTORY

High Street, Hamble-le-Rice, Southampton, Hampshire (023 80 453105).
Dogs allowed.
Pet Regulars: Sefton (Labrador), his 'usual' chew bars are kept especially.

HEREFORDSHIRE

THE GREEN MAN INN

Fownhope, Hereford, Herefordshire HR1 4PE (01432 860243).
Dogs welcome, but not in the restaurant.

HERTFORDSHIRE

THE BLACK HORSE

Chorly Wood Common, Dog Kennel Lane, Rickmansworth, Herts (01923 282252).
Dogs very welcome and allowed throughout the pub, on a lead.

THE ROBIN HOOD AND LITTLE JOHN
Rabley Heath, near Codicote, Hertfordshire (01438 812361).
Dogs allowed in non-food bar, car park tables, beer garden.
Pet Regulars: Bonnie (Labrador), beer-mat catcher. The locals of the pub have close to 50 dogs between them, most of which visit from time to time. The team includes a two Labrador search squad dispatched by one regular's wife to indicate time's up. When they arrive he has five minutes' drinking up time before all three leave together.

KENT

KENTISH HORSE
Cow Lane, Mark Beech, Edenbridge, Kent (01342 850493).
Dogs allowed in reserved area.

THE OLD NEPTUNE
Marine Terrace, Whitstable, Kent CT5 lEJ (01227 272262).
Dogs allowed in beach frontage.
Pet Regulars: Nut and Tory (Staffordshire Bull Terrier Crosses).

THE SWANN INN
Little Chart, Kent TN27 OQB (01233 840702).
Dogs allowed - everywhere except restaurant.

UNCLE TOM'S CABIN
Lavender Hill, Tonbridge, Kent (01628 483339).
Dogs allowed throughout.
Pet Regulars: Flossie, Pipa, Rusty. 10pm is dog biscuit time!

LANCASHIRE

ABBEYLEE
Abbeyhills Road, Oldham, Lancashire (0161 678 8795).
Dogs allowed throughout.

MALT'N HOPS
50 Friday Street, Chorley, Lancashire PR6 0AH (01257 260967).
Dogs allowed throughout pub.
Pet Regulars: Abbie (GSD), under-seat sleeper; Brandy (Rhodesian Ridgeback), at the sound of a bag of crisps opening will lean on eater until guest's legs go numb or he is offered a share; Toby (Labrador), valued customer in his own right, due to amount of crisps he eats, also retrieves empty bags; Mork – says please for bag of crisps and Zac - likes his pint of beer.

LEICESTERSHIRE

CHEQUERS INN
1 Gilmorton Road, Ashby Magna, Near Lutterworth, Leicestershire (01455 209523).
Dogs allowed in bar.
Pet Regulars: Suki – talking Samoyed.

LINCOLNSHIRE

THE HAVEN INN
Ferry Road, Barrow Haven, North Lincolnshire DN19 7EX (01469 530247).
Dogs allowed in the public bar, beer garden, and bedrooms on their own bed/blanket.
Pet Regulars: Jester the Collie.

THE BLUE DOG INN
Main Street, Sewstern, Grantham, Lincs NG33 5QR (01476 860097).
Dogs allowed.
Pet Regulars: The Guv'nor (Great Dane), best draught-excluder in history; Jenny (Scottie) shares biscuits with pub cats; Jemma (98% Collie), atmosphere lapper-upper. Spud and Nelson – Terriers.

MERSEYSIDE

AMBASSADOR PRIVATE HOTEL
13 Bath Street, Southport, Merseyside PR9 0DP (01704 543998).
Dogs allowed in non-food bar, lounge, guest bedrooms.

THE SCOTCH PIPER
Southport Road, Lydiate, Merseyside (0151 526 0503).
Dogs allowed throughout the pub.

MIDLANDS

AWENTSBURY HOTEL
21 Serpentine Road, Selly Park, Birmingham B29 7HU (0121 472 1258).
Dogs allowed.
Pet Regulars: Well-behaved dogs welcome.

NORFOLK

THE SPREAD EAGLE COUNTRY INN
Barton Bendish, Norfolk PE33 9DP (01366 347295).
Pet Regulars: Dirty Gertie, Pickles and Bosh.

MARINE HOTEL
10 St Edmunds Terrace, Hunstanton, Norfolk PE36 5EH (01485 533310).
Dogs allowed throughout, except dining room.
Pet Regulars: Many dogs have returned with their owners year after year to stay at The Marine Bar.

THE OLD RAILWAY TAVERN
Eccles Road, Quidenham, Norwich, Norfolk NR16 2JG (01953 888223).
Dogs allowed in non-food bar, beer garden.
Pet Regulars: Soshie (GSD); Annie (Labrador); and pub dogs Elsa (GSD). Elsa is so fond of sitting, motionless, on her own window ledge that new customers often think she's stuffed!

THE ROSE AND CROWN
Nethergate Street, Harpley, King's Lynn, Norfolk (01485 520577).
Dogs allowed in non-food bar, car park tables.
Pet Regulars: A merry bunch with shared interests – Duffy (mongrel); Tammy (Airedale); Dillon, all enjoy pub garden romps during summer and fireside seats in winter.

OXFORDSHIRE

THE BELL INN
High Street, Adderbury, Oxon (01295 810338).
Dogs allowed throughout the pub.
Owner's dogs; Bess and Elsa (Black Labradors).

SHROPSHIRE

THE TRAVELLERS REST INN
Church Stretton, Shropshire (01694 781275).
Well-mannered pets welcome - but beware of the cats!

LONGMYND HOTEL
Cunnery Road, Church Stretton, Shropshire SY6 6AG (01694 722244).
Dogs allowed in owners' hotel bedrooms but not in public areas.
Pet Regulars: Bruno and Frenzie; and owner's dogs, Sam and Sailor.

REDFERN HOTEL
Cleobury Mortimer, Shropshire SY14 8AA (01299 270395).
Dogs allowed in reception area and in guests' bedrooms.

SOMERSET

CASTLE OF COMFORT HOTEL
Dodington, Nether Stowey, Bridgwater, Somerset TA5 1LE (01278 741264).
Pet Friendly.

THE SPARKFORD INN
High Street, Sparkford, Somerset BA22 7JN (01963 440218).
Dogs allowed in bar areas but not in restaurant; safe garden and car park.
Pet Regulars: Holly (Jack Russell) and Stoner (Grizzly Bear)!

THE BUTCHERS ARMS
Carhampton, Somerset (01643 821333).
Dogs allowed in bar.

HALFWAY HOUSE
Pitney, Langport, Somerset TA10 9AB (01458 252513).
Dogs allowed.
Pet Regulars: Sam (Collie), Lotte (Otter Hound), Joe (Cocker Spaniel).

HOOD ARMS
Kilve, Somerset TA5 1EA (01278 741210)
Pets welcome.

THE SHIP INN
High Street, Porlock, Somerset (01643 862507).
Dogs allowed throughout and in guests' rooms.
Pet Regulars: Include Buster, Hardy (Jack Russell), terrorists from London; Bijoux (Peke), while on holiday at The Ship enjoys Chicken Supreme cooked to order every evening.

SUFFOLK

SIX BELLS AT BARDWELL
The Green, Bardwell, Bury St Edmunds IP31 1AW (01359 250820).
Dogs allowed in guest bedrooms and garden but not allowed in bar and restaurant.

THE COMPASSES INN
Wenhaston, Near Southwold, Suffolk IP19 9EF (01502 478319).
Dogs allowed throughout the pub and B&B (but not on the beds!). Bar open evenings only Tuesday to Sunday, and Sunday lunchtmes.
Pet Regulars: Raffles and Shadow (ex racing Greyhounds) who love all visiting dogs and crisps; Penny (Collie) and Cisco (young Doberman) who like to stand up at the bar.

SURREY

THE CRICKETERS
12 Oxenden Road, Tongham, Farnham, Surrey (01252 333262).
Dogs allowed in beer garden.

SUSSEX

THE FORESTERS ARMS
High Street, Fairwarp, Near Uckfield, East Sussex TN22 3BP (01825 712808).
Dogs allowed in the beer garden and at car park tables, also inside.
Owner's Dogs: Rascal and Sophie (Springer Spaniels).

THE INN IN THE PARK (CHEF & BREWER)
Tilgate Park, Tilgate, Crawley, West Sussex RH10 5PQ (01293 545324).
Dogs allowed in Patio area.

THE PLOUGH
Crowhurst, Near Battle, East Sussex TN33 9AY (01424 830310).
Dogs allowed in non-food bar, car park tables, beer garden.
Pet Regulars: Kai (Belgian Shepherd), drinks halves of Websters; Poppy and Cassie (Springer Spaniels), divided between the lure of crisps and fireside.

THE PRESTONVILLE ARMS
64 Hamilton Road, Brighton, East Sussex (01273 701007).
Dogs allowed in beer garden, throughout the pub (Pet Friendly).

QUEENS HEAD
Village Green, Sedlescombe, East Sussex (01424 870228).
Dogs allowed throughout the pub.

THE SLOOP INN
Freshfield Lock, Haywards Heath, West Sussex RH17 7NP (01444 831219).
Dogs allowed in public bar and garden.

THE SMUGGLERS' ROOST
125 Sea Lane, Rustington, West Sussex BN16 2SG (01903 785714).
Dogs allowed in non-food bar, at car park tables, in beer garden, family room.
Pet Regulars: Skip; Leo (Border Terrier), forms instant affections with anyone who notices him; Tim (King Charles Spaniel), quite prepared to guard his corner when food appears. The landlord owns a Great Dane and an Alsatian.

THE SPORTSMAN'S ARMS
Rackham Road, Amberley, Near Arundel, West Sussex BN18 9NR (01798 831787).
Dogs allowed throughout the pub.
Pet Regulars: Pippin, Spud Mollie and Nell.

WELLDIGGERS ARMS
Lowheath, Petworth, West Sussex GU28 0HG (01798 342287).
Dogs allowed throughout the pub.

WILTSHIRE

THE HORSE AND GROOM
The Street, Charlton, Near Malmesbury, Wiltshire (01666 823904).
Pet Regulars: P.D. (Pub Dog – Labrador).

THE PETERBOROUGH ARMS
Dauntsey Lock, Near Chippenham, Wiltshire SN15 4HD (01249 890409).
Dogs allowed in non-food bar, at car park tables, in beer garden, family room (when non-food).
Pet Regulars: Include Indy and Mac (West Highland Terriers).

THE THREE HORSESHOES
High Street, Chapmanslade, Near Westbury, Wiltshire (01373 832280).
Dogs allowed in non-food bar and beer garden.
Pet Regulars: Include Clieo (Golden Retriever), possibly the youngest 'regular' in the land - his first trip to the pub was at eight weeks. Westbury and District Canine Society repair to the Three Horseshoes after training nights (Monday/Wednesday). Five cats and four dogs in residence.

WAGGON AND HORSES
High Street, Wootton Bassett, Swindon, Wiltshire (01793 850617).
Dogs allowed throughout.
Pet Regulars: Include Gemma, a very irregular Whippet/Border collie cross. She likes to balance beer-mats on her nose, then flip them over and catch them, opens and shuts doors on command, walks on her hind legs and returns empty crisp bags. She is limited to one glass of Guinness a night.

YORKSHIRE

BARNES WALLIS INN
North Howden, Howden, East Yorkshire (01430 430639).
Guide dogs only

KINGS HEAD INN
Barmby on the Marsh, East Yorkshire DN14 7HL (01757 638357).
Dogs allowed in non-food bar.
Pet Regulars: Many and varied!

THE FORESTERS ARMS
Kilburn, North Yorkshire YO6 4AH (01347 868386).
Dogs allowed throughout, except restaurant.
Pet Regulars: Ainsley (Black Labrador)..

THE GREENE DRAGON INN
Hardraw, Hawes, North Yorkshire DL8 3LZ (01969 667392).
Dogs allowed in bar, at car park tables, in beer garden, family room but not dining room or restaurant.

NEW INN HOTEL
Clapham, Near Settle, North Yorkshire LA2 8HH (015242 51203).
Dogs allowed in bar, beer garden, family room.
Owner's dog: Time, (Rhodesian Ridgeback).

PREMIER HOTEL
66 Esplanade, South Cliff, Scarborough, North Yorkshire YO11 2UZ (01723 501062).
Dogs allowed throughout in non-food areas of hotel.

SIMONSTONE HALL
Hawes, North Yorkshire DL8 3LY (01969 667255).
Dogs allowed except dining area.
Pet Regulars: account for 2,000 nights per annum. More than 50% of guests are accompanied by their dogs, from Pekes to an Anatolian Shepherd (the size of a small Shetland pony!) Two dogs have stayed, with their owners, on 23 separate occasions.

THE SPINNEY
Forest Rise, Balby, Doncaster, South Yorkshire DN4 9HQ (01302 852033).
Dogs allowed throughout the pub.
Pet Regulars: Shamus (Irish Setter), pub thief. Fair game includes pool balls, beer mats, crisps, beer, coats, hats. Recently jumped 15 feet off pub roof with no ill effect. Josh; (Labrador) a guide dog. Indi and Jacques.

THE ROCKINGHAM ARMS
8 Main Street, Wentworth, Rotherham, South Yorkshire S62 7LO (01226 742075).
Dogs allowed throughout pub.
Pet Regulars: Sheeba (Springer Spaniel), Charlie and Gypsy (Black Labradors). Kate and Rags (Airedale and cross-breed), prefer lager to coffee; Holly (terrier and pub dog), dubbed 'the flying squirrel', likes everyone, whether they like it or not!

THE GOLDEN FLEECE
Lindley Road, Blackley, near Huddersfield, West Yorkshire (01422 372704).
Dogs allowed in non-food bar, at outside tables.
Pet Regulars: "Holly", (Border Collie).

CHANNEL ISLANDS/JERSEY

LA PULENTE INN
La Pulente, St Brelade, Jersey (01534 744487).
Dogs allowed in public bar..
Pet Regulars: Dusty (Old English Sheepdog)..

WALES

ANGLESEY & GWYNEDD

THE GRAPES HOTEL
Maentwrog, Blaenau Ffestiniog, Gwynedd LL41 4HN (01766 590365).
Pet Friendly.

PLAS YR EIFL HOTEL
Trefor, Caernarfon, Gwynedd LL54 5NA (01286 660781).
Pet Regulars: We have both dogs and cats

THE BUCKLEY HOTEL
Castle Street, Beaumaris, Isle of Anglesey LL58 8AW (01248 810415).
Dogs allowed throughout the pub, except in the dining room and bistro.
Pet Regulars: Cassie (Springer Spaniel) and Rex (mongrel), dedicated 'companion' dogs, also Charlie (Spaniel).

NORTH WALES

THE WEST ARMS HOTEL
Llanarmon Dyffryn Ceiriog, Llangollen, North Wales LL20 7LD (01691 600665).
Welcome Pets.

POWYS

SEVERN ARMS HOTEL
Penybont, Llandrindod Wells, Powys LD1 5UA (01597 851224).
Dogs allowed in the bar, but not the restaurant, and in the rooms - but not on the beds

---

Please mention *Recommended Wayside & Country Inns*
when enquiring about pubs and inns featured in these pages.

SCOTLAND

ABERDEEN, BANFF & MORAY

THE CLIFTON BAR
Clifton Road, Lossiemouth, Moray (01343 812100).
Dogs allowed throughout pub.
Pet Regulars: Include Zoe (Westie), has her own seat and is served coffee with two lumps; Milo (Jack Russel), Murphy (Minature Daushound) and Bob (Collie).

ROYAL OAK
Station Road, Urquhart, Elgin, Moray (01343 842607).
Dogs allowed throughout pub.
Pet Regulars: Mollie (Staffordshire Bull Terrier) – food bin. Biscuits (from the landlady), Maltesers (from the landlord), sausages and burgers (from the barbecue).

ARGYLL & BUTE

CAIRNDOW STAGECOACH INN
Cairndow, Argyll PA26 8BN (01499 600286).
Pet Regulars: Our own dog Rocky is a Golden Labrador.

THE BALLACHULISH HOTEL
Ballachulish, Argyll PA39 4JY (01855 811606).
Dogs allowed in the lounge, beer garden and guests' bedrooms, excluding food areas.
Pet Regulars: Thumper (Border Collie/GSD-cross), devoted to his owner and follows him everywhere.

BORDERS

CULGRUFF HOUSE HOTEL
Crossmichael, Castle Douglas, Kirkcudbrightshire DG7 3BB (01556 670230).
Dogs allowed in family room, guest bedrooms, but must be kept on leads outside.
Pet Regulars: A cross-section of canine visitors.

HIGHLANDS

ARISAIG HOTEL
Arisaig, Inverness-shire (01687 450210).
Dogs welcome.
Pet Regulars. Regulars in the public bar include Luar (Lurcher), Cindy (Collie), Whisky (Terrier).

PERTH & KINROSS

FOUR SEASONS HOTEL
St Fillans, Perthshire (01764 685333).
Dogs allowed in all non-food areas.

Tell us about YOUR favourite inn or pub

If you have visited an inn, pub or hotel which you think deserves to feature in this publication, then write and tell us about it!

Perhaps the food is particularly good, the landlord especially friendly (or a bit of a character!), or the beers and ales kept in tip-top condition. If children are made especially welcome, or pets allowed in and made a fuss of, then we would like to hear about it.

If you send us details, using the form below, then we will send you a FREE copy of one of our Year 2001 holiday guides (please choose from the list at the back of the book).

TO: FHG PUBLICATIONS LTD,
ABBEY MILL BUSINESS CENTRE, SEEDHILL, PAISLEY PA1 1TJ

Name & Address of Pub/Inn/Hotel ....

....

....

Telephone ....

Name of Licensee (if known) ....

Why this establishment is special

Your name & adddress (please PRINT) ....

....

....

Which one of our Year 2001 publications which you like? (totally free of charge) – see back of book for full list.

....

"Family-Friendly"
Pubs, Inns & Hotels

"FAMILY FRIENDLY"
Pubs, Inns and Hotels

This is a selection of establishments which make an extra effort to cater for parents and children. The majority provide a separate children's menu or they may be willing to serve small portions of main course dishes on request; there are often separate outdoor or indoor play areas where the junior members of the family can let off steam while Mum and Dad unwind over a drink. For more details, please see individual entries under county headings.

NB: Many other inns, pubs and hotels listed in the main section of the book but not included in this Supplement also welcome children – please see individual entries.

THE DUNDAS ARMS
Station Road, Kintbury,
Berkshire RG17 9UT
Tel: 01488 658263/658559
Fax: 01488 658263

THE INN ON THE GREEN
Old Cricket Common, Cookham
Dean, Berkshire SL6 9NZ
Tel: 01628 482638
Fax: 01628 487474

CHURCH HOUSE INN
Church Street, Bollington,
Macclesfield, Cheshire SK10 5PY
Tel: 01625 574014
Fax: 01625 576424

CHESHIRE CAT
Whitchurch Road, Christleton,
Chester, Cheshire CH3 6AE
Tel: 01244 332200
Fax: 01244 336415

SYCAMORE INN
Sycamore Road, Birch Vale, High
Peak, Cheshire SK22 1AB
Tel: 01663 742715
Fax: 01663 747382

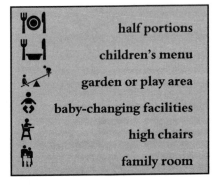

half portions

children's menu

garden or play area

baby-changing facilities

high chairs

family room

THE PHEASANT INN

Higher Burwardsley, Tattenhall,
Cheshire CH3 9PF
Tel: 01829 770434
Fax: 01829 771097

DRIFTWOOD SPARS HOTEL

Trevaunance Cove, St Agnes,
Cornwall TR5 0RT
Tel: 01872 552428/553323

SHIP INN

Lerryn, Lostwithiel,
Cornwall PL22 0PT
Tel: 01208 872374
Fax: 01208 872614

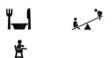

THE COPLEY ARMS

Hessenford, Torpoint,
Cornwall PL11 3HJ
Tel: 01503 240209
Fax: 01503 240766

CRUMPLEHORN MILL

Polperro, Cornwall PL13 2RJ
Tel: 01503 272348
Fax: 01503 272914

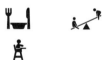

THE CORNISH ARMS

Pendoggett, Port Isaac,
North Cornwall PL30 3HH
Tel: 01208 880263
Fax: 01208 880335

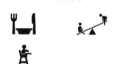

DRIFTWOOD SPARS HOTEL

Trevaunance Cove, St Agnes,
Cornwall TR5 0RT
Tel: 01872 552428/553323

THREE SHIRES INN

Little Langdale, Ambleside,
Cumbria LA22 9NZ
Tel: 015394 37215
Fax: 015394 37127

THE BLACKSMITH'S ARMS
Talkin Village, Brampton,
Cumbria CA8 1LE
Tel: 016977 3452
Fax: 016977 3394

SUN HOTEL & 16TH CENTURY INN
Coniston, Cumbria LA21 8HQ
Tel: 015394 41248
Fax: 015394 41219

THE BURNMOOR INN
Boot, Eskdale,
Cumbria CA19 1TG
Tel: 019467 23224
Fax: 019467 23337

QUEEN'S HEAD HOTEL
Main Street, Hawkshead,
Cumbria LA22 0NS
Tel: 015394 36271
Fax: 015394 36722

THE SWAN HOTEL
Thornthwaite,
Keswick,
Cumbria CA12 5SQ
Tel: 017687 78256

COLEDALE INN
Braithwaite,
Near Keswick,
Cumbria CA12 5TN
Tel: 017687 78272

	half portions
	children's menu
	garden or play area
	baby-changing facilities
	high chairs
	family room

WHITE LION HOTEL
Patterdale, Penrith,
Cumbria CA11 0NW
Tel: 01768 482214

POACHERS ARMS HOTEL
Castleton Road, Hope,
Derbyshire S33 6SB
Tel: 01433 620380
Fax: 01433 621915

BRIDGE INN
Bridge Street, Hatherleigh,
Devon EX20 3JA
Tel: 01837 810947
Fax: 01837 810614

BLACKCOCK INN
Molland,
South Molton,
Devon EX36 3NW
Tel & Fax: 01769 550297

THE TORS
Belstone,
Near Okehampton,
Devon EX20 1QZ
Tel: 01837 840689

THE PALK ARMS INN
Hennock,
Bovey Tracey,
Devon TQ13 9QS
Tel: 01626 836584

THE NEW INN
High Street, Clovelly, Near
Bideford, Devon EX39 5TQ
Tel: 01237 431303
Fax: 01237 431636

EXMOOR SANDPIPER INN
Countisbury, Near Lynmouth,
Devon EX35 6NE
Tel: 01598 741263
Fax: 01598 741358

THE SMUGGLERS
North Morte Road,
Mortehoe,
North Devon EX34 7DR
Tel & Fax: 01271 870891

THE POACHERS INN
Piddletrenthide, Dorchester,
Dorset DT2 7QX
Tel: 01300 348358
Fax: 01300 348153

KING'S ARMS INN
East Stour Common,
Near Gillingham,
Dorset SP8 5NB
Tel: 01747 838325

THE SCOTT ARMS
Kingston, Corfe Castle,
Dorset BH20 5LW
Tel: 01929 480270
Fax: 01929 481570

THE LANGTON ARMS
Tarrant Monkton, Near Blandford
Forum, Dorset DT11 8RX
Tel: 01258 830225
Fax: 01258 830053

THE OLD NEW INN
Bourton-on-the-Water,
Gloucestershire GL54 2AF
Tel: 01451 820467
Fax: 01451 810236

THE RAGGED COT INN
Cirencester Road, Hyde, Near
Stroud, Gloucestershire GL6 8PE
Tel: 01453 884643
Fax: 01453 731166

FALCON INN
Painswick,
Gloucestershire GL6 6UN
Tel: 01452 814222
Fax: 01452 813377

ROSE AND CROWN INN
Nympsfield, Stonehouse,
Gloucestershire GL10 3TU
Tel: 01453 860240
Fax: 01453 860900

THE COMPASSES INN
Damerham, Near Fordingbridge,
Hampshire SP6 3HQ
Tel: 01725 518231
Fax: 01725 518880

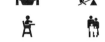

YE OLDE GEORGE INN
Church Street, East Meon, Near
Petersfield, Hampshire GU32 1NH
Tel: 01730 823481
Fax: 01730 823759

THE GREEN MAN
Fownhope,
Herefordshire HR1 4PE
Tel: 01432 860243
Fax: 01432 860207

THE NEW INN
Market Square,
Pembridge, Leominster,
Herefordshire HR6 9DZ
Tel: 01544 388427

THE INN ON THE WYE
Kerne Bridge, Goodrich, Near Ross-
on-Wye, Herefordshire HR9 5QS
Tel: 01600 890872
Fax: 01600 890594

THE NEW INN
St Owen's Cross,
Near Ross-on-Wye,
Herefordshire HR2 8LQ
Tel: 01989 730274

BUGLE HOTEL
The Square, Yarmouth,
Isle of Wight PO41 0NS
Tel: 01983 760272
Fax: 01983 760883

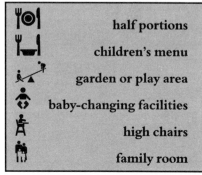

half portions

children's menu

garden or play area

baby-changing facilities

high chairs

family room

THE ST CRISPIN INN
The Street, Worth,
Kent CT14 0DF
Tel: 01304 612081
Fax: 01304 614838

THE OLD COACH-HOUSE
Dover Road (A2), Barham,
Kent CT4 6SA
Tel: 01227 831218
Fax: 01227 831932

THE EXETER ARMS
Wakerley, Oakham,
Rutland LE15 8PA
Tel: 01572 747817
Fax: 01572 747100

TALLY HO INN
Aswarby,
Near Sleaford,
Lincolnshire NG34 8SA
Tel: 01529 455205

LEA GATE INN
Lea Gate Road, Coningsby,
Lincolnshire LN4 4RS
Tel: 01526 342370
Fax: 01526 345468

THE MARQUIS OF GRANBY
High Street, Wellingore, Lincoln,
Lincolnshire LN5 0HW
Tel: 01522 810442
Fax: 01522 810740

THE RED LION INN
Main Road, Partney, Spilsby,
Lincolnshire PE23 4PG
Tel: 01790 752271
Fax: 01790 753360

FINCH HATTON ARMS
43 Main Street, Ewerby, Sleaford,
Lincolnshire NG34 9PH
Tel: 01529 460363
Fax: 01529 461703

THE SHIP HOTEL
Parkgate, Merseyside
Tel & Fax: 0151 336 3931

FEATHERS HOTEL
Manor Road, Dersingham,
King's Lynn,
Norfolk PE31 6LN
Tel & Fax: 01485 540207

THE HALF MOON INN
Rushall,
Near Diss,
Norfolk IP21 4QD
Tel & Fax: 01379 740793

THE JOHN H. STRACEY
West End, Briston, Melton
Constable, Norfolk NR24 2JA
Tel: 01263 860891
Fax: 01263 862984

SARACEN'S HEAD INN WITH ROOMS
Wolterton, Near Erpingham,
Norfolk NR11 7LX
Tel: 01263 768909

THE COTTAGE INN
Dunstan Village, Craster, Alnwick,
Northumberland NE66 3SZ
Tel: 01665 576658
Fax: 01665 576788

FHG PUBLICATIONS

FHG

publish a large range of well-known
accommodation guides.

We will be happy to send you details or you can use
the order form at the back of this book.

TANKERVILLE ARMS
Cottage Road, Wooler,
Northumberland NE71 6AD
Tel: 01668 281581
Fax: 01668 281387

THE PHEASANT INN
Stannersburn,
Falstone, Hexham,
Northumberland NE48 1DD
Tel & Fax: 01434 240382

SHEPHERDS HALL INN
Witney Road, Freeland,
Oxfordshire OX8 8HQ
Tel: 01993 881256
Fax: 01993 883455

THE KING'S HEAD INN AND RESTAURANT
Bledington, Near Kingham,
Oxfordshire OX7 6XQ
Tel: 01608 658365
Fax: 01608 658902

KILLINGWORTH CASTLE INN
Glympton Road, Wootton,
Woodstock, Oxfordshire 0X20 1EJ
Tel & Fax: 01993 811401

BOARS HEAD HOTEL
Church Street, Bishops Castle,
Shropshire SY9 5AE
Tel: 01588 638521
Fax: 01588 630126

STOKESAY CASTLE COACHING INN
School Road, Craven Arms,
Shropshire SY7 9PE
Tel: 01588 672304
Fax: 01588 673877

THE CHURCH INN
Buttercross, Ludlow,
Shropshire SY8 1AW
Tel: 01584 872174
Fax: 01584 877146

GASKELL ARMS HOTEL
Much Wenlock,
Shropshire TF13 6AQ
Tel: 01952 727212
Fax: 01952 728505

THE KINGS ARMS
Litton,
Near Bath,
Somerset BA3 4PW
Tel: 01761 241301

LION HOTEL
Bank Square, Dulverton,
Somerset TA22 9BU
Tel: 01398 323444
Fax: 01398 323980

THE HOOD ARMS
Kilve,
Somerset TA5 1EA
Tel: 01278 741210
Fax: 01278 741477

OLD POUND INN
Aller,
Langport,
Somerset TA10 0RA
Tel & Fax: 01458 250469

THE CATASH INN
North Cadbury,
Near Yeovil,
Somerset BA22 7DH
Tel & Fax: 01963 440248

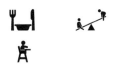

SPARKFORD INN
Sparkford, Yeovil,
Somerset BA22 7JN
Tel: 01963 440218
Fax: 01963 440358

CROSSWAYS INN
West Huntspill, Near Highbridge,
Somerset TA9 3RA
Tel: 01278 783756
Fax: 01278 781899

THREE HORSESHOES INN & RESTAURANT
Blackshaw Moor, Leek,
Staffordshire ST13 8TW
Tel: 01538 300296
Fax: 01538 300320

PEACOCK INN
37 The Street, Chelsworth,
Near Lavenham,
Suffolk IP7 7HU
Tel: 01449 740758

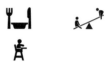

CHASE LODGE HOTEL
10 Park Road, Hampton Wick,
Kingston-upon-Thames,
Surrey KT1 4AS
Tel: 0208 943 1862
Fax: 0208 943 9363

THE QUEEN'S HEAD HOTEL
North Street,
Broad Chalke, Salisbury,
Wiltshire SP5 5EN
Tel & Fax: 01722 780344

THE OLD CROWN
Ogbourne St George,
Marlborough, Wiltshire SN8 1SQ
Tel: 01672 841445
Fax: 01672 841506

THE FOX AND HOUNDS COUNTRY INN
Main Street, Sinnington,
North Yorkshire YO62 6SQ
Tel: 01751 431577
Fax: 01751 432791

🍽	half portions
🍴	children's menu
🛝	garden or play area
👶	baby-changing facilities
🪑	high chairs
👪	family room

MAYPOLE INN
Long Preston, Skipton,
North Yorkshire BD23 4PH
Tel: 01729 840219
Fax: 01729 840456

DUKE OF WELLINGTON INN

West Lane, Danby, Near Whitby,
North Yorkshire YO21 2LY
Tel: 01287 660351

THE BUCK INN

Thornton Watlass, Near Bedale,
Ripon, North Yorkshire HG4 4AH
Tel: 01677 422461
Fax: 01677 422447

THE GANTON GREYHOUND

Ganton, Near Scarborough,
North Yorkshire YO12 4NX
Tel: 01944 710116
Fax: 01944 710705

GOLDEN FLEECE HOTEL

Market Place, Thirsk,
North Yorkshire YO7 1LL
Tel: 01845 523108
Fax: 01845 523996

LONG ASHES INN

Threshfield, Near Skipton,
North Yorkshire BD23 5PN
Tel: 01756 752434
Fax: 01756 752937

THE NEW INN MOTEL

Main Street, Huby, York,
North Yorkshire YO6 1HQ
Tel: 01347 810219

Visit the **FHG** website
www.holidayguides.com
for details of the wide choice of
accommodation featured in
the full range of FHG titles

INVER HOTEL
Crathie, By Balmoral,
Aberdeenshire AB35 5UL
Tel: 013397 42345
Fax: 013397 42009

MINMORE HOUSE HOTEL
Glenlivet, Ballindalloch,
Banffshire AB37 9DB
Tel: 01807 590378
Fax: 01807 590472

FINLAYSON ARMS
24 Hillhead, Coylton, Ayr,
Ayrshire KA6 6JT
Tel: 01292 570298
Fax: 01292 570298

LOCHNELL ARMS HOTEL
North Connel,
Argyll PA37 1RP
Tel: 01631 710408

TRAQUAIR ARMS
Traquair Road, Innerleithen,
Peeblesshire EH44 6PD
Tel: 01896 830229
Fax: 01896 830260

TIBBIE SHIELS INN
St Mary's Loch,
Selkirk,
Selkirkshire TD7 5LH
Tel: 01750 42231

THE CROOK INN
Tweedsmuir,
Peeblesshire ML12 6QN
Tel: 01899 880272
Fax: 01899 880294

THE POWFOOT HOTEL
Powfoot, Near Annan,
Dumfriesshire DG12 5PN
Tel: 01461 700254
Fax: 01461 700288

BLACK BULL HOTEL
Churchgate, Moffat,
Dumfriesshire DG10 9EG
Tel: 01683 220206
Fax: 01683 220483

FISHERMAN'S TAVERN HOTEL
Fort Street, Broughty Ferry,
Dundee DD5 2AD
Tel: 01382 775941
Fax: 01382 477466

LAIRD AND DOG HOTEL
5 High Street, Lasswade,
Near Edinburgh
EH18 1NA
Tel/Fax: 0131-663 9219

YE OLDE ORIGINAL ROSLIN INN
Main Street, Roslin,
Midlothian EH25 9LE
Tel: 0131-440 2384
Fax: 0131-440 2514

CASTLE ARMS HOTEL
Mey, By Thurso,
Caithness KW14 8XH
Tel & Fax: 01847 851244

STRATHCARRON HOTEL
Strathcarron, Ross-shire IV54 8YR
Tel: 01520 722227
Fax: 01520 722990

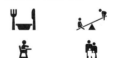

THE STRATHARDLE INN
Kirkmichael, Perthshire PH10 7NS
Tel: 01250 881224
Fax 01250 881373

THE MUIRS INN KINROSS
49 Muirs, Kinross,
Perth & Kinross KY13 8AU
Tel & Fax: 01577 862270

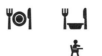

GOLDEN PHEASANT HOTEL
Glyn Ceiriog, Near Llangollen,
North Wales LL20 7BB
Tel: 01691 718281
Fax: 01691 718479

GALES HOTEL AND WINE BAR
18 Bridge Street, Llangollen,
North Wales LL20 8PF
Tel: 01978 860089
Fax: 01978 861313

GEORGE BORROW HOTEL
Ponterwyd, Aberystwyth,
Cardiganshire SY23 3AD
Tel: 01970 890230
Fax: 01970 890587

BLACK LION HOTEL
High Street,
Cardigan,
Cardiganshire SA43 1HJ
Tel: 01239 612532

SEVERN ARMS HOTEL
Penybont, Llandrindod Wells,
Powys LD1 5UA
Tel: 01597 851224/851344
Fax: 01597 851693

TREWERN ARMS HOTEL
Nevern, Newport,
Pembrokeshire SA42 0NB
Tel: 01239 820395

CLYTHA ARMS
Brecon Road,
Near Abergavenny,
South Wales NP7 9BW
Tel: 01873 840206

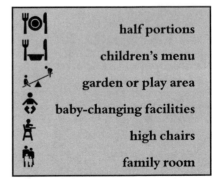

half portions

children's menu

garden or play area

baby-changing facilities

high chairs

family room

THE FHG DIPLOMA

HELP IMPROVE
BRITISH TOURIST STANDARDS

You are choosing holiday accommodation from our very popular FHG Publications.
Whether it be a hotel, guest house, farmhouse or self-catering accommodation, we think you will find it hospitable, comfortable and clean, and your host and hostess friendly and helpful.

Why not write and tell us about it?

As a recognition of the generally well-run and excellent holiday accommodation reviewed in our publications, we at FHG Publications Ltd. present a diploma to proprietors who receive the highest recommendation from their guests who are also readers of our Guides. If you care to write to us praising the holiday you have booked through FHG Publications Ltd. – whether this be board, self-catering accommodation, a sporting or a caravan holiday, what you say will be evaluated and the proprietors who reach our final list will be contacted.

The winning proprietor will receive an attractive framed diploma to display on his premises as recognition of a high standard of comfort, amenity and hospitality. FHG Publications Ltd. offer this diploma as a contribution towards the improvement of standards in tourist accommodation in Britain. Help your excellent host or hostess to win it!

FHG DIPLOMA

We nominate ....

....

Because

Name ....

Address..

....

Telephone No...

BOOKING

FOR THE
MUTUAL GUIDANCE
OF GUEST AND HOST

Every year literally thousands of holidays, short breaks and overnight stops are arranged through our guides, the vast majority without any problems at all. In a handful of cases, however, difficulties do arise about bookings, which often could have been prevented from the outset.

It is important to remember that when accommodation has been booked, both parties – guests and hosts – have entered into a form of contract. We hope that the following points will provide helpful guidance.

GUESTS: When enquiring about accommodation, be as precise as possible. Give exact dates, numbers in your party and the ages of any children. State the number and type of rooms wanted and also what catering you require – bed and breakfast, full board etc. Make sure that the position about evening meals is clear – and about pets, reductions for children or any other special points.

Read our reviews carefully to ensure that the proprietors you are going to contact can supply what you want. Ask for a letter confirming all arrangements, if possible.

If you have to cancel, do so as soon as possible. Proprietors do have the right to retain deposits and under certain circumstances to charge for cancelled holidays if adequate notice is not given and they cannot re-let the accommodation.

HOSTS: Give details about your facilities and about any special conditions. Explain your deposit system clearly and arrangements for cancellations, charges etc. and whether or not your terms include VAT.

If for any reason you are unable to fulfil an agreed booking without adequate notice, you may be under an obligation to arrange suitable alternative accommodation or to make some form of compensation.

While every effort is made to ensure accuracy, we regret that FHG Publications cannot accept responsibility for errors, omissions or misrepresentations in our entries or any consequences thereof. Prices in particular should be checked because we go to press early. We will follow up complaints but cannot act as arbiters or agents for either party.

Index of towns and counties.
Please also refer to Contents page 15

Abergavenny, SOUTH WALES
Aberystwyth, CARDIGANSHIRE
Acle, NORFOLK
Ainthorpe, NORTH YORKSHIRE
Alderminster, WARWICKSHIRE
Alnmouth, NORTHUMBERLAND
Alnwick, NORTHUMBERLAND
Alyth, PERTH & KINROSS
Ambleside, CUMBRIA
Applecross, HIGHLANDS
Ashbourne, DERBYSHIRE
Askham, CUMBRIA
Aswarby, LINCOLNSHIRE
Aysgarth, NORTH YORKSHIRE

Bainbridge, NORTH YORKSHIRE
Barham, KENT
Barton Bendish, NORFOLK
Bath, SOMERSET
Bedale, NORTH YORKSHIRE
Belstone, DEVON
Bildeston, SUFFOLK
Bilsborrow, LANCASHIRE
Birch Vale, CHESHIRE
Birch Vale, DERBYSHIRE
Bishop Wilton, NORTH YORKSHIRE
Bishops Castle, SHROPSHIRE
Blandford, DORSET
Bollington, CHESHIRE
Boscastle, CORNWALL
Boughton Aluph, KENT
Bourton-On-The-Water, GLOUCESTERSHIRE
Bovey Tracey, DEVON
Brampton, CUMBRIA
Bridgnorth, SHROPSHIRE
Brimfield, SHROPSHIRE
Broad Chalke, WILTSHIRE
Broughty Ferry, DUNDEE
Buckland, OXFORDSHIRE
Burlescombe, DEVON
Buxton, DERBYSHIRE

Cairndow, ARGYLL & BUTE
Candy, SHROPSHIRE
Cardigan, CARDIGANSHIRE
Cartmel, CUMBRIA
Castleton, DERBYSHIRE
Cawood, NORTH YORKSHIRE
Chelsworth, SUFFOLK
Chester, CHESHIRE
Chippenham, WILTSHIRE
Cholmondeley, CHESHIRE
Cirencester, GLOUCESTERSHIRE
Clapham, NORTH YORKSHIRE
Cley-Next-The-Sea, NORFOLK
Clovelly, DEVON
Coalbrookdale, SHROPSHIRE
Colchester, ESSEX
Coningsby, LINCOLNSHIRE
Coniston, CUMBRIA
Cookham Dean, BERKSHIRE
Countisbury, DEVON
Coylton, AYRSHIRE & ARRAN
Crathie, ABERDEEN, BANFF & MORAY
Craven Arms, SHROPSHIRE
Cricklade, WILTSHIRE

Danby, NORTH YORKSHIRE
Dartington, DEVON
Delph, LANCASHIRE
Devizes, WILTSHIRE
Ditchling, EAST SUSSEX
Donnington-on-Bain, LINCOLNSHIRE
Dorchester, DORSET
Dorchester-On-Thames, OXFORDSHIRE
Dulverton, SOMERSET
Dunbeath, HIGHLANDS
Dunsford, DEVON

East Coker, SOMERSET
Egloshayle, CORNWALL
Eskdale, CUMBRIA
Evercreech, SOMERSET

Falstone, NORTHUMBERLAND
Fordingbridge, HAMPSHIRE
Fort William, HIGHLANDS
Fownhope, HEREFORDSHIRE
Freeland, OXFORDSHIRE

Gillingham, DORSET
Glenlivet, ABERDEEN, BANFF & MORAY
Grassington, NORTH YORKSHIRE
Great Rissington, GLOUCESTERSHIRE

Haltwhistle, NORTHUMBERLAND
Harrietsham, KENT
Hartington, DERBYSHIRE
Hatherleigh, DEVON
Hawes, NORTH YORKSHIRE
Hawkshead, CUMBRIA
Hay-On-Wye, HEREFORDSHIRE
Hessenford, CORNWALL
Hexworthy, DEVON
High Post, WILTSHIRE
Hillington, NORFOLK
Holbeton, DEVON
Hook, HAMPSHIRE
Hook Norton, OXFORDSHIRE
Hope, DERBYSHIRE
Hopton Wafers, SHROPSHIRE
Horndean, HAMPSHIRE
Houghton Conquest, BEDFORDSHIRE
Huggate, EAST YORKSHIRE
Hutton Cranswick, EAST YORKSHIRE
Hyde, GLOUCESTERSHIRE
Hyde Heath, BUCKINGHAMSHIRE

Innerleithen, BORDERS
Ivybridge, DEVON

Keswick, CUMBRIA
Kilve, SOMERSET
Kingham, OXFORDSHIRE
King's Lynn, NORFOLK

Kingston, DORSET
Kingston-upon-Thames, SURREY
Kinross, PERTH & KINROSS
Kintbury, BERKSHIRE
Kirkbymoorside, NORTH YORKSHIRE
Kirkmichael, PERTH & KINROSS

Langport, SOMERSET
Lasswade, EDINBURGH & LOTHIANS
Ledbury, HEREFORDSHIRE
Leek, STAFFORDSHIRE
Leeming Bar, NORTH YORKSHIRE
Lenham, KENT
Leominster, HEREFORDSHIRE
Lichfield, STAFFORDSHIRE
Lincoln, LINCOLNSHIRE
Llangollen, NORTH WALES
Llangurig, POWYS
Llanwrtyd Wells, POWYS
Lostwithiel, CORNWALL
Loughborough, LEICESTERSHIRE
Ludlow, SHROPSHIRE
Lulworth Cove, DORSET
Lynmouth, DEVON
Lythe, NORTH YORKSHIRE

Malvern, WORCESTERSHIRE
Melton Constable, NORFOLK
Mevagissey, CORNWALL
Mey, HIGHLANDS (NORTH)
Mickleham, SURREY
Midhurst, WEST SUSSEX
Minehead, SOMERSET
Moffat, DUMFRIES & GALLOWAY
Molland, DEVON
Monkton Combe, SOMERSET
Mortehoe, DEVON
Much Wenlock, SHROPSHIRE

Newbury, BERKSHIRE
Newport, PEMBROKESHIRE

Newton Abbot, DEVON
North Brewham, SOMERSET
North Cadbury, SOMERSET
North Connel, ARGYLL & BUTE
North Dalton, EAST YORKSHIRE
North Perrott, SOMERSET
Norwich, NORFOLK

Oakham, LEICESTERSHIRE
Oban, ARGYLL & BUTE
Ogbourne St George, WILTSHIRE
Ossett, WEST YORKSHIRE
Outgate, CUMBRIA

Painswick, GLOUCESTERSHIRE
Parkgate, MERSEYSIDE
Partney, LINCOLNSHIRE
Penrith, CUMBRIA
Penybont, POWYS
Petersfield, HAMPSHIRE
Polperro, CORNWALL
Porlock, SOMERSET
Port Isaac, CORNWALL
Powfoot, DUMFRIES & GALLOWAY

Richmond, NORTH YORKSHIRE
Rosedale Abbey, NORTH YORKSHIRE
Roslin, EDINBURGH & LOTHIANS
Ross-on-Wye, HEREFORDSHIRE
Roydhouse, WEST YORKSHIRE
Rushall, NORFOLK
Rushyford, DURHAM

Salisbury, WILTSHIRE
Scarborough, NORTH YORKSHIRE
Sedbergh, CUMBRIA
Settle, NORTH YORKSHIRE
Shelf, WEST YORKSHIRE

Sinnington, NORTH YORKSHIRE
Skipton, NORTH YORKSHIRE
Slaidburn, LANCASHIRE
Sleaford, LINCOLNSHIRE
Snape, NORTH YORKSHIRE
St Agnes, CORNWALL
St Mary's Loch, BORDERS
Staple Fitzpaine, SOMERSET
Stonehouse, GLOUCESTERSHIRE
Strathcarron, HIGHLANDS
Sudbury, SUFFOLK

Tarrant Monkton, DORSET
Tattenhall, CHESHIRE
Taunton, SOMERSET
Tedburn St Mary, DEVON
Thirsk, NORTH YORKSHIRE
Thornham, NORFOLK
Threshfield, NORTH YORKSHIRE
Thurnham, LANCASHIRE
Timberland, LINCOLNSHIRE
Tintagel, CORNWALL
Tuddenham St Mary, SUFFOLK
Tweedsmuir, BORDERS

Ventnor, ISLE OF WIGHT
Veryan, CORNWALL

Wellington, SHROPSHIRE
Wells, SOMERSET
Wells-Next-The-Sea, NORFOLK
West Huntspill, SOMERSET
Winchcombe, GLOUCESTERSHIRE
Withypool, SOMERSET
Wolterton, NORFOLK
Woodstock, OXFORDSHIRE
Wooler, NORTHUMBERLAND
Worth, KENT

Yarmouth, ISLE OF WIGHT
Yeovil, SOMERSET
York, NORTH YORKSHIRE

Please mention *Recommended Wayside & Country Inns*
when enquiring about accommodation featured in these pages.

ONE FOR YOUR FRIEND 2001

FHG Publications have a large range of attractive holiday accommodation guides for all kinds of holiday opportunities throughout Britain. They also make useful gifts at any time of year. Our guides are available in most bookshops and larger newsagents but we will be happy to post you a copy direct if you have any difficulty. We will also post abroad but have to charge separately for post or freight. *The inclusive cost of posting and packing the guides to you or your friends in the UK is as follows:*

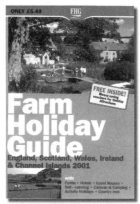

FARM HOLIDAY GUIDE
England, Scotland, Wales and Channel Islands.
Board, Self-catering, Caravans/ Camping, Activity Holidays.
£6.00 inc p&p

BED AND BREAKFAST STOPS.
Over 1000 friendly and comfortable overnight stops.
Non-smoking, Disabled and Special Diets Supplements.
£6.00 inc p&p.

BRITAIN'S BEST HOLIDAYS
A quick-reference general guide for all kinds of holidays.
£4.50 inc p&p.

SELF-CATERING HOLIDAYS
in Britain
Over 1000 addresses throughout for Self-catering and caravans in Britain.
£5.50 inc p&p.

Recommended
COUNTRY HOTELS OF BRITAIN
Including Country Houses, for the discriminating
£5.50 inc p&p

Recommended
SHORT BREAK HOLIDAYS
in Britain.
'Approved' accommodation for quality bargain breaks
£5.50 inc p&p

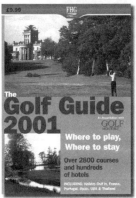  

GOLF GUIDE –
Where to play. Where to stay.
In association with GOLF MONTHLY.
Over 2500 golf courses in Britain
with convenient accommodation.
Holiday Golf in France, Portugal,
Spain,USA, South Africa and
Thailand.
£10.50 inc p&p.

The FHG Guide to CARAVAN &
CAMPING HOLIDAYS
Caravans for hire, sites and
holiday parks and centres.
£4.50 inc p&p.

B&B in Britain
Over 1000 choices for touring
and holidays throughout Britain.
Airports and Ferries Supplement.
£4.50 inc p&p.

CHILDREN WELCOME! Family Holidays and Attractions guide.
Family holidays with details of amenities for children and babies.   £5.50 inc p&p.

PETS WELCOME!
The unique guide for holidays for pet owners and their pets.   £6.50 inc p&p.

Tick your choice and send your order and payment to
••

FHG PUBLICATIONS, ABBEY MILL BUSINESS CENTRE, SEEDHILL, PAISLEY PA1 1TJ
TEL: 0141- 887 0428; FAX: 0141- 889 7204
e-mail: fhg@ipcmedia.com

FHG

Deduct 10% for 2/3 titles or copies; 20% for 4 or more.

Send to: NAME...

ADDRESS ....

....

....

POST CODE   ....

I enclose Cheque/Postal Order for £...

SIGNATURE ....DATE ....

Please complete the following to help us improve the service we provide. How did
you find out about our guides?:

☐Press   ☐Magazines   ☐TV/Radio   ☐Family/Friend   ☐Other

Map 1

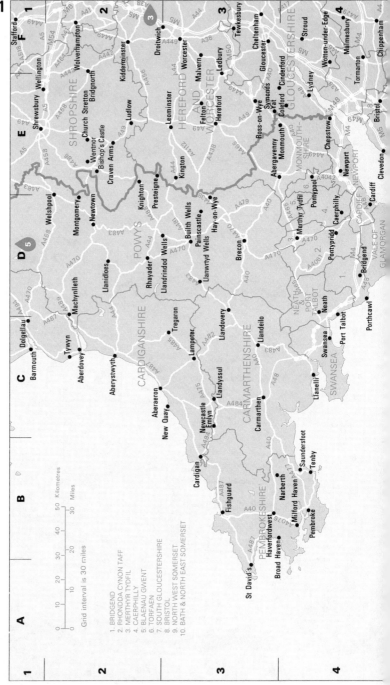

Map 2

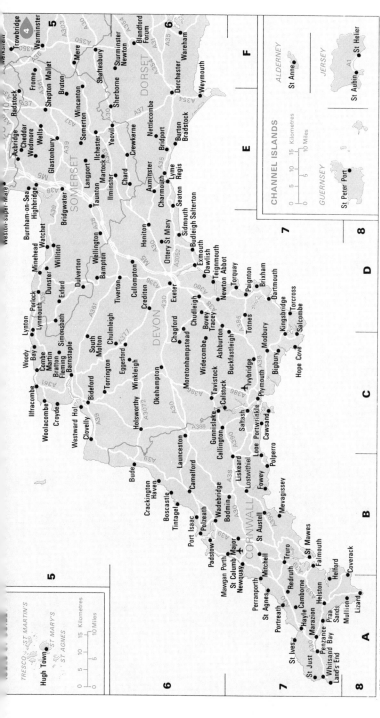

Map 3

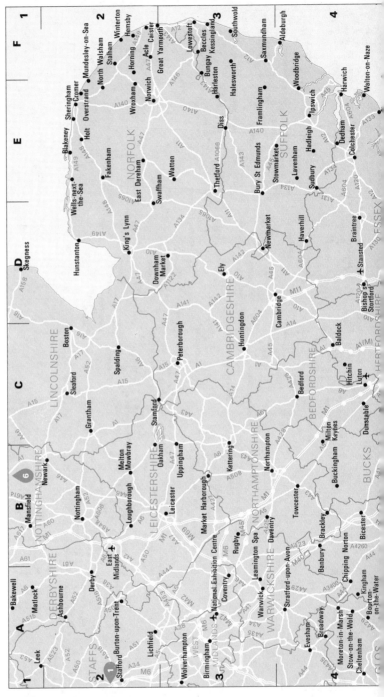

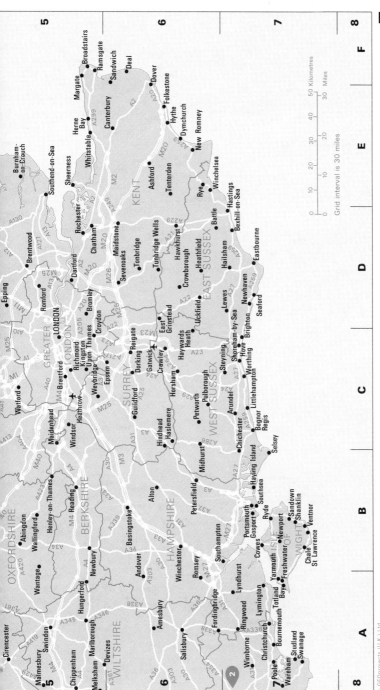

Map 4

Grid interval is 30 miles

Map 5

1 A   ●Girvan   B   A76   A701 A74   C   7   Langholm●   D   Belling●
                                                                                                                                                              NORT
              DUMFRIES AND GALLOWAY   A7
                        ●New Galloway   Dumfries●
                                                                                              Annan●   Gretna●   Longtown●
2   Newton   A75   A74   Brampton● A69   Greenhead●
              Stewart●   A75
                                                                                                        Carlisle●
     ●Wigtown   ●Castle Douglas   Silloth●   A689   ●Alston
              Gatehouse of Fleet●   ●Wigton   M6   A6   A686
                  ●Kirkcudbright   A596
     Port William●   ●Brampton
                                                   Maryport●   Penrith●
                                        Cockermouth●   ●Bassenthwaite   ●Brampton●
3   Workington●   Keswick●   Appleby●
                                                    A5086   A66   Shap●   ●Kirkby
                                 Whitehaven●   Ennerdale Ullswater●   CUMBRIA   ●Stephen
                                               Bridge●   Rydal●   A685
                                            Gosforth● Little Langdale● Ambleside●
                                          Seascale●   Hawkshead● Windermere●   ●Sedbergh
                                                         Coniston●   ●Kendal   A684   Kirkby Lonsda●
                               Broughton-in-Furness● Newby   A6   ●Inglet
4   ●Millom Bridge●   A65
                                                   Ulverston● Arnside●
                               Barrow-in-Furness●   Grange-over-Sands●   ●Settl
                                                   Morecambe●   A683
                                                   Lancaster●
                                               Fleetwood●
                                                                                   Clitheroe●
                                        Blackpool●   A585   M55   M6   A59   LANCASHIRE
5   Lytham St Annes●   ●Blackbur
                                                         Preston●
                                       Southport●   A570   Chorley●
                                                    A59   Bolton●
                                       Formby●   A565 A580 Wigan●   GREATER
                                                         M58   MANCHEST
                                                    MERSEYSIDE   ●Manche●
6   ●Amlwch   ANGLESEY   Hoylake● Liverpool●
    Holyhead● ●Llanerchymedd Llandudno● Rhyl● Prestatyn● Birkenhead●
       A5   Menai Beaumaris● Colwyn M53   Knutsford●
    Llangefni● Bridge● Conwy●   Bay Abergele● Holywell●   Northwich● CHESHIRE
              Bangor● ABERCONWY A55   M56   A54
         Caernarvon●   & COLWYN   Denbigh● Nannerch● Chester● A51
       Llanberis● Llanrwst●   FLINT-   A41
                    Ruthin●   SHIRE   Nantwich●
              Betws-y-Coed● DENBIGH-   Newcastle-under-Ly●
7   Nefyn● Portmadoc● GWYNEDD SHIRE
       Criccieth● Ffestiniog● Corwen● Wrexham●   A525
    Pwllheli● Penrhyndeudraeth● Bala● Llangollen● WREXHAM   A53
    Llanbedrog● Harlech●   Wem●   Market
    Abersoch●   Drayton●
    Aberdaron●   Oswestry●   ●Wellington
              Dolgellau●   SHROPSHIRE
         Barmouth●   A493 A458   A458   Shrewsbury●
     A   B   A487 Welshpool●   1   C   Shrewsbury● D
         Tywyn● ●Machynlleth   POWYS

Map 6

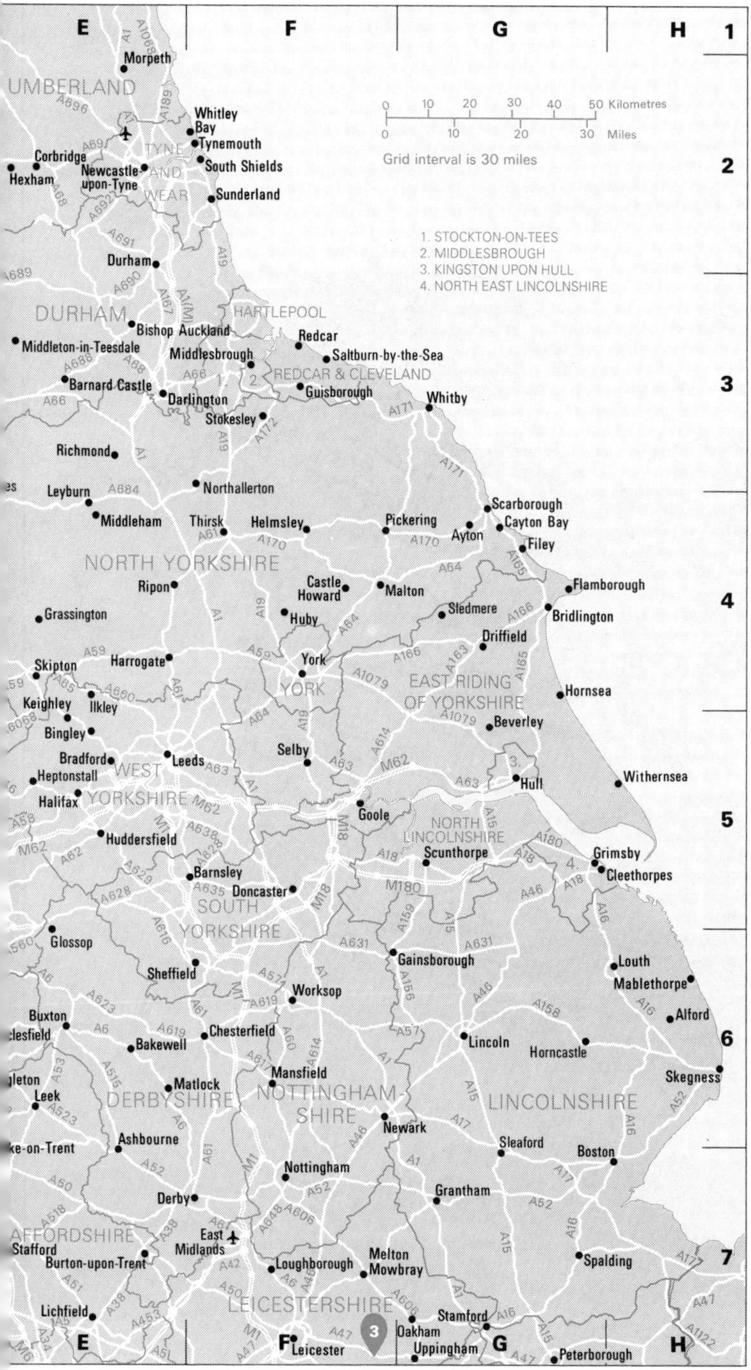

E F G H

1

2

3

4

5

6

7

Morpeth

UMBERLAND

Whitley
Bay
Tynemouth
South Shields
Sunderland

Corbridge
Hexham
Newcastle
upon-Tyne

TYNE AND WEAR

10 20 30 40 50 Kilometres
0 10 20 30 Miles
Grid interval is 30 miles

1. STOCKTON-ON-TEES
2. MIDDLESBROUGH
3. KINGSTON UPON HULL
4. NORTH EAST LINCOLNSHIRE

Durham

DURHAM

HARTLEPOOL

Bishop Auckland
Middleton-in-Teesdale
Barnard Castle
Darlington
Stokesley

Middlesbrough
REDCAR & CLEVELAND
Guisborough

Redcar
Saltburn-by-the-Sea

Whitby

Richmond

Leyburn
Middleham
Thirsk
Northallerton
Helmsley

Pickering
Ayton
Scarborough
Cayton Bay
Filey

NORTH YORKSHIRE

Ripon
Grassington

Castle
Howard
Huby
Malton
Sledmere
Driffield

Flamborough
Bridlington

Skipton
Harrogate

York

YORK

EAST RIDING
OF YORKSHIRE

Hornsea

Keighley
Ilkley
Bingley

Selby

Beverley

Bradford
Heptonstall
Halifax
Leeds

WEST
YORKSHIRE

Hull
Withernsea

Huddersfield

Goole

NORTH
LINCOLNSHIRE

Barnsley
Doncaster

Scunthorpe

Grimsby
Cleethorpes

SOUTH
YORKSHIRE

Glossop
Sheffield

Gainsborough

Louth
Mablethorpe

Buxton
clesfield
Bakewell
Chesterfield
Worksop

Lincoln
Horncastle

Alford

leton
Leek

Matlock
Mansfield

LINCOLNSHIRE

Skegness

ke-on-Trent
Ashbourne

DERBYSHIRE
NOTTINGHAM-
SHIRE

Newark
Sleaford
Boston

Derby

Nottingham

Grantham

AFFORDSHIRE
Stafford
Burton-upon-Trent

East
Midlands

Melton
Mowbray

Spalding

Lichfield

LEICESTERSHIRE

Loughborough

Stamford
Oakham
Uppingham

Peterborough

E F Leicester G H

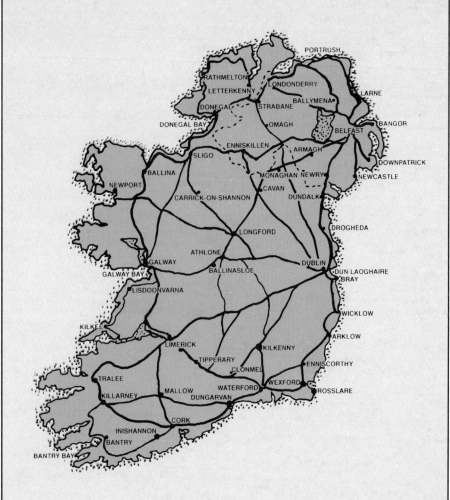